HOW FAITH COMES
(28 ways Faith Comes)

Dr Michael H Yeager

FRONT COVER MINISTERS

A/John Wesley (1703 – 1791)
B/George Whitefield (1714 – 1770)
C/Charles Grandison Finney (1792 – 1875)
D/Maria Woodworth-Etter (1844–1924)
E/John Alexander Dowie (1847 – 1907)
F/Smith Wigglesworth (1859–1947)
G/John Graham Lake (1870 – 1935)
H/William J. Seymour (1870–1922)
I/Charles Parham (1873–1929)
J/Fred Francis Bosworth (1877 – 1958)
K/Evan John Roberts (1878 – 1951)
L/Dr. Charles S. Price (1887-1947)
M/Aimee Semple McPherson (1890–1944)

N/Aiden Wilson Tozer (1897 - 1963)
O/Duncan Campbell (1898 -1972)
P/James Gordon Lindsay (1906–1973)
R/Kathryn Kuhlman (1907–1976)
S/Leonard Ravenhill (1907–1994)
T/William Branham (1909–1965)
U/Asa A. Allen (1911– 1970)
V/Kenneth Erwin Hagin (1917 – 2003)
W/Granville Oral Roberts (1918 – 2009)
X/Jack Coe (1918 – 1956)
Y/Tommy Lee Osborn (1923 – 2013)
Z/David Ray Wilkerson (1931 – 201

ISBN: 1499382243

ISBN-13: 9781499382242

DEDICATION

We dedicate this book to those who also face the dilemma of being human, to those who know what it's like to fall short of the glory and yet keep getting back up and striving by faith. We dedicate this to those who keep pressing towards the mark for the prize of the high calling of God in **Christ Jesus**; fellow believers who are on the journey of life, who stumble but never quit. They just keep getting back up and pressing on. It is only by the supernatural touch of God, the life of **Christ**, by which we are able to accomplish His will.

THE WHY OF THIS BOOK

1 John 5:For whatsoever is born of God overcometh the world: and this is the victory that overcometh the world, even our faith. 5 Who is he that overcometh the world, but he that believeth that Jesus is the Son of God?

Faith in **Christ** is the key to our victory! With this truth and reality in our heart, it is expedient that we become full of faith. As we connect the dots from Genesis to Revelation, it becomes quite clear that the cause of all of man's sorrows, shortcomings, immoralities, sicknesses, troubles are due to the fact that we are not truly trusting, looking, depending, relying and having faith in **Christ**! Based upon this fact we must do everything we can to attain more faith. Even the disciples as they watched the life of **Jesus** before their eyes, asked Him to help increase their faith. This is the whole purpose of this book. To provide biblical means by which we can have an increase of faith in **Christ** which causes us to overcome! Please open your heart, your mind, and your life to these realities. And let **Jesus Christ** become your all!

A Brief Description of Faith:
It is when God, His Word, His will is Supernaturally Quickened to you by the Holy Spirit! These realities become more real to you than anything in life. It is a revelation of Who Jesus Christ & God the Father really is & what He has done and is doing. It is a quickening in your heart when you know, that you know, that you know, that you know God is with you, then who can be against you? That Christ Jesus Himself, lives inside of you. Your mind, your will, your emotions, and every part of your being is overwhelmed with the reality of Jesus Christ! And you enter into the realm where all things are possible! This is where, by God's grace it is my hope and desire to take you.

FORWARD

28 WAYS THAT FAITH COMES!

For over 40 years of Ministry I probably have heard taught less than two biblical ways that faith comes. But in 2008 as I was in prayer early in the morning the spirit of God opened up my understanding, instantly downloading into me 28 major ways of **HOW FAITH COMES** within three minutes. I sat down at the dinner table absolutely flabbergasted, taking a pen and paper, and writing down what the Lord showed me. It took me days to write what I had seen in about three minutes. This revelation continues to flow to this day giving me deeper understandings on the important subject of faith in **Christ**! The Lord showed me supernaturally, and verified by Scriptures that there are approximately 28 ways that faith comes. This has been a progressive revelation. I am convinced that these are not the only ways that faith comes, but at this time it is the revelations that I have from God and his word.

How Faith Comes 28 Ways is not a new revelation, in the sense that it has always been there. Many of these 28 ways in which FAITH comes you will discover you have already been practicing, but now with a much clearer understanding you will be able to exercise yourself in these ways in a more persistent way in order to develop your FAITH in JESUS CHRIST!

Faith is like a diamond with many facets. And yet it is the same diamond!

Faith is spoken of in a very strong way (believe, trust, faith) over 800 times in the Bible. **Jesus** did more teaching on the subject of faith than anything else.

Heb11:6 WITH OUT FAITH IT IS IMPOSSIBLE TO PLEASE GOD!

I cannot over emphasize the importance of faith, but before we can really go any further I need to explain what I mean when I say faith. To me, as I read the word of God there is *only one true faith*, that is faith in **CHRIST JESUS**! All other faiths and beliefs, no matter what you may call them, according to the word of God, they are not truly faith at all! It may be a belief system a psychological philosophy, but it is not faith.

Hebrew 11 gives to us a description of faith, and its manifestations. Let's look very briefly at Hebrews 11: 1to 3

Hebrews 11:1-3 <u>Now faith</u> is the <u>substance</u> of things hoped for, the <u>evidence</u> of things not seen. ² For by it the elders obtained a good report. ³ Through <u>faith</u> we understand that the worlds were framed by the word of God, so that things which are seen were not made of things which do appear.

So we can boldly declare that faith is a substance --- that gives evidence -- by which the worlds were framed by the word of God. Only the Christian faith (faith in **CHRIST JESUS**) is what brought about, and continues to sustain creation, and all that exist.

Now this is very important what I'm about to say. There is only one faith! And this faith is the **only faith** that saves, heals, delivers, creates, pleases God, and makes all things possible!

Ephesians 4:4-6 There is one body, and one Spirit, even as ye are called in one hope of your calling; ⁵ one Lord, <u>one faith</u>, one baptism, ⁶ one God and Father of all, who is above all, and through all, and in you all. Did you hear that? There is only **one true faith**, and that is faith in **CHRIST JESUS**! There is no other name under heaven given among men whereby we must be saved, healed, delivered, set free, and transformed! **TRUE FAITH** always takes dominion over the world, flesh, and the devil! Faith in **Christ**

always produces positive results, and brings victory in every situation. Many people are operating in presumption, natural reasoning, mental acknowledgment, truly thinking that they are operating in faith (In **Christ Jesus**) when the truth of the matter is -- - **they are not!** *1 John 5:3-5 For this is the love of God, that we keep his commandments: and his commandments are not grievous. ⁴ For whatsoever is born of God overcometh the world: and this is the victory that overcometh the world, even our faith. ⁵ Who is he that overcometh the world, but he that believeth that Jesus is the Son of God?*

DID YOU KNOW THERE ARE 18 DECLERATIONS of FAITH!
<u>**18 Levels of Faith**</u>
 No faith
Lack of Faith
Little Faith
Weak Faith
Thy Faith
Common Faith
Mustard Seed Faith
Measure of Faith
Proportion of Faith
Unfeigned Faith
Precious Faith
Holy Faith
Abounding Faith
Rich Faith
Strong Faith
Great faith
 Full of Faith

DO YOU KNOW WHAT FAITH IS BASED UPON!

28 realities

God the Father, Father of lights
God his son, Jesus Christ
God the Holy Spirit
God's Ability
God's Authority
Blood of the Lamb
God's Character
God's Covenant
Crucifixion, Cross
God's Goodness
God's Holiness
God's Love
God's Mercy
The Name of JESUS
God's Nature
God's Omnipotence
God's Presence
God's Personality
God's Power
God's Promises
God's Redemption
Christ Resurrection
Christ Sacrificial Death
Stripes upon the back of Jesus
Sufferings and Agony of Jesus

Victory of Jesus
God's Will
God's Word

DID YOU KNOW THAT FAITH IN CHRIST IS CALLED!

<u>**Faith Revealed AS The**</u>

#1 Door of Faith
#2 Step of Faith
#3 Obedience of Faith
#4 Walk of Faith
#5 Household of Faith
#6 Unity of Faith
#7 Shield of Faith
#8 Joy of Faith
#9 Breastplate of Faith
#10 Fight of Faith
#11 Communication of Faith
#12 Life of Faith
#13 Law of Faith
#14 Common Faith
#15 Mystery of Faith
#16 Gift of Faith
#17 Circumcision of Faith
#18 Righteousness of Faith

DID YOU KNOW THAT FAITH HAS DIVISIONS

DIVISIONS OF FAITH!

#1 FAITH IN
#2 FAITH IS
#3 FAITH HAS
#4 FAITH DOES
#5 FAITH COMES
#6 FAITH TAKES
#7 FAITH BELIEVES

DID YOU KNOW THAT FAITH ALL WAYS JOINS ARM TO ARM WITH!

#1 Love
#2 Hope
#3 Grace
#4 Word
#5 Works
#6 Patience
#7 Obedience

CONTENTS

CHAPTER ONE   page 1
#1 Faith Given at Conception
#2 Hearing Jesus Christ Preached
#3 Meditation of the Word

CHAPTER TWO   page 27
#4 When You See Jesus
#5 BY Prayer and Fasting
#6 Sacrifice of Praise & Thanksgiving

CHAPTER THREE   page 55
#7 Assimilation by Associations
#8 Waiting upon God
#9 Being Doers of the WORD

CHAPTER FOUR   page 85
#10 Worship in Spirit & Truth
#11 When You Cry out for Mercy
#12 By Signs, Wonders & Miracles

CHAPTER FIVE   page 121
#13 Remembering what God has done
#14 Instant Obedience to Gods Voice
#15 Acknowledging Every Good Work

CHAPTER SIX   page 155
#16 Eating and Drinking Jesus Christ
#17 Abiding & Dwelling in Jesus Christ
#18 God Given Visitations, Visions & Dreams

CHAPTER SEVEN   page 187
#19 The Indwelling of Jesus Christ
#20 by Praying in the Holy Ghost

#21 by Seed Time and Harvest

CHAPTER EIGHT   **page 211**
#22 by the Prophetic Word!
#23 Impartation by the Laying on of Hands
#24 Exalting and Magnifying Jesus Christ

CHAPTER NINE   **page 229**
#25 Operating in the Gift of Faith
#26 God Will Touch Your 5 Senses
#27 Reading or Listening to Gods Word

CHAPTER TEN   **page 247**
#28 Delighting in the Word of God
Final Thoughts
How to Get More Books?

ACKNOWLEDGMENTS

*This is for our heavenly Father and His wonderful love.

*To our Lord, Savior and Master Jesus Christ, Who saved us and set us free because of His great love & Heart of obedience.

*To the Holy Spirit, who leads and guides us into the realm of faith every day.

*A special thanks to my Wife Kathleen, our precious children, Michael, Daniel, Steven, Stephanie, Catherine Yu, who is our precious daughter-in-law, and Naomi, who is now with the Lord. *And to the members of Jesus is Lord Ministries who have stayed the course with us through the good and the bad.

Dr Michael H Yeager

CHAPTER ONE

#1 Faith Given at Conception

Yes, at conception is the first way that faith comes to every human heart. Every human being when they were conceived within their mother's womb was invested with the divine seed of faith. It is extremely important that **we acknowledge this reality** in order that we do not allow our enemy (the devil) into deceiving us, into believing that we have no faith. Not only were we created with faith, but we were created by faith, by **Christ Jesus, God the Father, and the Holy Ghost!**

John 1:3 *All things were made by him; and without him was not anything made that was made.*

Let's take a look at the next two scriptures discovered in Genesis!

Genesis 1:26 *And God said, Let us make man in our <u>image</u>, after our likeness: and let them have dominion over the fish of the sea, and over the fowl of the air, and over the cattle, and over all the earth, and over every creeping thing that creepeth upon the earth.*

Genesis 1:27 *So God created man in his own <u>image</u>, in the image of God created he him; male and female created he them.*

Did you notice that man was created in the image of God! How does God operate, and function? We could talk about the character of God dealing with his love, mercy, forgiveness, long-suffering, gentleness, kindness, meekness, holiness, faithfulness, joy, goodness, faithfulness and many other attributes, but all of

1

these springs from the fact that he operates in faith. There is a very interesting Scripture that declares this found in the book of Timothy.

2 Timothy 2:13 If we believe not, yet he abideth faithful: he cannot deny himself.

And in Romans it declares..........

Romans 3:3 For what if some did not believe? Shall their unbelief make the faith of God without effect?

All of creation is sustained, maintained, and consists upon the reality of God having faith in **Himself**. We were created and made to walk in that realm of faith by trusting and having confidence, total reliance, complete dependence upon nothing but God. The only way the enemy could defeat men was by getting them out of the arena of faith. He had to sow the seed of unbelief into the soil of man's heart. Adam and his wife took the bait, thereby stepping out of the realm of faith, into a nightmare of death, poverty, fear, hate, lust, disobedience. A Pandora's Box had been opened.

Christ Jesus came to shut that box, by bringing men back into a position of absolute total faith, confidence, trust, obedience and dependence upon God.

Let's look in John 1:9 because within it is the evidence that at our conception God gave us faith.

John 1:9 That was the true Light, which lighteth <u>every man</u> that cometh into the world.

This light which lighteth up every man that comes into the world is the seed of faith, trust and confidence in God. **Jesus** boldly declared that in order to enter into the kingdom of heaven, we must have the faith of a child! Everything that **Jesus** ever spoke, was absolute truth. There was no exaggeration in anything he declared. Everything he spoke is absolute, complete, and total truth. We can and must base our life totally upon what he declared!

Matthew 18:3 And said, Verily I say unto you, Except ye be converted, and become as little <u>children</u>, ye shall not enter into the kingdom of heaven.

Mark 10:15 Verily I say unto you, Whosoever shall not receive the kingdom of God as a little <u>child</u>, he shall not enter therein.

Luke 18:17 Verily I say unto you, Whosoever shall not receive the kingdom of God as a little <u>child</u> shall in no wise enter therein.

Jesus was declaring unless you once again have the faith of a little child (this is true conversion) you will never be able to enter in! Of course we could look at all the attributes of a little child, which I believe is a natural manifestation of true faith in **Christ**!

Let us look at one more set of scriptures before we move on to the next reality of **how faith comes**! If you will believe this Scripture, It will clear up much confusion when it comes to regards to those who have not heard the gospel. Please understand faith simply takes God at his word without any argument or doubting. Now let us read Romans 1:20 -21

Romans 1:20-21 For the invisible things of him from the creation of the world are clearly seen, being understood by the things that are made, even his eternal power and Godhead; so that they are without excuse: [21] Because that, when they knew God, they glorified him not as God, neither were thankful; but became vain in their imaginations, and their foolish heart was darkened.

Did you notice that it says that man is without excuse because at some time he understood? I know this sounds extremely strange, but it's true. Well how would a child understand? Part of this mystery can be answered by Hebrews 11:3

Hebrews 11:3 Through faith we <u>understand</u> that the worlds were framed by the word of God, so that things which are seen were not made of things which do appear.

When faith is alive and active, it literally understands, not with human reasoning, but from the inner depths of the heart. At the conception of every human being, there was this invisible substance called faith. But the day came when a person knowingly, and willingly goes against the faith that is in his heart, thereby entering into a condition of what God calls death. Death is when you no longer have pure, holy faith in God in the sincerity of your heart. It is when you willingly and knowingly break the laws of God. Remember when Mary told Elizabeth her aunt that she was going to have a baby. That this baby was literally the son of God. What took place at that moment? It tells us that John within her womb as an infant leaped for joy. What caused this excitement in the heart of the unborn child John? He was **full of faith**. He understood in his mother's womb that **Jesus** was the son of God, the Lamb of God that he had come into the Earth. This brought tremendous joy to his heart. This is another reason why he could be filled with the spirit from his mother's womb. Because the Holy Ghost dwells in the atmosphere of faith.

Romans 7:9 For I was alive without the law once: but when the commandment came, sin revived, and I died.

Jesus Christ came to resurrect within the heart of every man complete and absolute faith, trust, confidence, dependence, reliance and obedience to God the **Father**! Do not allow the enemy to tell you that you were born without faith. Faith is your natural habitat, dwelling place, just like the birds in the air, and the fish in the sea. Step back in to your rightful position.

How Faith Comes

There are two experiences that I had as a child. I am convinced that all children have experiences with God, even if they do not remember them, because it is the faith of God in them that draws to them, supernatural visitations from heaven.

Touched as a Baby

Oral Roberts was conducting a large tent meeting in our area. My mother was desperate to get help for me, because of all my physical problems. She told me that Oral Roberts never laid hands on me. Yet, as she stood in the tent with a large crowd of people, something began to happen to me. She said that I began to shake uncontrollably as she was standing in the service. She did not understand what was happening. I am convinced the Spirit of God came upon me in that service over fifty-eight years ago. Never underestimate what God can do in the midst of a gathering of His saints!

How God uses Children in Heidi Baker's ministry

"I want anybody who is deaf to come to the front. Anybody who can't hear. God is going to heal tonight." Heidi Baker, who has short, swept-back blond hair, hawk-like blue eyes, speaks over a powerful sound system into a pitch-black African night.

We are in the dusty village of Mozambique, the 11th poorest nation on earth. No electricity or running water is available here. From their ragged clothes and bare feet, you can see that the people are destitute. Two trucks have brought students from Pemba, Baker's mission center. Setting up open-air screens and generator-powered projectors, they have just shown the Jesus film. Preaching followed. And now, a crowd of several hundred has gathered on the bare ground in front of the trucks for the climactic moment.

She encourages the villagers to bring all of those who are deaf because God is going to heal them. Responding to Baker's call, four people straggle to the front, standing uneasily. The audience crowds forward around them, blocking the view. Most of what happens is relayed over the booming sound system in Portuguese and translated into Makhuwa, the local language, with occasional explanations in English.

She now calls for all the children in the village to come to the front. She asked them if they believe what they just saw in the movie about Jesus. They all respond with an enthusiastic: YES! Through her interpreter she informs them that they are to lay their hands upon these deaf people. And then she is going to pray in the name of Jesus, and they will pray the exact same words, and Jesus will heal them! She asked the children: do you believe this? They respond with an enthusiastic YES!

She prays slowly with the interpreter repeating her words. The children enthusiastically pray the exact same words, commanding the deaf spirits to come out, and for their ears to be opened and healed. The atmosphere is filled with a tangible expectation. AND SURE ENOUGH EVERY ONE OF THE DEAF PEOPLE ARE HEALED. All we need is the faith of a little child.

#2 Hearing Jesus Christ Preached

*Romans 10:13 For whosoever shall call upon the name of the Lord shall be saved. 14 How then shall they call on **him** in whom they have not believed? and how shall they believe in **him** of whom they have not heard? and how shall they hear without a preacher? 15 and how shall they preach, except they be sent? as it is written, How beautiful are the feet of them that preach the gospel of peace, and bring glad tidings of good things!*

We need to begin this very important **truth in which faith comes** by looking at Romans chapter 10, starting with verse 13! *Whosoever shall call upon the name of the Lord shall be saved!* The word whosoever is important because **Jesus** also said *whosoever shall say unto this mountain*! Then in first John chapter 5 it says for *whatsoever is born of God overcomes the world, and this is the victory overcomes the world, even our faith. who is he that OVERCOMES the world, but he that believe that* **Jesus Christ** *is the son of God*. We are talking on the subject of faith in **Christ**, and **Jesus** says that he did not come to destroy, but says: *I am come that you might have life and have it more abundantly!* He was talking about his people, those called by his name. He says I want you to have life and have it more abundantly. The Greek word there for life is Zoe or life as God has it. God wants his divine life operating in you and me, but there is a lot of people in the church, (the body) that are not experiencing this abundant life. The reason why they're not experiencing this abundant life is because they are not walking by faith. They are walking by their feelings, emotions, circumstances and situations. They are slaves of their 5 senses and the elements of the world. They are not walking or living by faith, yet **Christ** wants us to have life and have it more abundantly. It can only be done by **the one who comes** to God. And **He** must believe that God is a rewarder of them that diligently seek **Him.** Now we need to look at verse 17, this is the **second way that faith comes!**

Romans *10:17 So then faith cometh by hearing, and hearing by the word of God.*

This particular verse is used quite often by people who are under the misconception that this is the only way that faith comes, and even the way they interpret it is basically wrong. In order to properly understand this Scripture, we must keep it in context. Let us look at what it says in Hebrews 11: 6

Hebrews 11:6 But without faith it is impossible to please him: for he that cometh to God must believe that he is, and that he is a rewarder of them that diligently seek him.

Notice if you truly believe, **YOU** will come to God! He that cometh to God must believe, and if you believe, you will come. You will pursue God because your faith is alive and active, thereby you will seek the face of God, if he is working in you. You will go after God like a deer after water in a dry and thirsty land! But to fully grasp this concept we must look at Romans 10 verse 13! *For whosoever shall call upon the name of the Lord shall be saved!* I want to emphasize the word Lord! We are talking about the **Lord Jesus.** *How shall they believe in <u>him</u> of whom they have not heard? And how shall they hear without a preacher?* So really the context of this particular declaration in Romans is that faith comes by hearing and hearing by the word of God that is coming out of the mouth of a preacher. Notice it did not say faith cometh by reading, faith cometh by you hearing yourself, that's another subject which we will speak about in another chapter. But this particular Scripture says that faith is going to come by hearing from a preacher. And then it tells us something about this preacher.

Romans 10:15 and how shall they preach, except they be sent? As it is written, How beautiful are the feet of them that preach the gospel of peace, and bring glad tidings of good things!

#2 **Faith comes by hearing and hearing by the preaching of a minister of the gospel, who is under the divine influence of the Holy Ghost, speaking by the Holy Spirit.**

This is a very important declaration, because **Jesus** said *my words are spirit and they are life.* For faith to be ministered by the preaching of the word, it must be done by a man who is operating in true, authentic, living, active, dynamic faith.

Hebrews 10:17 So then faith cometh by hearing, and hearing by the word of God.

Another translation does not say the word of God, but it says: *by the declaration of Jesus Christ!*

I can prove to you that biblical faith comes by hearing the proclamation of **Jesus Christ**! Faith will come by the preaching of **Jesus Christ**, who **Jesus Christ** is, what **Jesus Christ** has done and what he is about to do! Please notice the contents of Romans chapter 10 is.

Romans 10: 6 But the righteousness which is of faith speaketh on this wise, Say not in thine heart, Who shall ascend into heaven? (that is, to bring Christ *down from above:) 7 or, Who shall descend into the deep? (that is, to bring up* Christ *again from the dead.) 8 But what saith it? The word is nigh thee, even in thy mouth, and in thy heart: that is, the word of faith, which we preach; 9 that if thou shalt confess with thy mouth the* Lord Jesus, *and shalt believe in thine heart that God hath raised* him

9

from the dead, thou shalt be saved. 10 For with the heart man believeth unto righteousness; and with the mouth confession is made unto salvation. 11 For the scripture saith, Whosoever believeth on **him** *shall not be ashamed.*

Now not every minister preaches the **word of faith** which is **Jesus Christ**! Okay so you have to have the name of **Jesus Christ** on your lips, and believe in your heart that **Jesus Christ** is Lord, and that God has raised Him from the dead. We who preached **Jesus Christ** must believe that he overcame principalities, powers and made a show over the devil and demons triumphing over them in it! And this minister must have made **Jesus** Lord of his life.

The word of faith which we preach and believe, Will cause **Jesus** to be Lord over my life. **Jesus** is Lord of my hands. **Jesus** is Lord of my thoughts. **Jesus** Is Lord of my feet. **Jesus** Is Lord of my heart. **Jesus** Is Lord of my emotions. **Jesus** Is Lord of my feeling. **Jesus** Is Lord of my circumstances. **Jesus** Is Lord of my eyes. **Jesus** Is Lord of my finances. In every area of life he must be Lord! If you truly have made **Jesus** Lord of your life as a minister, then as you preach, the words you speak will be filled with the spirit and power of **Christ**.

John 6:63 It is the spirit that quickeneth; the flesh profiteth nothing: the words that I speak unto you, they are spirit, and they are life.

What is the conclusion of faith comes #2?

Faith comes by hearing, and hearing by the declaration of who Jesus Christ is, from the lips of a person who has been enabled by the ability of God to preach Jesus Christ. A person who has made Jesus Lord of their life, thereby the spirit of faith is released into the hearts of the hearers!

ALL FELL TO THE FLOOR, AS I WAS PREACHING

I was ministering in a German-speaking church called The Industrial Center of Germany. This church was situated about five stories up in a high-rise office complex. They did not have a pastor in this church at the time. They had a board of elders, and I understood one of the men was an oil tycoon. He was the one who supported all the activities and outreaches of the church. I had an interpreter with us who was a famous German worship leader and singer. When I preached at the church, I ministered a radical message on being one hundred percent, completely and totally sold out to **Jesus Christ**. I shared that there was a price to be paid to enter in to the deeper things of God, and that you had to die to the flesh in order to live in the Spirit. **Jesus** gave His everything and now it was our turn to give everything. About two-thirds of the way through this message, something amazing happened.

As I was speaking, everyone in that church literally fell out of their chairs. The Spirit of God fell in such a mighty way. Everyone in the congregation was on the floor weeping and wailing under the influence of the Spirit. I no longer had their attention so I quit preaching, got down on my knees, and started praying along with them. This continued for quite a while. Eventually the weeping and crying stopped, and people began to trickle away from the meeting. No one was talking. There was a Holy hush upon the whole congregation. One of the leaders of the church invited us down to the next floor where there had been a meal prepared for us in the fellowship hall. As we sat down to eat, I could tell that they were staring at me. I spoke to one of the men about the meeting we just came out of and asked him if this happened very often.

He replied, "Does what happen very often?"

I said, "Where all the people suddenly fall on the floor and start crying and praying?" He looked at me as if this was a dumb question. He told me they had never seen or experienced anything like this before.

Men, woman, children and babies COULD NOT MOVE or SPEAK for 2 1/2 hours

My family and I traveled out West ministering in different churches and visiting relatives in Wisconsin. We were invited to speak at a church in Minneapolis, Minnesota. The pastor actually had two different churches that he pastored. One of these churches was in the suburbs, and the other one was in the heart of Minneapolis. The larger of the two churches was in the suburbs. I was to minister at the larger church first, and then immediately go to his other church downtown. The whole congregation was in the same service that morning. There were approximately 140 to 160 people including women, men, children, and babies in the sanctuary. As I began to speak, I found myself unexpectedly speaking on the subject of: **The year that King Uzia died**, I saw the Lord high and lifted up, and his glory filled the Temple, which is found in the book of Isaiah! The unction of the Holy Ghost was upon me so strong, that it just flowed out of my belly like rivers of living water. To this day I do not remember exactly everything I said. As I was speaking, I sensed an amazing heavenly touch of God's presence upon myself and on everyone in the sanctuary.

The spirit of God was upon me in a mighty way, and yet I was aware of the time factor. In order to get to pastor bills sister church downtown Minnesota, I was not going to have time to lay hands on, or pray for anyone. If God was going to confirm his word with signs following, then he would have to do it without me being there. It turns out this is exactly what God wanted to do! When I was about at the limit of the amount of the time allotted to me, I quickly closed with a prayer. I did not say anything to the pastor, or anyone else as I grabbed my Bible to leave the sanctuary. My family was already loaded up and waiting for me in our vehicle. As I ran out the door I perceived something strange, awesome and wonderful was beginning to happen to the congregation. There was a heavy, amazing and holy hush that had come upon them.

How Faith Comes

By the time I arrived at the other church, their worship had already begun. As I went up to the pulpit to minister God's word, the Holy Spirit began to speak to me again giving me a completely different message then I had spoken at the Mother Church. God did wonderful things in the sister church downtown that afternoon as I preached a message on being radical sold out and committed to **Christ**. **Everyone ended up falling out of their chairs unto the floor to their faces, weeping and crying before the Lord**. This is not something which I have ever encouraged any congregation to do. I have seen this happen numerous times where I simply have to stop preaching because the presence of God is so strong, and so real that people cannot stay in their seats. I stopped preaching, getting on my face, and just waiting upon God, as he moved upon the people's hearts.

After that service we went back to our fifth wheel trailer at the local campgrounds where we were camping. Later in the day, I received a phone call from this pastor. He was acting rather strange and speaking very softly in a very hushed manner.

He asked me with a whisper: does that always happen after you are done preaching? I said to him, tell me what happened? He said: **as you were headed out the door, I began to melt to the floor, I could not keep standing, and I found myself pinned to the floor of the sanctuary**. I could not move or speak. Now all of the children (including babies) were in the sanctuary with the rest of the congregation. He said he personally could not move for 2 ½ hours. During this whole experience of 2 1/2 hours he did not hear another sound in the facility. For over 2 1/2 hours he just simply laid there not being able to move or speak a word under the presence and mighty hand of God. After 2 ½ hours pastor Bill was able to finally move, and to be able to get up. He had thought for sure that he was the only one still left in the church. Everybody must have gone home a long time ago, and that he was there by himself.

To his complete shock and amazement everybody was still there, laying on the floor. Nobody could move or speak for over 2 1/2 hours! Men, women, children and even the babies were still lying on the floor, not moving, talking, or crying! God was

in the house!" The tangible overwhelming solemn presence, holiness of God had come!

Pastor Bill asked me to come over to his house in order that we could talk about what happened that day in his church service. My family and I arrived, with him inviting us inside. He asked if this normally happened wherever I went. I informed him, no, but many wonderful and strange things do take place. That it did not always happen, except when I got myself into a place of complete absolute surrender and submission to **Jesus Christ**. This submission included not putting anything else but the word of God into my heart. That when I would simply seek the face of God, by pray, giving myself completely to the word, meditation, singing and worship, intimacy with the **Father**, Son and Holy Ghost, that this was the results! God is not a respecter of people, what he does for one, he will do for others!

#3 Meditation of the Word

If you study the context of Romans chapter 10 it is literally talking about the preaching of **Jesus Christ**! When ministers preach **Jesus Christ** out of a heart filled with faith, that faith is **contagious**. That's why we need to preach **Jesus Christ** because it is all about **Jesus**, through him, to him, and by him. This is why in the New Testament from Matthew to the end of the book of Revelation about 163 pages, 7,957 Scriptures, **Jesus Christ** himself is referred to in a personal intimate way over 9000 times!

At this moment we are living in an actual physical world, with our feet on the ground. This planet we are on is spinning around the sun, the moon is spinning around the earth, and we have Jupiter, Mars and Venus, all these other planets spinning around the sun. Now we call this invisible power gravitation. Gravitation is an amazing invisible force that scientists still do not fully understand. Scripture declares that **God upholds all things by the power of His Power.** I believe the invisible force we call gravitation is **God's faith** manifested. In the New Testament you can go to any chapter, and discover the subject of faith! Why because it's all about faith in **Jesus Christ!**

Acts 17:28 For in him we live, and move, and have our being; as certain also of your own poets have said, For we are also his offspring.

In the book of Romans chapter 12, we will see the **third way in which faith comes**, but first I need to give you a word of warning. Let's look in Romans chapter 14.

Romans 14:22 Hast thou faith? have it to thyself before God. Happy is he that condemneth not himself in that thing which he alloweth.

Your faith in God is not dependent upon any other person. You can go as high and deep in God by faith as you want. **Romans** chapter **14:22** is a warning, in which it is talking about the Sabbath days, holy days, meats. It is talking about the convictions of what people perceive to be the will of God. Now here is the danger, you can have convictions about what you believe to be the will of God, when it is not really his will, but now you will have to live under these convictions because anything that is not of faith is sin.

1 Timothy 4:3-5 forbidding to marry, and commanding to abstain from meats, which God hath created to be received with thanksgiving of them which believe and know the truth. 4 For every creature of God is good, and nothing to be refused, if it be received with thanksgiving: 5 for it is sanctified by the word of God and prayer.

There are many Christians who are weak in their faith. Who is weak in the faith but people who take to themselves convictions that really do not make a difference? They get caught up in all kind of crusades dealing with meats, holy days, Sabbath days, clothing, when it's really all about the character, nature, and divine attributes of God.

Romans 14:1-3 Him that is weak in the faith receive ye, but not to doubtful disputations. 2 For one believeth that he may eat all things: another, who is weak, eateth herbs. 3 Let not him that eateth despise him that eateth not; and let not him which eateth not judge him that eateth: for God hath received him. To verse :5 One man esteemeth one day above another: another esteemeth every day alike. Let every man be fully persuaded in his own mind. 6 He that regardeth the day, regardeth it unto the Lord; and he that regardeth not the day, to the Lord he doth not regard it.

The perfect will of God is revealed to us through **Jesus Christ**. He is the brightness of God's glory, the express image of his person. If you have seen **Jesus Christ**, then you have seen the **Father**. Let us now adventure into the **third way in which faith comes**.

How Faith Comes

Romans 12:12 I beseech you therefore, brethren, by the mercies of God, that ye present your bodies a living sacrifice, holy, acceptable unto God, which is your reasonable service. 2 And be not conformed to this world: but be ye transformed by the renewing of your mind, that ye may prove what is that good, and acceptable, and perfect, will of God. What is that good, and acceptable, and perfect, will of God.

The third way in which faith comes is by the renewing of your mind by meditating on Scriptures! There must be a transformation in your thinking processes by the means of meditation. You have to take your head and your heart and give them to God. I mean all of who you are, needs to be given to God.

Isaiah 26:3 Thou wilt keep him in perfect peace, whose mind is stayed on thee: because he trusteth in thee.

Proverbs 3:5 Trust in the LORD with all thine heart; and lean not unto thine own understanding.6 In all thy ways acknowledge him, and he shall direct thy paths.

The Scriptures declare that if **two be not agreed together, they cannot walk together**. Faith is when you come into complete agreement with God, his Word, and his will. Paul said by the spirit of God, be not conformed to this world, but be ye transformed (**metamorphosis**) this means being changed by the renewing of our mind.

Before your mind is transformed, renewed we are like a **caterpillar**. The number of legs and feet that a **caterpillar** has varies. There is one type of caterpillar that has 16 legs, and 16 feet, which they use to hold on to anything, and everything they can. When that **caterpillar** becomes a **Butterfly**, everything changes. Including the number of feet they have, and their purpose. All Butterflies end up with SIX legs and feet. In some species such as the monarch, the front pair of legs remains tucked up under the body most of the time. Their legs become long and slender, and something amazing happens to their feet, because within their feet are now taste buds. That means that whatever their feet touch they taste. It prevents them from eating anything that is not good for them. When they were **caterpillars** they were willing to eat everything their little feet took a hold of. You see the **Butterfly** which came from the caterpillar now lives in a completely different world. It is no longer bound by earthly things. It no longer has feet that cling to the Earth! It is free to fly above all the worries, fears, anxieties, enemies, and circumstances of life. It literally can see into the future, where it is going. It has overcome the law of gravitation, by a superior law. It is called the law of aerodynamics. We as believers, as we renew our minds leave behind the law of sin and death, entering into a new world called: **The Law of the Spirit of Life in Christ Jesus**! We need to be very picky at what we eat mentally. Whatever we place in our minds and our hearts, is what we will meditate upon. As *a man thinketh, so is he!*

Romans 8:2 For the law of the Spirit of life in Christ Jesus hath made me free from the law of sin and death.

To operate in God's kingdom, you need to **renew your mind**. Your faith level cannot be higher than that of the **renewing of your mind**. Everything that is contradictory to the word, the will, the divine nature of **Jesus Christ** must be dealt with. As we bring every thought captive to the obedience of **Christ**, our faith will soar like an eagle. Listen to what James the brother of **Jesus** said about the renewing of the mind.

James 1:21Wherefore lay apart all filthiness and superfluity of naughtiness, and receive with meekness the engrafted word, which is able to save your souls.

WE CAN NOT BE DEFEATED WHEN WE ARE LIVING, WALKING & MOVING IN FAITH!

How Faith Comes

What if I told you that your usefulness to God can only equal the level of faith you have in Christ! The faith I am referring to, is true faith. This is a faith that will take a hold of God (like Jacob wrestling with the Angel) refusing to let go, until there is a wonderful transformation in your Heart and in your Mind!

There are so many Scriptures dealing with the renewing of your mind, and the meditation of your heart, that many books could easily be written on this subject. I will share with you only a small number of Scriptures that are important to this particular chapter. Then I will share with you how you meditate.

Joshua 1:8 This book of the law shall not depart out of thy mouth; but thou shalt meditate therein day and night, that thou mayest observe to do according to all that is written therein: for then thou shalt make thy way prosperous, and then thou shalt have good success.

Psalm 1:2 But his delight is in the law of the Lord; and in his law doth he meditate day and night.

Psalm 63:6 when I remember thee upon my bed, and meditate on thee in the night watches.

Psalm 77:12 I will meditate also of all thy work, and talk of thy doings.

Psalm 119:148 Mine eyes prevent the night watches, that I might meditate in thy word.

Psalm 104:34 My meditation of him shall be sweet: I will be glad in the Lord.

Psalm 119:97 O how love I thy law! it is my meditation all the day.

Psalm 119:99 I have more understanding than all my teachers: for thy testimonies are my meditation.

1   Timothy 4:15 Meditate upon these things; give thyself wholly to them; that thy profiting may appear to all.

Psalm 39:3 My heart was hot within me, while I was musing the fire burned: then spake I with my tongue,

2   Samuel 23:2 The Spirit of the Lord spake by me, and his word was in my tongue.

What Is Meditation?

To meditate means to Muse, to Ponder, to Think Upon, To Mutter, Recite, To Talk to Yourself. It is way more than just memorization. In the most basic form it would be what we call to worry, but it's the opposite of worry. When you worry about something, it is like a record stuck in a groove that keeps playing over and over. Have you ever had a song that just would not leave your mind? You sang it to yourself in your mind, and even with your lips, because it got into your head, and your heart. This is what meditation is. We need to meditate upon the word, the will, the personality of **Jesus Christ** day and night. This will bring about a wonderful transformation.

In nature God has given to us many examples that can be applied to spiritually. I think one of the greatest examples of meditation is revealed to us through the process of dairy cows, turning green grass into wonderful white and creamy milk.

How do Cows Make Milk?

Or we could say:

How do Believers Produce Faith?

#1 First A cow only starts to produce milk once her first calf is born.

(Even so we must become impregnated by the word of God, being born again by the spirit and the water, in order to walk where Jesus walked)

#2 A cow will only produces milk for as long as she keeps eating massive amounts of living green grass, chewing the cud, and is milked. If any of these processes are stopped, she will stop producing milk.

(The believer must keep eating the living word of God, chewing it, and then doing it! Doing it would equal that of the dairy cow being milked!)

John 6:53 Then Jesus said unto them, Verily, verily, I say unto you, Except ye eat the flesh of the Son of man, and drink his blood, ye have no life in you. 54 Whoso eateth my flesh, and drinketh my blood, hath eternal life; and I will raise him up at the last day. 55 For my flesh is meat indeed, and my blood is drink indeed.

#3 Cows belong to a group of animals called ruminants. All of these animals have **four stomach compartments,** and each compartment has a specific part in digesting food. [Amazingly sheep are included in this animal group.] The transformation of grass into milk is not instantaneous, or accomplished quickly. It will take about **70 hours** for a cow to turn grass into milk!

(Even so is it with faith. As you begin to meditate upon the word consistently hour after hour, day after day, faith will begin to be produced in your heart and your life! Many believers do not have this understanding. They chew a little bit of the word, for a little bit of time, and then are disappointed when faith dose not pour out of their hearts like a mighty river)

#4 Blood has a significant part of the cow producing milk. For every **2 to 3 cups of milk** a cow makes, more than **105 gallons** of blood must travel around her udder to deliver the nutrients and water for making milk. In total a cow has about **12 gallons** of blood in her body, so her blood is always **on the move** around the udder to keep making milk.

Even so with the believer, there must be continual moving of the Holy Spirit in our lives for us to produce faith. This is why Jesus asked: will there be any faith left on the earth when he returns? It is because there is very little moving of the spirit in many church gatherings today, much less in a believer's everyday life. And yet in Ephesians it tells us to be filled with the spirit beginning in chapter 5 verse 17. It will take massive amounts of the word and the moving of the spirit to produce the faith that is necessary to live the same life that Jesus did!

#5 To produce milk, cows must eat a variety of grasses, clover and bulky fodder, which make them feel full, plus food rich in protein and energy. If the pasture (**pastor**) they are eating from is not providing the right kind of foods, it will cause the cow to produce dismal results. It only takes the cow to be eating one wrong type of vegetation for it to ruin its milk. And it can have dire consequences to the health of the cow. It could even die!

(Even so is it with the believer. If the pastor (pasture) is not providing healthy, spiritual truths, preaching the reality of Jesus Christ, His will and His purposes, it will not produce faith that prevails and overcomes the obstacles of life)

How Faith Comes

Now let us look at the four stomach compartments (digestive compartments) and their special functions:

The stomach: The heart of man, his mind, will, emotions, attitude, disposition, purpose for living could be likened unto the cows stomach.

1. The rumen

When cows graze on grass they swallow the grass half-chewed and mix it with water in their first stomach - the rumen - which can hold about **13 gallons** of chewed grass. It is here that the digestive process begins. The rumen softens and breaks down the grass with stomach juices and microbes (or bacteria).

(Even so with the believer, we begin to hide Scriptures within our heart. We memorize these Scriptures. This is the first process. The Holy Spirit can do very little with the Scriptures unto they are memorized)

2. The reticulum

In the reticulum the grass is made even softer and is formed into small wads called cuds. Each cud is then returned to the mouth where the cow chews it **40 to 60** times (for about one minute). Each card is chewed for almost an hour!

(After the believer has memorized the Scripture it now must be spoken (chewed) for at least an hour. Within this time frame the Holy Spirit begins to change the word of God from letter into spirit.)

3. The omasum

The chewed cud is swallowed into the third stomach, the omasum, where it is pressed to remove water and broken down further.

(This is where things really begin to get interesting, because now the word begins to be assimilated into your heart. It begins to take

upon it a reality that you have never known. It begins to renew and transform your mind).

King David said: My heart was hot within me, while I was musing the fire burned: then spake I with my tongue,

4. The abomasum

The grass then passes to the fourth stomach, called the abomasum, where it is digested. The digested grass then passes through the small intestine, where all the essential nutrients the cow needs to stay healthy and strong are absorbed, and some are transported to the udder.

(Life is now beginning to flood the believer. Divine wisdom and strength is beginning to overtake him or her. The reality of Christ is exploding in their minds, their thoughts, their deeds, and their actions. Even as the milk comes forth from the utter of the cow, so now the works of the kingdom are being produced through our lives. People are beginning to see, hear, and experience Jesus Christ in and through us!)

Walking through the Fire by Meditation of the WORD!

In 1979 we ended up being pastors at a little church in Three Springs, Pennsylvania. The parsonage that we lived in was very old and dilapidated. There was a large porch deck over a garage area. One day my wife was walking on this deck when she broke through the flooring. Praise God, she didn't get hurt. The church did not have very much money. The amount of fuel oil we went through to keep it warm was ridiculous. I decided to put a wood stove in the parsonage. I put it in the half-basement of the house. The floor of the basement was nothing but rocks and dirt. The wood-burning stove was a long, deep, cast-iron outfit. There was an existing chimney in the basement, so I hooked the wood stove into this chimney. It was a very old system, however, and there was so very little draft, that it was extremely hard to get a good fire going. In the process of trying to keep the fire going, I would consistently somehow place my hands against the stove. I do not know how many blisters I got from that wood stove. It seemed as if I could not help but burn my hands! You would have thought that I would have begun to believe God for wisdom not to burn my hands, but that's not what I did! Instead, I began to confess verses about the fire not being able to burn me.

This went on for a number of weeks, and sure enough, without fail, I would touch the stove by accident, and yet I was getting burned less and less. My hand or fingers would simply turn red. One day, I again touch the stove when it was literally glowing red, that's how hot the stove was. Instantly my hand hurt. I put my other hand over the burnt part of my hand and commanded the pain to cease. I confessed that I would have no blister. Sure enough, the pain left and my hand was only slightly pink.

I was cooking breakfast one morning, having just put cooking oil in a cast-iron skillet. I was making eggs, bacon, and hash browns. As I was busy making breakfast, there was a knock on the door. When I opened up the door, one of my parishioners named Paul was there. Paul and I were good friends and we would spend hours together praying and witnessing. He probably was fifteen years my senior. I invited him into the house and we began to talk about the things of God. I had completely forgotten about the cast-iron skillet on the stove. The next thing I knew; my wife was screaming. I went into the kitchen and saw that the oil in the skillet had exploded into fire, with flames reaching as high as the old pine wood kitchen cupboards. I knew if I did not move fast the whole house would go up in flames. The house was a firetrap waiting to happen. I was not thinking. I yelled for Paul to open the outside door as I was running for the stove and the skillet. I scooped the red-hot skillet up into my hands, spun around, and carried it out the door. Paul was standing out of the way and my wife was watching everything as it happened. I ran outside and flipped the pan upside down on the ground.

After a while the flames went out. I was standing and looking down at the cast-iron skillet when I suddenly realized what I had done. I looked down at my hands in complete amazement. They should have been severely burned. All that happened was that they became a little red. Not only that, but how come the flames of the burning oil did not burn me? In just a brief period of time, all the pain and the redness in my hands were gone.

Who through faith subdued kingdoms, wrought righteousness, obtained promises, stopped the mouths of lions, Quenched the violence of fire, escaped the edge of the sword, out of weakness were made strong, waxed valiant in fight, turned to flight the armies of the aliens.

CHAPTER TWO

#4 When You See Jesus

The **fourth way for faith to come** is by seeing **Jesus**! What exactly am I referring to? Am I talking about physically seeing **Jesus**? [it could include this] No, I am talking about seeing **Jesus** by a revelation of the Holy Ghost! In order to exactly understand this spiritual principle, we will take a look at a number of moments of enlightenment in people's lives in the New Testament, and how these experiences caused a radical transformation, with a tremendous increase of their faith in **Jesus Christ**. In *Matthew chapter 14* after **Jesus** had fed the multitude he instructed his disciples to enter their boat to meet him on the other side. **He** himself went up into the mountains to pray to the heavenly **Father**.

Matthew 14: 22 And straightway Jesus constrained his disciples to get into a ship, and to go before him unto the other side, while he sent the multitudes away. 23 And when he had sent the multitudes away, he went up into a mountain apart to pray: and when the evening was come, he was there alone. 24 But the ship was now in the midst of the sea, tossed with waves: for the wind was contrary. 25 And in the fourth watch of the night Jesus went unto them, walking on the sea. 26 And when the disciples saw him walking on the sea, they were troubled, saying, It is a spirit; and they cried out for fear. 27 But straightway Jesus spake unto them, saying, Be of good cheer; it is I; be not afraid. 28 And Peter answered him and said, Lord, if it be thou, bid me come unto thee on the water. 29 And he said, Come. And when Peter was come down out of the ship, he walked on the water, to go to Jesus. 30 But when he saw the wind boisterous, he was afraid; and beginning to sink, he cried, saying, Lord, save me. 31 And immediately Jesus stretched forth his hand, and caught him, and said unto him, O thou of little faith, wherefore didst thou doubt? 32 And when they were come into the ship, the wind ceased. 33 Then they that were in the ship came and worshipped him, saying, Of a truth thou art the Son of God.

When you are moving in faith you will be operating in **immediate obedience**. There will be no discussing, no arguing, or hesitation. There will be no let's think about this! You notice that **Jesus** called these men to follow him, and **immediately** they forsook everything. Some might think they were just yes men, and that's exactly what we need to be when it comes to God. All the promises in **Christ** are yes and Amen.

Now in the midst of the sea, tossed by waves, with the wind contrary to where they were trying to get, something happened. The Scriptures say that in the fourth watch of the night **Jesus** went on to them walking on the water. To me this is absolutely amazing because **Christ** is walking on the water like it's nothing in the darkness of night, in the midst of a storm. **Christ** has also proclaimed that greater works than this will we do because he was going to his **Father** which is in heaven!

When the disciples saw him walking on the water, they cried out in fear. When you are not operating in faith the very first thing that will be manifested is a tormenting, dreadful, peace robbing fear. Yet the Scriptures clearly declare that *God has not given us a spirit of fear, but of power, love, and a sound mind*. Notice what happens next, straightway **Jesus** speaks unto them saying: be of **good** cheer. He actually tells them to be happy and rejoice. Why? Because it was **Him**, **Jesus Christ**! When **Jesus** arose from the dead he told his disciples to be of *good cheer* for *I have overcome the world*. In the old covenant God told Joshua - *only be strong and courageous*! As believers in **Jesus Christ** we need to stop being afraid, don't be afraid no matter what happens, don't be afraid because the worst thing that can happen to you and me is that we could die, and be with **Christ** forever is that really so bad?

How Faith Comes

Do you know being afraid of dying early is causing a lot of believers to go through unnecessary torment, trying desperately to keep on living? I believe our fight should not be one to keep on living, but one to be trusting in **Christ** even in the mist of dying. If we just get our hearts right with God and say to the Lord, if you heal me fine, if you don't fine. In the old covenant when Nebuchadnezzar threatened to throw the three Hebrew children into the fire we can see how they responded. They said we will not bow down to you even if you throw us into the fire. When they took that stand of faith, and Nebuchadnezzar threw them into the fire, the **fourth man** showed up. If you and I will take a stand of faith, **Jesus Christ** himself will show up.

I believe at that very moment when Peter saw **Jesus** walking on the water he had a revelation of who **Jesus** was for the first time!
John 8:56 Your Father Abraham rejoiced to see my day: and he saw it, and was glad.

The old covenant saints saw **Jesus Christ** by faith. They had a revelation by the spirit and the prophetic words of the prophets pertaining to the coming of **Christ**. The faith that is revealed to us in Hebrews 11 is literally the faith they had in the coming Messiah. I cannot emphasize enough the importance of having a revelation of **Jesus Christ**. That the eyes of our understanding must be enlightened for we can see **Jesus** as he really is! **Jesus** never did anything by mistake, or accident. Every question, and every statement he made to his disciples was of the utmost importance. Let's take a look at what he said to the disciples.

Matthew 16:13 When Jesus came into the coasts of Cæsarea Philippi, he asked his disciples, saying, Whom do men say that I the Son of man am? 14 And they said, Some say that thou art John the Baptist: some, Elias; and others, Jeremias, or one of the prophets. 15 He saith unto them, But whom say ye that I am? 16 And Simon Peter answered and said, Thou art the Christ, the Son of the living God. 17 And Jesus answered and said unto him, Blessed art thou, Simon Bar-jona: for flesh and blood hath not revealed it unto thee, but my Father which is in heaven. 18 And I say also unto thee, That thou art Peter, and upon this rock I will build my church; and the gates of hell shall not prevail against it. 19 And I will give unto thee the keys of the kingdom of heaven: and whatsoever thou shalt bind on earth shall be bound in heaven: and whatsoever thou shalt loose on earth shall be loosed in heaven.

Within the context of this story there contains a treasure of wealth and revelation. Peter knew by the spirit who **Jesus** was. He seen him by the eyes of his heart. It was faith speaking out of the mouth of Peter. This faith came when he saw who **Jesus** really was. When we see who **Jesus** really is, or I should say when we see **Jesus**, we will begin to operate in faith that moves mountains. Upon this revelation of seeing who **Jesus** is, the Gates of hell will not prevail.

Let's now take a look at another very important event. Saul of Tarsus was on his way to persecute the church when out of the blue, **Jesus** appeared to him.

Acts 9:1 And Saul, yet breathing out threatenings and slaughter against the disciples of the Lord, went unto the high priest, 2 and desired of him letters to Damascus to the synagogues, that if he found any of this way, whether they were men or women, he might bring them bound unto Jerusalem. 3 And as he journeyed, he came near Damascus: and suddenly there shined round about him a light from heaven: 4 and he fell to the earth, and heard a voice saying unto him, Saul, Saul, why persecutest thou me? 5 And he said, Who art thou, Lord? And the Lord said, I am Jesus whom thou persecutest: it is hard for thee to kick against the pricks. 6 And he trembling and astonished said, Lord, what wilt thou have me to do? And the Lord said unto him, Arise, and go into the city, and it shall be told thee what thou must do.

How Faith Comes

When he saw **Jesus** His whole life was forever radically changed. Up to this moment he had no faith in his heart that **Jesus** was the **Christ**, the Messiah. But now that he has seen **Jesus**, faith explodes in his heart, causing him to confess him as Lord. He completely surrenders himself to the will of the **Father** because he has seen **Jesus**. When we truly see **Jesus** we also will experience an explosion of faith that causes us to surrender all, and to follow him!

Acts 26:14And when we were all fallen to the earth, I heard a voice speaking unto me, and saying in the Hebrew tongue, Saul, Saul, why persecutest thou me? it is hard for thee to kick against the pricks. 15 And I said, Who art thou, Lord? And he said, I am Jesus whom thou persecutest. 16 But rise, and stand upon thy feet: for I have appeared unto thee for this purpose, to make thee a minister and a witness both of these things which thou hast seen, and of those things in the which I will appear unto thee;

Did you notice he declared I have appeared unto you for this purpose? This is why **Christ** will appear unto you and me in order to radically transform and change us. That we may go forth and set the captives free. Of course there are different levels of seeing **Jesus**. When we finally lay our Eyes upon him at his return, or at our departure to heaven, we will be completely like him because we will see him as he is.

1   John 3:2 Beloved, now are we the sons of God, and it doth not yet appear what we shall be: but we know that, when he shall appear, we shall be like him; for we shall see him as he is.

As we look upon **Christ** we are changed from glory to glory. Our faith begins to dramatically increase.

2   Corinthians 3:18 But we all, with open face beholding as in a glass the glory of the Lord, are changed into the same image from glory to glory, even as by the Spirit of the Lord.

The day of our complete transformation is almost upon us. But the glorious good news is that we do not have to wait until that moment. That if we will cry out to God, he will open up the eyes of our understanding, in order that we will see **Christ** in all of his glory.

#4 Seeing Jesus is the fourth major way that faith comes.

1 Corinthians 13:12 For now we see through a glass, darkly; but then face to face: now I know in part; but then shall I know even as also I am known.

Go Tell My Children

I was standing in my office in the midst of prayer one day looking towards the east, which was nothing but my office wall. To my shock and amazement, **Jesus Christ** stepped right through the wall and into my office! This happened so fast that it frightened me. I was only about four feet away from this wall. When He stepped into my room, He did not say a word to me, but just kept walking right toward me.

The next thing I knew, **Jesus** walked right into my body. It was one of the strangest experiences I have ever had. My body did not resist in the least. It was as if my body was made for Him to dwell in. It was almost like when someone comes home to their house, opens the door, and simply steps in. When **Jesus** stepped into me, His face would've been looking out of the back of my head. I know this is hard to believe, but I literally felt Him turn around inside of me. His arms and hands went into my arms and hands. His legs and feet went into my legs and feet. The moment **Jesus** was in His proper position; I instantly grew a hundred feet tall! I was gigantic in size. My head and more than half of my body was outside of the building I was in, and I was looking down upon everything. My whole being was filled with amazing power, authority, and knowledge. All the problems and difficulties of this world were laughable compared to the One who was within me. All of creation itself could not compare to Him!

As fast as this experience began, it was over. The next thing I knew, I was back to normal size. Then the Spirit of the Lord spoke something to me that would change the course of my life forever. He said to me, *Go tell my children who they are! They know not who they are!*

The reason why so many Christians walk around defeated is because they've never had a quickening of the Spirit of the revelation of who **Christ** really is. They do not realize that the same **Jesus Christ** who overcame principalities and powers, rulers of darkness, and spiritual wickedness in high places now lives in them. The very one who brought all things into existence now lives in us? **Christ** in us the hope of glory!

To whom God would make known what is the riches of the glory of this mystery among the Gentiles; which is Christ in you, the hope of glory: Whom we preach, warning every man, and teaching every man in all wisdom; that we may present every man perfect in Christ Jesus: Where unto I also labour, striving according to his working, which worketh in me mightily (Colossians 1:27

Dr Michael H Yeager

#5 BY Prayer and Fasting

We need to understand the importance of faith. I think that most believers have not really grasped the importance of Faith.

Hebrews 11:6 ***But without faith it is impossible to please him: for he that cometh to God must believe that he is, and that he is a rewarder of them that diligently seek him.***

Hebrew Chapter 11 is considered the **Faith Hall of Fame**. These are those who by faith fulfilled the will of God. And because they had faith that produced obedience and action, they accomplished amazing and impossible task. Of course Hebrews 11 is an account of the Old Testament saints. How much greater can be accomplished now with the New Testament, based upon better promises through the blood of **Jesus Christ**. This book is specifically written to help you enter into that realm of faith where all things are possible. Let us now look at the fifth way that faith comes beginning in Matthew 17:14

*Matthew 17:14 **And when they were come to the multitude, there came to him a certain man, kneeling down to him, and saying, 15 Lord, have mercy on my son: for he is lunatick, and sore vexed: for ofttimes he falleth into the fire, and oft into the water. 16 And I brought him to thy disciples, and they could not cure him. 17 Then Jesus answered and said, O faithless and perverse generation, how long shall I be with you? how long shall I suffer you? bring him hither to me. 18 And Jesus rebuked the devil; and he departed out of him: and the child was cured from that very hour. 19 Then came the disciples to Jesus apart, and said, Why could not we cast*** *him out? 20 And Jesus said unto them, Because of your unbelief: for verily I say unto you, If ye have faith as a grain of mustard seed, ye shall say unto this mountain, Remove hence to yonder place; and it shall remove; and nothing shall be impossible unto you. 21* **Howbeit this kind goeth not out but by prayer and fasting.**

We need to look very carefully at the attitude of **Jesus** when it came to unbelief. He said that his generation was faithless, which equates to being rebellious, obstinate, stubborn, and unbelieving. He said how long I will have to suffer you. Unbelief is completely opposite from that of faith, trusting and believing. When you and I do not trust God and what he has said, we are literally calling him a liar. It is hard for us to wrap our carnal minds around this truth. The greatest offense to God is our refusal to trust and believe him. It literally cuts us from all that God desires to do in, through, and by us.

Hebrews 6:18 That by two immutable things, in which it was impossible for God to lie, we might have a strong consolation, who have fled for refuge to lay hold upon the hope set before us:

James 1:17 Every good gift and every perfect gift is from above, and cometh down from the Father of lights, with whom is no variableness, neither shadow of turning. God is not a man that he should lie, nor the son of man that he should repent. As he said it, and will he not do it. Has he spoken it, and will he not bring it to pass.

He told his disciples if you had faith the size of a grain of mustard seed........*nothing would be impossible unto you!* **Christ** was not exaggerating when he declared this truth. Every word he spoke was absolute, pure, unadulterated truth. We can stake our eternal and immortal souls upon his words. They asked him: why could we not cast these devils out? Notice unequivocally **because of your unbelief**! Or you could say: because you are not operating in faith that is in me.

How Faith Comes

Yeah but in verse 21, did not **Jesus** say that this kind only comes out by prayer and fasting? I think we need to ask ourselves, was he really speaking about the devil, or the unbelief. One reason the disciples were moving in unbelief was because of what they were hearing from the father about his son's condition. If you look at the other Gospels you'll notice in them that the father of this demon possessed boy, was obsessed with the manifestations and shenanigans of the demons that were in his son. Listen very carefully! Any time somebody brags about the devil, in whatever circumstance they find themselves in, they are not operating in faith. **Jesus** in one of the other Gospels simply asked this man, when did this come upon your son? **Christ** knew that somehow the door had been opened for the demons to come into this young boy. But the father began to go on in a braggadocio's manner of the manifestations of these devils. That's when **Jesus** declared they were a faithless generation. Please get it deep into your heart, **never brag about the devil**, your problems, or evil. Notice, I'm not telling you to ignore them, I'm simply saying do not boast or brag about them.

Ephesians 5:11 And have no fellowship with the unfruitful works of darkness, but rather reprove them. 12 For it is a shame even to speak of those things which are done of them in secret. 13 But all things that are reproved are made manifest by the light: for whatsoever doth make manifest is light.

The spirit of unbelief is so deep in every one of us that it will take prayer and fasting for it to come out. Now let us for just a moment break down these two words.

#1 Prayer

When we are talking about prayer, I am not referring to some type of religious ceremony. Let us get right to the nitty-gritty. It is divine intimate fellowship with the **Father**, **Son** and **Holy Ghost**. It is that invisible umbilical cord connected to God. And what is it that we pray? We pray the known will and purposes Of the **Father**! We pray the word of God, within biblical context.

1 Thessalonians 5:17 Pray without ceasing.

2 Timothy 1:3 I thank God, whom I serve from my forefathers with pure conscience, that without ceasing I have remembrance of thee in my prayers night and day;

Philippians 4:6 Be careful for nothing; but in everything by prayer and supplication with thanksgiving let your requests be made known unto God.

Many erroneously teach that there is power in prayer, but in truth there isn't. The power is not in prayer, for many pray to false deities, idols, and religions. The power is not in the prayer, but in the one we are praying to. And he is the one that has all power, authority and dominion. As we are speaking to God, as we pray his will and his word, faith will begin to rise in our heart. When we pray the spirit of the Lord will begin to fall upon us like rain. And even as rain causes the seed to bud, and to bring forth fruit, so our faith will begin to grow. The more intimate we grow with God, the greater our faith will become. Now let us look at fasting!

#2 Fasting

Dealing with the subject of fasting could be a book within itself. Many have taught mystical things upon this subject. There are books that are attributing things to fasting which the Scriptures do not teach. In this particular context we are dealing with the subject of denying our flesh! I am talking about driving out unbelief. We must say **no** to our flesh, by faith. This fasting does not only deal with the subject of food, but desires and actions that are against the will of God. Denying our flesh is actually an act of faith even as prayer is an act of faith in **Christ**. Faith is like your physical muscles in your body. If you do not use them, they begin to shrivel up and become useless. But if you will exercise them on a daily basis, they will become strong and powerful. As we exercise our faith by prayer and fasting, it will become strong and solid in **Christ**.

Matthew 16:24 Then said Jesus unto his disciples, If any man will come after me, let him deny himself, and take up his cross, and follow me.

Mark 8:34 And when he had called the people unto him with his disciples also, he said unto them, whosoever will come after me, let him deny himself, and take up his cross, and follow me.

Titus 2:12 Teaching us that, denying ungodliness and worldly lusts, we should live soberly, righteously, and godly, in this present world;

Let us delve a little bit deeper into the subject of unbelief by looking at what Paul declared in the book of Romans. It is important that we recognize that unbelief must not be allowed to live in our lives. It is the seed of unbelief that is the root cause of all of man's wickedness and sin.

Romans 11: 19 Thou wilt say then, The branches were broken off, that I might be graffed in. 20 Well; because of <u>unbelief</u> they were broken off, and thou standest by <u>faith</u>. Be not highminded, but fear: 21 for if God spared not the natural branches, take heed lest he also spare not thee. 22 Behold therefore the goodness and severity of God: on them which fell, severity; but toward thee, goodness, if thou continue in his goodness: otherwise thou also shalt be cut off. 23 And they also, if they abide not still in <u>unbelief,</u> shall be graffed in: for God is able to graff them in again.

Unbelief is extremely demonic and diabolical. It says: I do not have to obey God! Unbelief is literally the voice of the devil speaking to all of us, accusing God, and making him a liar. But let God be true, and everything else a lie. Did you know that the Bible says whatever is not of faith is sin! The reason why the **Father** said about the son; **This Is My Son in Whom I Am Well Pleased**, is because he had no unbelief operating in his mind or heart. He gave absolutely no place to the devil. Now that same **Jesus** is in us. We need to put our faith and confidence in him, by allowing him to rise up within us to overcome every work of unbelief.

*Faith is the voice of God!   *Unbelief is the voice of the devil!

Luke 4:4 And Jesus being full of the Holy Ghost returned from Jordan, and was led by the Spirit into the wilderness, 2 being forty days tempted of the devil. And in those days he did eat nothing: and when they were ended, he afterward hungered....................14 And Jesus returned in the power of the Spirit into Galilee: and there went out a fame of him through all the region round about. 15 And he taught in their synagogues, being glorified of all.

If we closely examined Luke chapter 4, we would discover that **Jesus** was deep in prayer during this whole time of testing. He was in constant communion with his Heavenly **Father**. During these 40 days, he denied his flesh any earthly food. And then in verse 14 it says he returned in the power of the spirit. Where people are full of faith, they will be full of power, and of the Holy Ghost. To have this type of faith, there must be continual communion with God, and a denial of your flesh. I'm not saying that you will have to go 40 days without natural food.

There must be a lifestyle of self-denial. We must deny ourselves from anything that is displeasing to the heavenly **Father**. We must also deny ourselves anything that would get between us, and God's divine plan for our lives. After **Jesus** came out of the wilderness, by passing the test, denying the flesh, he was filled with the power of the spirit and he set the captives free. From then on miracles began to flow like a mighty river out of his innermost being. Now you might say, it was the Holy Ghost, and you would be absolutely correct. The Holy Ghost uses vessels that are prepared for the master's use, full of faith in **Christ**.

Acts 6:8 And Stephen, full of faith and power, did great wonders and miracles among the people.

Acts 11:24 For he was a good man, and full of the Holy Ghost and of faith: and much people was added unto the Lord.

How Faith Comes

God did move upon those within the early church to pray and fast. Prayer and fasting does not change the mind or the heart of God, but it brings us into a place of harmony with God! **It is a place of Faith and Power!**

Acts 10:30 And Cornelius said, Four days ago I was fasting until this hour; and at the ninth hour I prayed in my house, and, behold, a man stood before me in bright clothing,

Acts 13:2 As they ministered to the Lord, and fasted, the Holy Ghost said, Separate me Barnabas and Saul for the work whereunto I have called them.

Acts 13:3 And when they had fasted and prayed, and laid their hands on them, they sent them away.

Acts 14:23And when they had ordained them elders in every church, and had prayed with fasting, they commended them to the Lord, on whom they believed.

Let us look at one more example of the life of **Jesus** in the Gospel of Luke chapter 22. **Jesus** is our supreme example of walking, living, moving and operating in faith.

Luke 22:39 And Jesus came out, and went, as he was wont, to the mount of Olives; and his disciples also followed him. 40 And when he was at the place, he said unto them, Pray that ye enter not into temptation. 41 And he was withdrawn from them about a stone's cast, and kneeled down, and prayed, 42 saying, Father, if thou be willing, remove this cup from me: nevertheless not my will, but thine, be done. 43 And there appeared an angel unto him from heaven, strengthening him. 44 And being in an agony he prayed more earnestly: and his sweat was as it were great drops of blood falling down to the ground. 45 And when he rose up from prayer, and was come to his disciples, he found them sleeping for sorrow, 46 and said unto them, Why sleep ye? rise and pray, lest ye enter into temptation.

Jesus told his disciples that they must pray (Have Communion with the **Father**) lest they enter into temptation. First John chapter 5 says that is faith (in **Christ**) that overcomes the world!

#5 Prayer and fasting is the fifth way that God has provided for faith to come, grow, and mature!

Jesus in the time of his greatest test and trial, prayed without ceasing. When he said, not my will be done, but yours **Father**. This was self-denial, fasting that which was not God's will, that the **Father**'s will might be done. Notice the Scripture says an angel came to strengthen him. Why? Because he was operating in pure, holy faith. Faith is an invisible magnet that will draw God to you. The angelic world will come rushing to a man or woman moving in this type of faith. It's like the attraction of a flower to a honeybee. You want God to show up in your life? Then you need to begin to move in this realm of faith. How can this be accomplished? **By prayer and fasting!**

Where Is the Man I Married?

I began to grow a little bit cold and lukewarm in my spiritual walk with God. Now I still was very much active in the church as a pastor, but I wasn't flowing in the Holy Ghost. My wife became very concerned about me. Unbeknownst to me, she began to pray and intercede on my behalf.

Kathee's Perspective:

My heart yearned for the man I married. Michael was not on fire for God like he once was. He had become burdened by the woes and cares of life and the church. He was miserable, and making us all miserable with him! My prayer to God was to bring back the man I had married, and make him more on fire for God. I began anointing everything that Mike touched with oil: his truck, his clothes, even his computer.

However, my prayers did not appear to be very effective, that is, until the day the Spirit of God came upon me! A supernatural spirit of travail overtook me. This time as I prayed, I anointed his pillows and things with my tears instead of oil. I had truly touched heaven, because that very night when Mike returned home, God was waiting for him!

Back to Michael :

When I came home from church, Kathee was already in bed asleep. I slipped out of my clothes and crawled into bed. The minute I laid my head upon my pillow, the overwhelming power of God's conviction hit me. It didn't seem fair! Kathee was sleeping peacefully, but I was about to lose my sleep, and so much more!

Immediately I began to weep and cry. The conviction of God so overwhelmed me, I had to get out of bed and begin to pray. I prayed all night long in this spirit of conviction. I kept praying through the next whole day. It was so strong upon me that I was not able to stop.

Not only could I not stop praying, but I had no desire for physical food. It wasn't as if I decided not to eat, it was because I could not eat. The only thing I could do was drink water and pray. This went on one whole day. After the first day it did not lift, but instead it increased. I went two days; then three days. This continued for the next forty days and nights. All I could basically do was pray and fast.

I do not want you to be led to believe that I did not drive my car, preach in the pulpit, check the mail, or do the necessary natural things; I did all those things. However, the Spirit of God was on me in a mighty way. Right after God dealt with me this way, we had a wonderful move of God in our home and church.

My little children, of whom I travail in birth again until Christ be formed in you

#6 The Sacrifice of Praise & Thanksgiving

Many ministers today are declaring that everything that happens to people is God's fault. This is one of the most grievous and ridiculous lies propagated by the devil. People teach that God is in control of everything, which is absolutely not the truth. Yes, if God so desired he could stop humanity in its tracks, and he will someday. But at this moment in time he has given us a choice to make. We can choose to follow him, or disobey. And based upon these decisions we will reap either life or death! When people declare that God is in control of everything, it simply reveals their utter ignorance of the workings, the dealings of God. Many bad things take place because we are not submitted, yielded, and obedient to the Lord. It is also because of the fact that many are ignorant of God's will, or they are not taking the authority which is given to us. The thief comes to steal, kill, and destroy. **Jesus** said: I am come that you might have life, and have it more abundantly. We overcome the world, the flesh and the devil by faith in **Jesus Christ**!

The purpose of this book is to help you increase and grow in faith that is in **Christ Jesus**. Many have realized that they need an education to be successful in the world, so that pay whatever price they need to, and do whatever it takes to get one. Many today are in desperate need of medical help, and are willing to do whatever it takes in order to get better. There are many other examples I could use pertaining to people giving all they have to possess something they need. The greatest need of all is for us to have faith in **Christ**.

1 John 5:3 For this is the love of God, that we keep his commandments: and his commandments are not grievous. 4 For whatsoever is born of God overcometh the world: and this is the victory that overcometh the world, even our faith. 5 Who is he that overcometh the world, but he that believeth that Jesus is the Son of God?

God has given to us amazing tools, weapons, and spiritual truths in order that we might become partakers of his divine nature. His divine nature will only be manifested in us to the degree of our Faith in **Christ Jesus**.

Heb 10:15 By him therefore let us offer the <u>sacrifice</u> of praise to God continually, that is, the fruit of our lips giving thanks to his name.

Notice the word sacrifice in this Scripture. Hebrews is a tremendous book that reveals the sacrifice that **Christ** made for our salvation. Within this book is also revealed that God requires us to continue to sacrifice, not as in the old covenant with the shedding of the blood of animals, but in our life and conduct. It takes faith in order for us to **give thanks and praise to God** when in the natural there seems to be no reason why we should rejoice. I can honestly tell you that this has been one of the number one ways that God has allowed me to receive many miracles. As I have rejoiced, praised, thanked and worshiped God in the midst of the hardship, faith has risen up within my heart in order for me to possess that which God had promised. At the end of this chapter I will share with you numerous experiences I've had over 40 years pertaining to this truth.

In the old covenant sacrifices were extremely important beginning with Able, Abraham, Isaac, Jacob, and all the patriarchs of old. This sacrifice of praise and thanksgiving is extremely important in the development of our faith in **Christ Jesus**. Let us take a moment and look at some of the definitions for the words revealed to us in verse 15.

Praise: to speak highly of, complement, applaud, standing ovation, salute, or we could simply say YEA to Jesus!

Sacrifices will always cost you something which your flesh will not want to give. When I am in dire circumstances my emotions and feelings do not want to praise God in the mist of the terrible situation. But if I will simply do this by faith, it will bring about a miraculous change in me, which will bring glory to the **Father**. This will be well pleasing to our Heavenly **Father**, causing God to take notice of us. You see faith has a divine fragrance that will attract the attention of heaven. This is not in any way exaggerated, but absolute truth. God is looking for those whose hearts are in agreement (in faith) with him!

2 Chronicles 16:9For the eyes of the Lord run to and fro throughout the whole earth, to shew himself strong in the behalf of them whose heart is perfect toward him.

Hebrews 10:15 also says we are to offer unto God the sacrifice continually! It is not to be spasmodic, temporary, or when we feel like it, but continually offering onto God praise and thanksgiving. Let us look at this work continually.

Continually: at all times, endlessly, always, evermore, forevermore, perpetually, on a regularly basis!

This word **continually** implies that it must be a daily, moment by moment lifestyle. I cannot emphasize the importance of this act of faith sufficiently. Many are defeated because they will not due the word of God. Faith cannot and will not grow in an atmosphere of disobedience.

Psalm 34:1 I will bless the Lord at all times: his praise shall continually be in my mouth.

Acts 16:25 And at midnight Paul and Silas prayed, and sang praises unto God: and the prisoners heard them.

Ephesians 5:20 Giving thanks always for all things unto God and the Father in the name of our Lord Jesus Christ;

Psalm 145:1 I will extol thee, my God, O king; and I will bless thy name for ever and ever.2 Every day will I bless thee; and I will praise thy name for ever and ever.

1 Thessalonians 5:18 In everything give thanks: for this is the will of God in Christ Jesus concerning you.

Colossians 3:17 And whatsoever ye do in word or deed, do all in the name of the Lord Jesus, giving thanks to God and the Father by him.

Psalm 71:8 Let my mouth be filled with thy praise and with thy honour all the day.

Let us take a look at another set of very important scriptures.

Colossians 2: ⁵For though I be absent in the flesh, yet am I with you in the spirit, joying and beholding your order, and the stedfastness of your faith in Christ.⁶ As ye have therefore received Christ Jesus the Lord, so walk ye in him: ⁷ rooted and built up in him, and stablished in the faith, as ye have been taught, abounding therein with thanksgiving.

Our roots must go deep into **Christ**. He is the vine, and we are the branches. All of our life flows from **Christ** into us, into every fiber of our being. **Christ** lives in our hearts by faith, this is why it is so important that our faith in **Jesus Christ** must increase on a daily moment by moment basis. Please notice that Paul said that we abound with **Thanksgiving**. This is an amazing revelation, that if you will take a hold of this truth, it will transform your life. The definition for abounding means: overflowing, increasing, multiplication! There are many Scriptures that confirm this in the New Testament and in the Old Testament.

Psalm 23:5 Thou preparest a table before me in the presence of mine enemies: thou anointest my head with oil; my cup runneth over.

How was David's cup running over? It was by the fact that he constantly was giving thanks to God. Those who are consistently, moment by moment giving thanks to God, no matter what the circumstances they find themselves in, the Scripture declares that they are constantly partaking of a continual feast.

Proverbs 15:15All the days of the afflicted are evil: but he that is of a merry heart hath a continual feast.

Thanksgiving reveals a heart that is filled with appreciation, gratitude, gratefulness which Actually is an expression of faith. **Thank you Lord, I just want to thank you**: sang by Andre Crouch is one of my favorite songs. Not only is it faith in action, but it literally will cause you to take off like a rocket in the development of your faith.

Acts 16: 23 And when they had laid many stripes upon them, they cast them into prison, charging the jailor to keep them safely: 24 who, having received such a charge, thrust them into the inner prison, and made their feet fast in the stocks.25 And at midnight Paul and Silas prayed, and sang praises unto God: and the prisoners heard them. 26 And suddenly there was a great earthquake, so that the foundations of the prison were shaken: and immediately all the doors were opened, and every one's bands were loosed.

Not only did Paul and Silas operate in the realm of Faith, but through this experience their Faith had a sudden spurt of growth. When we operate in faith God will always supernaturally divinely intervene and show up. Let us look at another Scripture.

Psalm 100:4 Enter into his gates with thanksgiving, and into his courts with praise: be thankful unto him, and bless his name.

We could expand on this Scripture a little bit deeper, even change it slightly to have a correct understanding and interpretation. Let's do that for a moment.

Psalm 100:4 Enter into his gates (of faith) with thanksgiving, and into his courts (of trust) with praise: be thankful unto him, and bless his name.

With the sacrifice of praise and thanksgiving we enter into a new world, the divine spiritual world of the heavenly realm where all things are possible

Psalm 100:3 Know ye that the Lord he is God:it is he that hath made us, and not we ourselves;we are his people, and the sheep of his pasture.4 Enter into his gates with thanksgiving,and into his courts with praise:be thankful unto him, and bless his name.5 For the Lord is good; his mercy is everlasting;and his truth endureth to all generations.

This is why our hearts should be filled with thanksgiving and praise, because the **Lord** is good, yes good, and his mercy is everlasting. Let the sacrifice of thanksgiving flow out of our bellies like rivers of living water. Then there will rise up within us a faith that will overcome the world, the flesh, and the devil. Our faith cannot but help to grow when our hearts are filled with the atmosphere of praise, and thanks giving. The flip side of this coin is that unbelief cannot help but grow like a weed when there is grumbling, griping, complaining, faultfinding, an unappreciative and thankless hearts! Out of over 40 years of ministry you cannot believe how many people I run into that call themselves Christians who are Grumblers, Gripers, complainers, faultfinders and just simply negative. And yet they do not understand why they are living such defeated lives.

Colossians 1: 12 giving thanks unto the Father, which hath made us meet to be partakers of the inheritance of the saints in light: 3:15 And let the peace of God rule in your hearts, to the which also ye are called in one body; and be ye thankful. 16 Let the word of Christ dwell in you richly in all wisdom; teaching and admonishing one another in psalms and hymns and spiritual songs, singing with grace in your hearts to the Lord. 17 And whatsoever ye do in word or deed, do all in the name of the Lord Jesus, giving thanks to God and the Father by him.

How Faith Comes

The word of God is full of Scriptures commanding us to give thanks, over and over. This is good rich soil in which your faith will grow exceedingly, and become strong and great in **Christ Jesus**.

1 Thessalonians 5:18 In everything give thanks: for this is the will of God in Christ Jesus concerning you.

Ephesians 5:20 Giving thanks always for all things unto God and the Father in the name of our Lord Jesus Christ;

Philippians 4:6 Be careful for nothing; but in everything by prayer and supplication with thanksgiving let your requests be made known unto God.

Psalm 34:1 I will bless the Lord at all times: his praise shall continually be in my mouth.

Psalm 95:2 Let us come before his presence with thanksgiving, and make a joyful noise unto him with psalms.

Psalm 100:2 Serve the Lord with gladness: come before his presence with singing.

Now believe me when I tell you that I have hundreds of stories I could tell you, but this is only one of them.

Victory over Tumors by Sacrifice of Thanks Giving!

I woke up one morning with tremendous pain in my lower abdomen. I lifted up my shirt and looked down where the pain was. There was a lump on my abdomen about the size of an acorn. I laid my hands on it immediately, commanding it to go.

I said "You lying devil, by the stripes of **Jesus** I am healed and made whole." After I spoke to the lump, the pain became excruciating and overwhelmingly worse. All that day I walked the floor crying out to God, and praising him that His Word is real and true. I went for a walk on the mountain right behind the parsonage. It was a long day before I got to sleep that night. When I awoke the next morning the pain was even more severe. It felt like somebody was stabbing me in my gut with a knife. I lifted up my shirt and looked and there was another lump. Now I had two lumps in my lower abdomen. I laid my hands on them, commanding them to go. Tears were rolling down my face, as I spoke the Word. I lifted my hands toward heaven and kept praising God that I was healed. Even though I did not see any change, I kept praising God. All the symptoms were telling me that God's Word is a lie, and that I was not healed by the stripes of **Jesus**. But I knew that I was healed. It was another long day. It seemed as if I could never get to sleep that night. The pain was continual and non-stop!

When I got up the next morning the pain had intensified even more. Once again I looked at my abdomen and to my shock there was another lump the size of an acorn. Now I had three of these nasty lumps and each were about the size of an acorn. I did not think that the pain could get any worse, but it was. Once again I laid my hands on these tumors, commanding them to go in the name of **Jesus Christ** of Nazareth. I declared that by the stripes of
Jesus I am healed! It felt like a knife sticking in my gut all that day and night. I lifted my hands, and with tears rolling down my face, kept praising God that I was healed. By faith I began to dance before the Lord a victory dance, praising God that I was healed by the stripes of **Jesus**. I went to bed that night hurting worse than ever. All night I tossed and turned and moaned, all the while thanking God that I was not going to die but that I was healed. I got up the next morning, and all of the tumors and pain were gone. They have never come back.

Thanking God for Food & Money WE Did Not Have

I was up early in the morning, as my routine was. It was time for me to talk to God about our needs. We were in Germany doing missionary work, and the apartment we were in had a very small front room with sliding doors. When you came through the front door you had to go down a long hallway. Then on the right-hand was a small kitchen, the left-hand was the bedroom. Straight ahead was the front room. I was in this front room praying and crying out to God. I never complain, gripe, or tell God what is wrong when I pray. Prayer, supplication, and thanksgiving are the order of the day, so I was talking to the **Father** in the name of **Jesus**. I knew He already knew what we needed. Still, He tells us in His Word to let Him know what we need. After I was done talking to the **Father**, I stepped into the realm of praise and thanksgiving. I lifted my hands and began to dance before the Lord. My dance is not an elaborate orchestrated symbolic performance. It is just me lifting my feet, kind of kicking them around and jumping a little bit in a rather comical, childlike fashion. Some people really think they've got to get some kind of elaborate system of swinging arms and bodies. I just keep it really simple, sincere, and from my heart. You see we were completely out of food, money and gas for our car. Our one year old son was having to depend on mom for all of his nourishment.

While I had been seeking God, my wife was in the kitchen cleaning up. In the midst of me singing in tongues and dancing before the Lord, there was a knock on the apartment door, which I did not hear. My wife did hear the knocking, put down her dishes, and headed for the door. Now as far as we knew no one knew where we were staying. My wife opened the door, and there standing at the door was a tall, distinguished-looking German gentleman. He informed her that he had been looking for us. He said that had been hunting us down because God had used us in a service where he had experienced his first supernatural encounter.

Dr Michael H Yeager

My wife came to the front room informing me about the gentleman who was at the door. I walked down the skinny hallway to where this gentleman was standing to speak to him. I did have a recollection of meeting him at a previous service. I had prayed for him to be filled with the Holy Ghost, and I remember him speaking in tongues, at the time I had no idea of his background. He then began to give me quite an impressive resume of who he was. It turns out that he was a college professor at a local German college. He shared with us how he struggled with believing in the supernatural because of his superior intellect, but when he came to the service were I was ministering, his world was turned upside down. He had experienced God! After he had left that meeting, he said the Spirit of the Lord was upon him. He said the Lord spoke to him for the first time he could ever remember. The Lord told him specifically that he was to find me and give me a specific amount of money.

Ever since the Lord had spoken to him a number of days previously, he had been trying to discover where we were. He had just learned the address here we were at from someone at a church we had been ministering. Now here he was at our door, during the exact same time when I had been praying—praising and thanking God for the finances and food we needed. Before he left that day he handed us an envelope. After he was gone we opened up the envelope, and it was exceedingly abundantly above all that we could ask or hope for. We did not have any more financial needs until we left Germany.

CHAPTER THREE

#7 Assimilation by Associations

1 John 5:3 For this is the love of God, that we keep his commandments: and his commandments are not grievous. ⁴ For whatsoever is born of God overcometh the world: and this is the victory that overcometh the world, even our faith. ⁵ Who is he that overcometh the world, but he that believeth that Jesus is the Son of God?

We overcome by the blood of lamb and the word of our testimony. We must have faith that overcomes the world, the flesh, and the devil. The Scriptures imply that there's nothing impossible to those who believe. Throughout the New Testament we are called believers.

Matthew 17:20
And Jesus said unto them, Because of your unbelief: for verily I say unto you, If ye have faith as a grain of mustard seed, ye shall say unto this mountain, Remove hence to yonder place; and it shall remove; and <u>nothing shall be impossible</u> unto you.

We were created and made to walk in this realm of Faith where all things are possible. Every believer needs to study and read very carefully **Hebrews 11**. This particular chapter gives to us over 50 different major events that happened in the lives of people who lived and walked by faith in **Christ Jesus**. Yes we are saved by grace through faith and not by works, but read the next verse, which declares we are created unto good works. These good works proceed from, and are given birth to by trusting in **Christ Jesus**. It is all by faith and without faith in **Christ Jesus** it is impossible to overcome. We need to begin this particular chapter by looking at the children of Israel as they come to the Jordan River, and are getting ready to enter into the Promised Land. The 12 spies have just returned from spying out the land, and bringing back a large cluster of grapes.

Numbers 13: ²⁷ And they told him, and said, We came unto the land whither thou sentest us, and surely it floweth with milk and honey; and this is the fruit of it. ²⁸ Nevertheless the people be strong that dwell in the land and the cities are walled, and very great: and moreover we saw the children of Anak there. ²⁹ The Amalekites dwell in the land of the south: and the Hittites, and the Jebusites, and the Amorites, dwell in the mountains: and the Canaanites dwell by the sea, and by the coast of Jordan. ³⁰ And Caleb stilled the people before Moses, and said, Let us go up at once, and possess it; for we are well able to overcome it.

They reported that the land really does flow with milk and honey, there is fruit and wealth in abundance. They said: yes Moses everything you said about Canaan it is, but there is only one major problem. The People that live in this land are extremely vicious and violent. They are mighty people, even giants, and we are nothing but grasshoppers in their site.

Now God had already told them these facts about the inhabitants of the land when they were still in Egypt. God had told them that the Hittites were there, the Amorites, the Jebusites, the Amalekites and the Philistines were there. He also said: do not be afraid because they are bread for you to eat. And even though God had already previously told them these things they still brought up an **evil report**. Now let us listen to Caleb and Joshua because they had a different spirit.

Numbers14: ⁶ And Joshua the son of Nun, and Caleb the son of Jephunneh, which were of them that searched the land, rent their clothes: ⁷ and they spake unto all the company of the children of Israel, saying, The land, which we passed through to search it, is an exceeding good land. ⁸ If the LORD delight in us, then he will *bring us into this land, and give it us; a land which floweth with milk and honey. ⁹ Only rebel not ye against the LORD, neither fear ye the people of the land; for they are bread for us: their defence is departed from them, and the LORD is with us: fear them not. ¹⁰ But all the congregation bade stone them with stones.*

You see Caleb and Joshua had a spirit of faith. A **spirit of faith always brags about God, exalts God, and belittles the devil!** When you are operating in a spirit of faith you will always exalt **Christ** and make your problems look little, because in comparison to God, our problems are insignificant. There is nothing you or I have ever been confronted with in this world that is anything at all next to God. I mean He is holding everything together with the power of His word!

Caleb stilled the people before Moses and said let us go up at once and possess the land, because God is with us, and we are well able to overcome these adversaries. Notice faith is always now. The substance of things hoped for, the evidence of things not seen. Caleb declares by the spirit of faith to the people, we are well able to overcome it, we can do it. The message for the church today is still the same: We can do all things through **Christ** which strengthens us. There is no weapon formed against that can prosper!

Psalm 91:7 A thousand shall fall at thy side, and ten thousand at thy right hand; but it shall not come nigh thee.

Caleb is not talking about his ability, but he is talking about the ability that **Christ** has given to every one of us! He is talking about what we can do in **Christ**! In and by myself I'm an absolute and utter failure. On my own I can do nothing that pleases God! My righteousness is as filthy rags, but in **Christ Jesus** I can do all things that please the **Father**, as I put my faith In Him! Caleb has another spirit according to numbers chapter 14 verse 24. *Caleb has another spirit*, and will fully follow **Christ**'s commandments, will and purpose. Faith always agrees with God by saying what He says about you and your circumstance, doing exactly as he commanded you.

Numbers 14: ²⁴ but my servant Caleb, because he had another spirit with him, and hath followed me fully, him will I bring into the land where into he went; and his seed shall possess it.

If two be not agreed together then you cannot walk together. Faith always agrees with the word and the spirit of God. Let us look at Chapter 13 in verse 31 which reveals the evil report!

13:³¹ But the men that went up with him said, We be not able to go up against the people; for they are stronger than we. ³² And they brought up an evil report of the land which they had searched unto the children of Israel, saying, The land, through which we have gone to search it, is a land that eateth up the inhabitants thereof; and all the people that we saw in it are men of a great stature.

Even though we know without a shadow of a doubt that God is greater than any enemy that could ever confront us, to these men Caleb was stupid and living in a make-believe land. It's almost like there's two different worlds divided by an invisible fence. On one side is the land of faith, on the other side is the land of unbelief. We need to ask ourselves which side are we living on? People who live in the realm of unbelief will think that there is something wrong with those who live on the side of faith, but those who live in the realm of faith fully understand those who live on the side of unbelief, and they will try to encourage them to come over to the side of faith. Now those who live on the side of unbelief, unless their eyes are opened up, will eventually attack and try to kill those who live in the realm of faith.

God performed all of those miracles in the land of Egypt in order to destroy the spirit of unbelief, which is a lack of trust. This spirit of unbelief will be manifested by rebellion and disobedience to God, His will and His word. With all the mighty signs and wonders that God did for the children of Israel, there was no excuse for them not trusting, following and obeying all that was commanded of them. If that is true with the children of Israel in the days of Moses and Joshua, then how much more is it for us that are on the other side of the resurrection of **Jesus**?

What people completely have misunderstood and distorted is what **Jesus Christ** accomplished for us does not give us the right to live in sin and unbelief, but it actually takes away all of our excuses.

FAITH is the voice of God! Unbelief is the voice of the devil!

Jesus said when he came back to the earth would there be any men and women who really would know how to trust him? God is looking for people who are in agreement with him. That's exactly what faith is. It is when you are in complete agreement with God, his word, and his will. Your agreement with God is expressed in your words, deeds, thoughts, actions and lifestyle.

2 Chronicles 16:9 For the eyes of the Lord run to and fro throughout the whole earth, to shew himself strong in the behalf of them whose heart is perfect toward him.

The word Perfect means to be in complete agreement. A heart that is perfect towards the Lord, means that it is filled with faith and trust in all that God has proclaimed and commanded.

A perfect heart is one that Loves, Trust, Agrees, Follows, and Obeys Christ!

Joshua and Caleb were men of faith. Joshua was a man of the WORD. Hebrews 11 were men and women of faith, Abel was a man of faith, Enoch was a man of faith, who walked with God and was not. Abraham was a man of faith; he walked with God following all of his instructions. Faith is not a New Testament principle. It was before the beginning of time. And it flows from the heart of God into the heart of those who will receive it. A person of faith does not deny the problems, they do not deny the circumstance, but to them God is so much greater than the problem that the problems and circumstances are not worth talking about.

People who bring up an evil report are bragging about the devil, bragging about the Giants, bragging about their problems, glorifying the enemy. This unbelief is contagious and will cause you to have a grasshopper complex. Understand that our victory is not in our wisdom, it is not in our strength, it is not in our intelligence, it is not in our financial resources: it is in **Jesus** alone. Whenever we listen to people who are full of unbelief and doubt, you will end up losing what little bit of faith you had. Let us look in Numbers chapter 14:

Numbers 14:1 And all the congregation lifted up their voice, and cried; and the people wept that night.

These poor people have now become contaminated by these ten leaders who are full of unbelief. These people who had seen God do so much and yet they would not believe God to enter into the land of promise. The mightiest nation of the world (Egypt) had been brought to its knees through the mighty hand of God. They walked on dry land over the Red Sea. They had a fire by night and a cloud by day. Manna came from heaven every morning to feed all the descendants of Abraham.

her they are now weeping with fear and self-pity because they have been contaminated by leaders filled with unbelief. Whether you know it or not unbelief is contagious. And if you catch a case of unbelief from other people it could be the end of your life as you have known it. The majority of the medical world is permeated with unbelief.

Hebrews 12:15 looking diligently lest any man fail of the grace of God; lest any root of bitterness springing up trouble you, and thereby many be defiled;

Two years after I was born again, (1975) I started pastoring. More times than I care to count I have watched as a spirit of bitterness, a spirit of fear, a spirit of despair contaminated whole congregations, by people who were not walking with God. These 10 spies by operating in a spirit of fear, destroyed their whole generation. You better use wisdom what pastor and spiritual leaders you're sitting underneath. They can only take you to the place where they are living. If they are teaching deception it will get in you! If their life is full of sin and unbelief, this is where they will take you. If covetousness is their God, you will end up worshiping at the altar of materialism.

Let us take a deeper look at Caleb and Joshua who were the only ones from the first generation that entered into the land of promise! Please believe me when I tell you that faith can be caught because it is contagious!

#7 This is the **seventh way that faith comes, it comes by Association and Assimilation.**

Numbers 14:16 And Joshua the son of Nun, and Caleb the son of Jephunneh, which were of them that searched the land, rent their clothes: ⁷ and they spake unto all the company of the children of Israel, saying, The land, which we passed through to search it, is an exceeding good land. ⁸ If the LORD delight in us, then he will bring us into this land, and give it us; a land which floweth with milk and honey. ⁹ Only rebel not ye against the LORD, neither fear ye the people of the land; for they are bread for us: their defence is departed from them, and the LORD is with us: fear them not. ¹⁰ But all the congregation bade stone them with stones. And the glory of the LORD appeared in the tabernacle of the congregation before all the children of Israel.

Caleb and Joshua were endeavoring to bring the children of Israel into the realm of faith. Those who are operating in faith will always try to bring those who are operating in the spirit of unbelief and death over unto God side. Remember you can only take people where you yourself live. As you read the whole chapter you will discover that they were not able to help the first generation. But the second-generation was drastically affected by Caleb and Joshua. They embraced the reality of victory by faith in God. How this second-generation spoke and acted was completely different than how their parents spoke and acted. Thank God there is hope for us. Let's look there in Joshua chapter 1 at how the second generation spoke.

Joshua 1: ¹⁶ And they answered Joshua, saying, All that thou commandest us we will do, and whithersoever thou sendest us, we will go. ¹⁷ According as we hearkened unto Moses in all things, so will we hearken unto thee: only the LORD thy God be with thee, as he was with Moses. ¹⁸ Whosoever he be that doth rebel against thy commandment, and will not hearken unto thy words in all that thou commandest him, he shall be put to death: only be strong and of a good courage.

What a difference when we associate with those who are filled with a spirit of faith. The second-generation was rescued because they caught a good case of faith from Joshua, Caleb and of course Moses. We desperately need to find people of faith that we can be in fellowship with.

I think another amazing example of this is King David. The armies of Israel were facing the Philistines, and a champion came forth from the enemies ranks by the name of Goliath, nobody was willing to face him accept a young shepherd by the name of David. Think about it none of the fighting men of Israel had enough faith to face Goliath, not even King Saul. David had tremendous faith in God and in the covenant that God had made with Abraham, Isaac, and Jacob.

1Samuel 17: ³² And David said to Saul, Let no man's heart fail because of him; thy servant will go and fight with this Philistine. ³³ And Saul said to David, Thou art not able to go against this Philistine to fight with him: for thou art but a youth, and he a man of war from his youth. ³⁴ And David said unto Saul, Thy servant kept his Father's sheep, and there came a lion, and a bear, and *took a lamb out of the flock: [35] and I went out after him, and smote him, and delivered it out of his mouth: and when he arose against me, I caught him by his beard, and smote him, and slew him. [36] Thy servant slew both the lion and the bear: and this uncircumcised Philistine shall be as one of them, seeing he hath defied the armies of the living God. [37] David said moreover, The LORD that delivered me out of the paw of the lion, and out of the paw of the bear, he will deliver me out of the hand of this Philistine. And Saul said unto David, Go, and the LORD be with thee.*

I want you to notice that David not only declared that by faith in God he could deal with Goliath, but he also had life experiences. You will discover that within the body of **Christ** there is a lot of hot air, but true faith always produces works. I love the book of James because it boldly declares that faith without works is dead. James reveals this truth by wonderful examples of Abraham and the prophets.

David comes exploding into the pages of the Bible with the defeat of Goliath. Later he is challenged by Saul to take on the Philistines for the right to marry his daughter, in which he personally over comes two hundred of them. From then on other men began to follow him, and before everything is said and done David had over **300 mighty men** of war that were virtually invincible. Where did these 300 mighty men who all accomplished great feats come from? They were called mighty men because of the fact that great faith was operating in them, the faith that overcomes the world, the flesh, and the devil. These men did not have faith in the beginning, but as they associated with David, the faith that was on him, got on them!

1Samuel 23:8 These be the names of the mighty men whom David had.... etc.

Dr Michael H Yeager
We must give ourselves over to God and to a spirit of faith!

It is the spirit of FAITH that takes a hold of you when you cry out to **Jesus Christ** for your salvation. When I got gloriously born again it was because the **fear of the Lord** fell on me which is actually the spirit of faith. The Scripture says the fear of the Lord is the beginning of wisdom. We could also call it the spirit of faith, because it takes faith to believe that God means what he says, and says what he means. God does what he says he will do, including his judgments.

Galatians 6:7 Be not deceived; God is not mocked: for whatsoever a man soweth, that shall he also reap.

Out of the blue all of a sudden here I was about to commit suicide and then I have a visitation from Heaven. The spirit of faith entered into me and **I cried out to Jesus, being gloriously born again, giving myself over to Jesus through a spirit of faith in Christ Jesus.**

2 Corinthians 4:13 We having the same spirit of faith, according as it is written, I believed, and therefore have I spoken; we also believe, and therefore speak;

Now once the spirit of faith in **Christ Jesus** took a hold of me, it began to spread like a contagious disease through the Navy base I was stationed at. Young man after young man was gloriously born again and filled with the Holy Spirit. Here it is over 40 years later and I'm still hearing reports of what God is doing because the spirit of faith got a hold of me.

#7 FAITH comes by Association and Assimilation!

When **Jesus** came to the earth at his appointed time his purpose was to bring us into the realm of faith. You see one man committed sin, and unbelief entered into his heart. Unbelief is spread through the DNA of the human flesh. Faith is of the spirit, and it is in the soul and spirit of every human being. It is when a person gives himself freely and willingly over to the spirit of unbelief (that is in his flesh) that the human soul dies. **Christ** came to resurrect the dead, those who are dead because of unbelief. It is time to catch a good case of faith. Even **Jesus** when he ministered in certain situations would put out those from the room that were full of unbelief. Numerous times he kept Peter, James and John next to him, in order that they might catch a case of divine faith.

Luke 8: 49 While he yet spake, there cometh one from the ruler of the synagogue's house, saying to him, Thy daughter is dead; trouble not the Master. [50] But when Jesus heard it, he answered him, saying, Fear not: believe only, and she shall be made whole. [51] And when he came into the house, he suffered no man to go in, save Peter, and James, and John, and the Father and the mother of the maiden. 52 And all wept, and bewailed her: but he said, Weep not; she is not dead, but sleepeth. [53] And they laughed him to scorn, knowing that she was dead. [54] And he put them all out, and took her by the hand, and called, saying, Maid, arise.

We are not greater than **Jesus**, therefore we must study and meditate upon how **HE** operated in faith. A famous declaration is **What Would Jesus Do?** This statement is more profound then I think many have realized. We see that the faith that was in **Jesus Christ** eventually got into his disciples, spreading to other men and women. As we look in the book of Acts we see a complete full-blown case of contagious faith, caught by many through the aspect of Association and Assimilation. Let us now begin to look for those who are full of faith, that we may allow it to get on US for we can spread it to others!

Satanic Worshiper Delivered, Saved & Filled with Holy Ghost!

One night I was witnessing in my dormitory room to three men. While sharing biblical truths with these three men, another man entered my room. We called him TJ. This individual had always been very different and strange. He was kind of out there. I had never even spoken to him up to that time, except one night when he showed a really nasty movie to the guys in his dorm. I had walked out of his room in disgust.

When TJ entered my room he began to preach some off-thewall weird things about the devil. He said he was from California where he had been part of a satanic church. He showed us the ends of his fingers in which some of the ends were missing from the first joint out. He told us he had eaten them for power and drank human blood within satanic worship services. As he spoke, there seemed to be an invisible power speaking through him. He had come under the influence of a demonic presence, one of the guys who were in my room, Hussein, declared this was too much and left the room. The other two, Bobby and Willie, sat and listened.

I had never encountered anything as sinister and evil as this ever before. I honestly didn't know what to do at that time so I went downstairs to the barracks right below me. There was a fellow Christian I had the opportunity of working with who lived there. After I had given my heart to **Jesus Christ**, Willie, the cowboy, told me he was a born again Christian. I had yet to see the evidence of this in Willie's life but I didn't know where else to go. I knocked on Willie's door. When he opened the door I explained to him what happened in my room. He agreed to come to my room. When he stepped into my dormitory he saw that TJ was up on a wooden stool preaching under the power of the devil. Willie, turned tail and ran out of my room. He said he had no idea what to do and he couldn't handle this. He left me standing outside by my door.

I went back into my room and did the only thing I could - I cried out to **Jesus**. The minute I cried out, a bright light from heaven shone through my ceiling. I don't know if anyone else saw this bright light, all I know is what I needed to say was placed within me. I began to preach **Jesus** to TJ! As I began to speak, the power of God fell into the room and TJ dropped to the floor, squirming like a snake. Willie and Bobby fell on their knees crying out to **Jesus** and gave their hearts to the Lord. I found myself kneeling over the top of TJ. I placed my hands upon him. Willie and Bobby came over and laid their hands upon him. With a voice of authority inspired by the Spirit, I commanded the demons to come out of the man. As God is my witness, three to five different voices came screaming out of TJ! After the demons were gone TJ gave his heart to **Jesus Christ** right then and there. All of these three men were filled with the Holy Ghost and spoke in tongues. The next Sunday they all went to church with me.

Amazing Conviction began to Fall upon the Community

Kathleen and I had a burden for souls (1980). We prayed about what to do and where to go. In order to reach sinners, we knew we had to go where they were. It was Quickened in our hearts to go to a town called Mount Union, which was about fifteen miles away. I knew we would have to believe for a bus, but so be it. We began to go door-to-door to the people in the low income housing projects in this town. They were basically African-American people. There were already two other churches running their buses through this area. We would simply go to each door, and knock on it. When a person opened up the door, we introduced ourselves and told them that if they had any needs, we would love to pray for them. We began to see wonderful results immediately. A miniature revival erupted in that community. People were getting saved and healed everywhere! They were also getting filled with the Holy Ghost.

One day I was out with another brother instead of my wife. As we were working our way down the street, I saw an African-American lady about five apartments ahead of us. She was hanging laundry out to dry on a clothesline behind her apartment. At that very moment, she looked up and saw us. Our eyes made contact for a brief second, and then she dropped her clothes and literally ran into her house. I knew instantly that something strange was happening. We continue going door to door.

About 20 minutes later we arrived at her door. Her regular solid door was open, with just her screen door closed. I knocked on her door when a woman's voice yelled from upstairs. She told us to come on in. I did not want to just step into her house, being a total stranger, so I yelled through the screen door and asked her if she knew who we were. She yelled back down at us, "Yes she said: your men of God." We stepped into her house not knowing exactly what to expect. She appeared at the top of the stairs with wet hair and a completely different set up close on.

The next thing we knew she came down the stairs to the bottom step. The minute she got to the bottom of the stairs, she literally fell to her knees weeping and crying. She asked us to lead her to Jesus Christ. I led her into the sinner's prayer and then I perceived she was ready for the Holy Ghost. So I prayed right then and there for her to be filled with the Holy Ghost. Immediately she began to speak in a brand-new heavenly language. We were awestruck on how God had moved upon this precious lady so fast. She later informed us what had happened. She said that when she saw us going door-to-door, she knew in her heart that she was not right with the Lord. An overwhelming conviction came upon her, and she knew that she was filthy and lost. She felt so dirty at that moment that she said she had to go in to her house, and go upstairs and take a quick shower. She felt as if she needed to put on clean clothes before we arrived. And put on some clean clothes. God was working so strongly in her that by the time we got to her house, she was ready to be saved and filled with the Holy Ghost. Thank God for the convicting and quickening power of the Holy Ghost.

#8 Waiting upon God

I cannot declare to you strong enough and boldly enough the importance of having faith in **Jesus Christ**! As we continue looking into the word of God from Genesis to Revelation, we see that God is a God of faith! Faith is an invisible spiritual force that holds everything together. In Hebrews 1 it declares that God upholds all things by the word of his power. Hebrews 11 declares that by faith every miracle, every sign and wonder, all of creation was accomplished and brought into existence by faith. That is God having faith in **himself**.

2 Timothy 2:12 if we suffer, we shall also reign with him: if we deny him, he also will deny us: 13 if we believe not, yet he abideth faithful: he cannot deny himself.

Man himself is a creation of faith, and we were created and made to move in the realm of Faith. Adam lived and moved in the realm of faith until he committed sin, which is called unbelief. Sin is the opposite of faith, just like darkness is the opposite of light, or hate is the opposite of love, torment is the opposite of peace, deep sorrow is the opposite of joy. When you function by faith you will enter into another world, another realm were all things are possible.

All things are possible to him that believeth.

Nothing is impossible to those who are living, walking and moving by faith in **Christ Jesus**. When we talk about all things are possible to him that believeth, what we're talking about is that all things that are based upon the known will and character of God, because that's what faith is. Faith is given to us to draw close to God, and to become partakers of the divine nature of **Jesus Christ**. When you walk by faith it will cause God to come rushing towards you, because **like draws onto like**. The law of Genesis declares everything produces after its own kind. Therefore, faith is a spiritual magnetic power that will draw God toward you.

James 4:8 Draw nigh to God, and he will draw nigh to you.

Faith in Christ Jesus will draw miracles to you, healing to you, deliverance to you, freedom to you, and victory to you. Causing God himself to draw close to you.

I was lying in bed back in 2012 when I literally heard the audible voice of God, and he said to me: **the violent take it by force**! For a while now this has been marinating in my soul. Sometimes when God speaks to me it takes time for it to become a reality. It could be four years later or maybe decades as the spirit of God will be at work on my inside. You could say that it is like a woman when she gets pregnant, life is growing inside of her womb. Even so faith begins as a seed, and must grow within us, in our hearts. We have a lot to do with that faith growing, expanding, enlarging and becoming mature.

Please understand everybody has faith, everybody was born with a measure, a proportion of faith. When **Jesus** shared the parables about the 10 virgins who were asleep, they all woke up when the trumpet sounded! But **Jesus** said there were five foolish and five wise. The Five that were wise had enough oil to take them to the arrival of their husband to be. I believe that the oil that **Jesus** was speaking about is the oil of faith; I believe it's faith in God and **Jesus Christ**. People who do not have faith in this time period are really going to have it bad. They're going to try to find somebody that has faith, but it will be too late. And then there are those who have faith which has been in hibernation. Faith can be lying dormant inside of you for many years, and then all of a sudden something supernatural happens and it begins to come forth like a bear coming out of hibernation!

Let us now look at the eighth way that faith comes!
Isaiah 40: ³¹ but they that wait upon the LORD shall renew their strength; they shall mount up with wings as eagles; they shall run, and not be weary;

and they shall walk, and not faint.   We are looking at the end of Isaiah chapter 40: verse 31

But they that wait upon the Lord shall renew their strength.

Notice there is a very specific clarification in this particular set of Scriptures. It does not say that all of God's people, but only they that **wait upon the Lord**. They that wait upon Jehovah, they shall renew their strength, they will mount up with wings as eagles, they shall walk and not faint. This is not referring to those who are taking time to soak in the presence of God. I'm not against this resting in God's presence, but the word to wait in the Hebrew is referring to that of a **slave** or a servant. In the King James Version and many other translations, it always says servant instead of slave. As you look in the Old and the New Testament it talks about being a servant many times. Paul began his epistles many times as a servant of **Jesus Christ**, Peter a servant of **Jesus Christ**, John a servant of **Jesus Christ**.

In our culture (in which I praise God) we do not have slaves, but in many parts of the world today slavery is probably more rampant than it ever has been before. There are all kinds of slaves, because a slave is a person who really has lost their free will to some extent. According to the word of God every one of us are slaves, you might say servants, but still in reality slaves. We either are Slaves to **Jesus Christ** or you're a slave to your flesh, you're a slave to the devil, a slave to feelings and emotions that are against the will of God.

Do you not know, that to whom YOU present yourselves slaves to obey, YOU ARE THAT ONES SLAVE WHOM YOU OBEY, whether of SIN leading to death or of OBEDIENCE leading to righteousness!

You can be a slave (servant) to the spirit of **Christ** or you can be a slave to the world, the flesh and the devil. It is totally up to you, but you will either be a slave to the devil or a slave of God. It will be one of the two! In verse 31 it says that they that wait upon the Lord. They who are looking to the Lord, listening for his voice with anticipation. They are waiting for God to tell them what to do.

71

#8th way that faith comes is by having a servant's heart! Waiting upon the LORD!

Philippians 2: ⁵ Let this mind be in you, which was also in Christ Jesus: ⁶ who, being in the form of God, thought it not robbery to be equal with God: ⁷ but made himself of no reputation, and took upon him the form of a servant, and was made in the likeness of men: ⁸ and being found in fashion as a man, he humbled himself, and became obedient unto death, even the death of the cross.

At 12 years old **Jesus** revealed the secret of his great faith and success when he declared to Mary and Joseph: **I Must Be about My Father's Business!**

Hebrews 10:6-8 & Psalm 40:6 Sacrifice and offering thou didst not desire; mine ears hast thou opened: burnt offering and sin offering hast thou not required. 7 Then said I, Lo, I come: in the volume of the book it is written of me, 8 I delight to do thy will, O my God: yea, thy law is within my heart.

The whole purpose of the life of **Christ**, was to be a servant to his **Father**. He did not come to be served, but to serve. Over and over he gave examples to his disciples. He said that those who wanted to be the greatest of all, must become the servant of all. As you and I apprehend a servant's heart towards the Lord, and towards others, our faith will grow exceedingly.

Psalm 123:1 Unto thee lift I up mine eyes, O thou that dwellest in the heavens.2 Behold, as the eyes of <u>servants</u> look unto the hand of their <u>masters,</u> and as the eyes of a maiden unto the hand of her mistress; so our eyes <u>wait</u> upon the Lord our God, until that he have mercy upon us.

Over and over the Scriptures declare that those who **come** to do the will of the Heavenly **Father**, will be filled with a faith that overcomes the world. This is a radical God pleasing type of faith. **Jesus** boldly declared: not my will, but his will be done!

Now let us take a look at the Centurion who **Jesus** declared had great faith. As you read Matthew chapter 8 beginning with verse five, you'll discover that the Centurion and had an amazing attitude towards **Christ**. Faith will cause us to apprehend the same type of attitude, which will cause us to have great faith in **Jesus Christ**.

Matthew 8:5 And when Jesus was entered into Capernaum, there came unto him a centurion, beseeching him, 6 and saying, Lord, my servant lieth at home sick of the palsy, grievously tormented. 7 And Jesus saith unto him, I will come and heal him. 8 The centurion answered and said, Lord, I am not worthy that thou shouldest come under my roof: but speak the word only, and my servant shall be healed. 9 For I am a man under authority, having soldiers under me: and I say to this man, Go, and he goeth; and to another, Come, and he cometh; and to my servant, Do this, and he doeth it. 10 When Jesus heard it, he marvelled, and said to them that followed, Verily I say unto you, I have not found so great faith, no, not in Israel.

First notice the Centurion who was a Roman soldier could've commanded **Christ** to come, but he actually approached him as an inferior. He came begging and pleading with **Jesus** to have mercy on his servant, because he knew he did not deserve healing. Yes, I realize that **Jesus** took the stripes upon his back for our healing, and yet in our own righteousness, we do not deserve his help.

Jesus of course responded that he would come, the centurion said he was not worthy for **Jesus** to come under his roof. This man had an incredible insight into how the kingdom of God works. He said to **Jesus**: **speak the word only**, and my servant **shall be healed**. And then he explains this attitude by declaring that he himself was a servant under authority of another master. This centurion had a servant's heart which is one of the most important elements that a believer needs to have. **Jesus** marveled at this man's faith! Faith cannot help but grow, increase and prosper in the heart of a man or a woman who has a **servant** attitude. One who submits to the authority that is over them. In the last set of Scriptures, we are about to use in this section, we need to recognize that the apostles perceived the absolute necessity to have faith. Therefore, they inquired of the Lord how to increase their faith. Let us read very carefully what the disciples said to the Lord **Jesus** in Luke chapter 17.

Luke 17:5 And the apostles said unto the Lord, Increase our faith. 6 And the Lord said, If ye had faith as a grain of mustard seed, ye might say unto this sycamine tree, Be thou plucked up by the root, and be thou planted in the sea; and it should obey you. 7 But which of you, having a **servant plowing or feeding cattle, will say unto him by and by, when he is come from the field, Go and sit down to meat?** *8 And will not rather say unto him, Make ready wherewith I may sup, and gird thyself, and serve me, till I have eaten and drunken; and afterward thou shalt eat and drink? 9 Doth he thank that* **servant** *because he did the things that were commanded him? I trow not. 10 So likewise ye, when ye shall have done all those things which are commanded you, say, We are* **unprofitable servants***: we have done that which was our duty to do.*

This must get deep into our hearts, that we are servants of **Jesus Christ**. We are here to please him, by fulfilling his divine will, in whatever he calls us to do. This is the whole purpose of living. We must be about our **Father**'s business. In verse nine, it declares that our master commands us, he does not ask us. Then in first 10 it seals the reality of God's attitude towards us as people.

10 So likewise ye, when ye shall have done all those things which are commanded you, say, We are **unprofitable** *servants: we have done that which was our duty to do.*

In the gospel of John, **Jesus** reveals to us and astounding transformation from servant hood, to friendship, because his disciples simply did what they were told to do.

John 15:15 Henceforth I call you not **servants***; for the* **servant** *knoweth not what his lord doeth: but I have called you friends; for all things that I have heard of my Father I have made known unto you.*

Let us as quickly as possible make this transition so that God can use us in a powerful way for his glory and honor. That our faith may take off like a rocket towards the moon in its spiritual development and growth.

HOW I ENDED UP WORKING FOR KENNETH HAGIN!

I had been working for the Broken Arrow school district for about six months in 1978. During that time, I had shared **Christ** with all of the other janitors at the elementary school. The man who was over me was a very large and nasty fellow. He seemed to be antagonistic against the things of God. I did not preach at him, but I did share as the Lord allowed. All of these people spent a lot of time in the coffee room talking and backbiting. I would only go there to eat my lunch, and then only when needed, then I would be back to cleaning. We all had a schedule to keep when it came to maintenance work and waxing and buffing hallways and classrooms. I was way ahead of my schedule and doing extra things just to keep busy. The reason I did this, was because I was working as onto the Lord, not unto men. **Christ** had a servant's heart, and it was my greatest desire to be just like **Jesus**. Ever since I've been born again wherever I have worked God has prospered me. He has supernaturally elevated me into positions much faster than those around me! Why would this be? It is because I'm doing it heartily to the Lord and not for men. We can see this in the life of Joseph before God elevated him into the second-highest position in Egypt. Well this attitude seemed to extremely aggravated my boss. At times he would follow me around trying to intimidate and mock me. To be honest, it did not really bother me. I had been through so many rough situations that this was simply like a little aggravating fly buzzing around my head. It was nothing compared to the times when people had tried to kill me for my faith.

One day I went to work as usual, not knowing this would be my last day of employment with the school district, because God was about to elevate me. I was waxing and buffing a classroom floor when this man came storming into the room. He asked me what in the #@!#@ did I think I was doing. I just looked at him and kept working. He became more aggravated, yelling and screaming like he had lost his mind. (He actually was quite demon oppressed.) I knew he was living a perverted and very twisted lifestyle, because he talked and bragged about it. I had not condemned him, but simply strove to live a holy life in front of him and the others. He finally got in my face and tried to push me around. As I was standing there, I heard the Lord say, ***It's time to quit; you have done all that you can here.*** Now, in the natural I really needed this job for my wife and I to keep going to Bible school and to pay bills and food. However, the Spirit of the Lord said to me, ***Your job is done here***.

I have learned through the years that if God tells you to do something, then you better do it, because He is my boss. Whenever I have ignored the voice of God, the results have always been tragic. So right on the spot I turned off the floor buffer, looked at this man and said," I quit!"

He said, "What?" I said, "I quit!" He said to me, "You can't quit!" I said, "Oh, yes I can, and I just did!" I walked right past him out into the hallway of the school. He was yelling and screaming at me as I walked down the hallway. I simply ignored him and kept walking. What was I going to do now? I went home and told Kathleen what I had done. She took the news with a gentle acknowledgment that God would provide. That's one wonderful thing about my lovely wife. She has been in very difficult situations with me, and yet she just keeps on loving. God will give you the desires of your heart, especially when those desires are led and directed by his Spirit. I asked the Lord if I could have a job working at the Bible school (Rhema) we were attending. It would be the perfect place to work because I wanted to be around Godly people and get more connected to the ministry.

A number of days later as Kathee and I sat in class, there was an announcement over the loudspeaker that the school was hiring people to work with their yard and maintenance crew. My heart leapt for joy. Immediately after that class was out, I went to the main office and filled out an application. The next day, I went back to the office and they informed me that I had been hired, and they wanted me to start that very day. Working for the Broken Arrow school district had prepared me for this job. If I had not quit when the Spirit of the Lord had quickened me, I would have missed this opportunity. I worked right alongside of Dad Hagins older brother Dub who before he was born again used to drive the getaway car for gangsters. I also helped Dad Hagin move into a new house that someone had donated to him.

#9 Being Doers of the WORD

1 John 5:4 For whatsoever is born of God overcometh the world: and this is the victory that overcometh the world, even our faith. 5 Who is he that overcometh the world, but he that believeth that Jesus is the Son of God?

In the book of Revelation over and over, it declares that we must overcome. Those who overcome will be clothed in white raiment, and their names will be written down on white stones that no man knows but God himself. **Jesus** has already overcome all principalities and powers. He said to his disciples in Matthew: behold all authority has been given to me in heaven & in earth, go therefore in to the entire world and preach the gospel to every creature. For whatsoever is born of God, overcomes the world! John is very specific about who overcomes. This is John who was the beloved of **Jesus**, the one who laid his head upon the chest of **Jesus** at the last meal. He was the only Apostle who was there at the cross when **Christ** suffered and died. He was the first of the 11 apostles who arrived at the tomb on resurrection morning. John boldly declared that the victory that overcomes the world is **faith** in **Jesus Christ**. Faith is the declaration of trust, reliance, and dependence upon **Christ**. To overcome means to conquer, triumph, prevail, subdue and have victory. Hebrews chapter 11 reveals to us 50 major events that were accomplished by faith in **Jesus Christ**.

What's amazing is that if you look up the word faith in the four Gospels, it appears many times in Matthew, Mark, and Luke, but in the gospel of John the word faith does not appear even one time. Instead we see the emphasis on the word **believe**! Believe and faith are really the same, but the word to **believe** has a deeper and more personal connotation to it than the word faith. It brings to mind a much more intimate relationship.

1 John 5:1 Whosoever believeth that Jesus is the Christ is born of God: and every one that loveth him that begat loveth him also that is begotten of him. 2 By this we know that we love the children of God, when we love God, and keep his commandments. 3 For this is the love of God, that we keep his commandments: and his commandments are not grievous.

In verse three it declares that we keep his commandments. This is a faith that works by love. This is the declaration of our faith in **Jesus Christ**. In one situation **Jesus** asked the multitudes: *why do you call me, Lord, Lord, and do not the things I say?* In another situation, he said: *who is my mother brother and sister, but they that do the will of my Father which is in heaven!*

We are called to keep the commandments of **Christ** and **to do them**! James declares that faith without works is dead. What we do with our time, resources, energy, mind, and body reveals who we really are. Because what you love reveals who you are, and that which you love possesses you. **Jesus** declared: *for where your heart is there your treasuries is also.* There is a song I love to sing that declares: *I love to praise him!* There are many Scriptures that declare the love that God's people have for his word.

Jeremiah 15:16 Thy words were found, and I did eat them; and thy word was unto me the joy and rejoicing of mine heart: for I am called by thy name, O Lord God of hosts.

Psalm 119:47 And I will delight myself in thy commandments, which I have loved.

Psalm 119:16 I will delight myself in thy statutes: I will not forget thy word.

Psalm 1:2 But his delight is in the law of the Lord; and in his law doth he meditate day and night.

This is where we come to the **ninth way** that faith will come. It is revealed to us from Genesis to Revelation. It is extremely important that we get this deep down into our hearts, this reality of how faith will come.

James 1:22 But be ye doers of the word, and not hearers only, deceiving your own selves.

#9 The ninth way that faith will come is by: **doing whatever the word of God tells us to do!**

Let us read the Scriptures very carefully, taking heed to them.

Romans 2:13 (for not the hearers of the law are just before God, but the doers of the law shall be justified.

James the brother of **Jesus**, who knew **Christ** in a very personal intimate way reveals to us amazing realities of faith.

James 1:23 For if any be a hearer of the word, and not a doer, he is like unto a man beholding his natural face in a glass: 24 for he beholdeth himself, and goeth his way, and straightway forgetteth what manner of man he was. 25 But whoso looketh into the perfect law of liberty, and continueth therein, he being not a forgetful hearer, but a doer of the work, this man shall be blessed in his deed.

Back in 1996 I memorized the book of James word for word because I desired to have these truths within my heart. We must be doers and participators of the word of God. **Faith will come as we act upon the simple principles of the word of God**. In the New Testament alone it talks about doing the word **373** times. When I gave my heart to **Jesus** I determined within my heart that whatever I read in the New Testament, that I would do it. Unbeknownst to me I stepped into a major way in which faith will come. Some of the practical and elemental ways of doing the word of God is as follows. **#1** pray **#2** forgive **#3** raise your hands toward heaven **#4** share **Christ** with others **#5** gathered together with believers on a regular basis **#6** give when possible **#7** do good **#8** give thanks **#9** love at all times **#10** never complain **#11** do not speak evil of anyone **#12** casting all of your cares upon the Lord!

In order to do all of these things it will require faith. We need to understand that faith is like a muscle in your physical body, the more you use it the stronger it becomes. Faith is a spiritual muscle, and if you do not work it, then you will lose it!

1   Timothy 4:8 For bodily exercise profiteth little: but godliness is profitable unto all things, having promise of the life that now is, and of that which is to come.

James 4:17 Therefore to him that knoweth to do good, and doeth it not, to him it is sin.

2   Corinthians 11:3 But I fear, lest by any means, as the serpent beguiled Eve through his subtilty, so your minds should be corrupted from the simplicity that is in Christ.

James also declared that if we do not do the word then we will end forgetting what kind of person we are meant to be. I am not saying that it is easy to do the will of God. We understand when it comes to the development of our physical muscles that in itself it is a challenge. To develop our spiritual muscle called faith will take even more effort than it does to develop your physical muscles, but it is well worth it. Even **Jesus** struggled to stay within the will of the **Father** at times.

Luke 22:44 And being in an agony he prayed more earnestly: and his sweat was as it were great drops of blood falling down to the ground.

Matthew 26:42 He went away again the second time, and prayed, saying, O my Father, if this cup may not pass away from me, except I drink it, thy will be done.

Thank the **Father** that **Jesus** did not fail to obey the will of the Father by Faith. Because of his obedience even to death upon the cross, the **Father** has highly exalted him, and given him a name that is above every name!

James 1:24 for he beholdeth himself, and goeth his way, and straightway forgetteth what manner of man he was. 25 But whoso looketh into the perfect law of liberty, and continueth therein, he being not a forgetful hearer, but a doer of the work, this man shall be blessed in his deed. 26 If any man among you seem to be religious, and bridleth not his tongue, but deceiveth his own heart, this man's religion is vain.

How Faith Comes

There are many that call themselves believers, but their religion is in vain because they are not exercising any faith when it comes to obeying the word, the will, the plans, and the purposes of God. This is extremely displeasing to our heavenly **Father**. When **Jesus** himself returns with the angelic host he will separate the sheep from the goats. And he will take vengeance on them that have not obeyed the gospel.

2 Thessalonians 1:8 in flaming fire taking vengeance on them that know not God, and that obey not the gospel of our Lord Jesus Christ:

Where Faith Is Alive - The Flesh Will Die!

Jesus declared heaven and earth shall pass away, but my words will never pass away. Every promise, provision, and blessing that **Christ** spoke over his church can be trusted. Now on the other side of the coin I can also guarantee that every warning he spoke will come to pass upon those who will not exercise faith to hear and obey.

Matthew 7:21 Not every one that saith unto me, Lord, Lord, shall enter into the kingdom of heaven; but he that doeth the will of my Father which is in heaven. 22 Many will say to me in that day, Lord, Lord, have we not prophesied in thy name? and in thy name have cast out devils? and in thy name done many wonderful works? 23 And then will I profess unto them, I never knew you: depart from me, ye that work iniquity.

How I Received a Victory over depression

In my earlier days, God was supernaturally quickening my mind to memorize scripture. The gifts of the Spirit were flowing with the word of knowledge, wisdom, prophecy, tongues, and interpretation. My life used to be filled with extreme depression and self-pity. and this depression was trying to sneak its way back into my life in a strong way. I fought it constantly. One morning I got up early to pray. I was fed up with the feelings and emotions of depression that were trying to overwhelm me. I took my large Bible (I know this sounds disrespectful but I was still young in the Lord) and put it on the floor. I physically stood upon the Word of God as an act of faith. I spoke to the depression and declared: "In the name of **Jesus Christ** of Nazareth, from this day forward I will not believe what my feelings or emotions are telling me. Let God's Word be true and everything else a lie." From 1977 to now I have been living in this reality. God gave me glorious victory over depression on that day that I stood upon my Bible and declared I was free! I have continued to walk in this victory through the most difficult times one could ever imagine. Yes, depression tries to come back upon me, but I put it under my feet by faith every time. We must be doers of the word, and not hearers only!

How God Taught Me How to Live by Faith and Not by Feelings

I learned this lesson within the first two months I was saved. When I gave my heart to Jesus his presence overwhelmed me. For close to two months I lived, walked and moved in his tangible presence. I was constantly experiencing the quickening power of His spirit.

Now one morning I awoke with the total absence of God's presence. I did not know what to do in this particular situation. I examined my heart to make sure I was not out of God's will. After much agonizing I came to the conclusion that there was nothing in my life I was knowingly or willingly doing to grieve the **Father**, **Son**, or **Holy Ghost**!

Right then and there I decided that regardless of how I felt, that I would continue to pray, read my Bible, share the gospel, and do God's will. This experience of the lack of God's presence lasted for about two weeks. Every day I would cry out to God asking him what I had done wrong, and yet I did not back off in my prayer time, meditation, reading my Bible, going to church, or sharing Christ with others. Actually I increased my pursuit after God. I had determined in my heart that I was not going to let go no matter how I felt.

How Faith Comes

One day while I was in prayer, God's tangible presence came flooding in upon me in like a mighty wave of the ocean. I started laughing, crying and rejoicing. When I was finally able to get my composure I asked the Lord "Where have you been?" The Spirit of the Lord spoke to my heart saying: *I never left you.* I said Lord but your presence was not with me? I heard the voice of God reply: *I wanted you to learn how to live by faith and not by your feelings.*

If My Son Would Not Obeyed Instantly, He would Have Died!

This actually happened to my son Michael a number of years ago. If you ever visit our facilities, you will see in our parking lot real tall metal streetlights. We installed these streetlights almost 25 years ago. Now, one day Michael, my son was out in the parking lot, with his back to one of these heavy steel streetlights. He was just standing there minding his own business looking across the parking lot, when out of the blue there was a Divine quickening in his heart to take a step over to the right hand side. He told me: dad I wasn't even thinking, I just in my heart I knew I had to obey this inclination instantly to step over to the right-hand side. Now the very moment that he moved to the right, something came whizzing past him very close to his left shoulder and arm. Then there was a loud crack of something hitting the ground.

Here in less than a second after Michael moved that tall, heavy and large steel streetlight, fell over. It slammed down right next to him. If he would not have moved exactly at that moment, he would' have been slammed in the head by that heavy falling steel lamp post. In all probability it would have killed him instantly on the spot. Thank God for the quickening of the Holy Spirit, and Michael's quick response to that quickening. Many people die early deaths because they do not hearken to the moving of the spirit. Just a matter of inches made all the difference in the world between life and death for my son Michael. I am convinced that when we get to Heaven we will discover that many of Gods people will tell us that they died early deaths because they did not, or were not in tune with the Holy Ghost. When God puts a quickening in your heart, you need to obey immediately, without thinking.

CHAPTER FOUR

#10 Worship in Spirit & Truth

I have been ministering and teaching on the subject of **how faith comes**! Most People have been taught only one way that faith comes. God Quickened to my heart in 2008 over 28 different ways that faith comes. I believe that having faith in **Jesus Christ** is one of the most important subjects of the Bible. Faith is when God and his will is quickened by the Holy Spirit, becoming more real to you than any circumstance, or situation that you or I will ever find ourselves confronted with. When you walk by faith, when you live by faith, you are actually living and walking in the spirit. If you live in the spirit you will not fulfill the lust of the flesh, this is the law of the spirit of life in **Christ Jesus**. I believe that the law of the spirit of life in **Christ Jesus** is literally walking, breathing, thinking, and functioning in faith.

Now I am talking about a faith that is absolutely centered, based and built upon nothing but **Jesus Christ**. To me there is no other type of faith. Every other type of faith is nothing but a lie, an imitation, and a deception. Faith in **Jesus Christ** is when he is your all in all, he has become everything, and in him you live and move and have your being. When you are truly living by faith in **Christ Jesus** you do not see things the way that most people see them, you do not even really care about the things that most people care about. You do not respond to, or even act the way that most people do. Now the enemy of our soul is doing everything he can to destroy the faith that we have in our hearts, but we need to also realize that **Christ Jesus** is more than enough to defeat any work of the enemy.

THE WORD OF GOD, this BOOK (THE BIBLE) MUST BECOME MORE REAL TO US THEN THE FLESH & BLOOD WORLD WE ARE LIVING IN RIGHT NOW!

#10 Let us now take a look at the **10ᵗʰ Way** God has provided for faith to come.

The champion of the Philistine army, Goliath by name is a giant of a man who from his youth up has been a killing and murdering machine. I mean he is one tough hombre who has come to defeat the Israelites! Now David was a Shepherd boy (he was also a man of war if you study the Scriptures) who had not gone down to the battle like his other seven brothers, but as he came down to the battlefield with food for his family, Goliath came forth challenging the army of Israel. None of the men of Israel had the courage, or faith to meet this giant. Now when David saw this Philistine he spoke up and said: let no man's heart fail because of this uncircumcised Philistine. Because of David's speech they brought him before King Saul, and David gave this amazing testimony to King Saul. In verse 34

:34 And David said unto Saul, Thy servant kept his Father's sheep, and there came a lion, and a bear, and took a lamb out of the flock:35 And I went out after him, and smote him, and delivered it out of his mouth: and when he arose against me, I caught him by his beard, and smote him, and slew him.36 Thy servant slew both the lion and the bear: and this uncircumcised Philistine shall be as one of them, seeing he hath defied the armies of the living God.37 David said moreover, The Lord that delivered me out of the paw of the lion, and out of the paw of the bear, he will deliver me out of the hand of this Philistine.

Amazing Faith is manifested in David with an absolute unwavering confidence in God. Listen to the courage and faith filled words of David and his attitude towards Goliath.

45 Then said David to the Philistine, Thou comest to me with a sword, and with a spear, and with a shield: but I come to thee in the name of the Lord of hosts, the God of the armies of Israel, whom thou hast defied.46 This day will the Lord deliver thee into mine hand; and I will smite thee, and take thine head from thee; and I will give the carcases of the host of the Philistines this day unto the fowls of the air, and to the wild beasts of the earth; that all the earth may know that there is a God in Israel.47 And all this assembly shall know that the Lord saveth not with sword and spear: for the battle is the Lord's, and he will give you into our hands.

David had faith in God that overcame the enemy.

48 And it came to pass, when the Philistine arose, and came, and drew nigh to meet David, that David hastened, and ran toward the army to meet the Philistine.49 And David put his hand in his bag, and took thence a stone, and slang it, and smote the Philistine in his forehead, that the stone sunk into his forehead; and he fell upon his face to the earth.50 So David prevailed over the Philistine with a sling and with a stone, and smote the Philistine, and slew him; but there was no sword in the hand of David.51 Therefore David ran, and stood upon the Philistine, and took his sword, and drew it out of the sheath thereof, and slew him, and cut off his head therewith. And when the Philistines saw their champion was dead, they fled.

Within this confrontation David mentioned God **seven** times. God declared that he was going to make David King because King Saul would not listen and obey the orders given to him by Samuel the Prophet. When your heart is filled with faith in God you will have a heart of obedience like unto David, who had a heart after God.

1 Samuel 13:14 But now thy kingdom shall not continue: the Lord hath sought him a man after his own heart, and the Lord hath commanded him to be captain over his people, because thou hast not kept that which the Lord commanded thee.

The question that we need to ask is **how did David get all of this amazing faith in God**? This question is very important because however David apprehended this faith is the same way we will have to apprehend it. Let us take a quick journey to the New Testament were the **10ᵗʰ Way** that **faith comes** will be made alive to us. **Jesus** is speaking to the woman at the well about spiritual realities.

John 4:6 Now Jacob's well was there. Jesus therefore, being wearied with his journey, sat thus on the well: and it was about the sixth hour. 7 There cometh a woman of Samaria to draw water: Jesus saith unto her, Give me to drink. 8 (For his disciples were gone away unto the city to buy meat.) 9 Then saith the woman of Samaria unto him, How is it that thou, being a Jew, askest drink of me, which am a woman of Samaria? for the Jews have no dealings with the Samaritans……………….:19 The woman saith unto him, Sir, I perceive that thou art a prophet. 20 Our fathers worshipped in this mountain; and ye say, that in Jerusalem is the place where men ought to worship. 21 Jesus saith unto her, Woman, believe me, the hour cometh, when ye shall neither in this mountain, nor yet at Jerusalem, worship the Father. 22 Ye worship ye know not what: we know what we worship: for salvation is of the Jews. 23 But the hour cometh, and now is, when the true worshippers shall worship the Father in spirit and in truth: for the Father seeketh such to worship him. 24 God is a Spirit: and they that worship him must worship him in spirit and in truth.

The 10ᵗʰ Way that faith will come to us is by worshiping Christ in spirit and in truth!

You see the principles of the old and New Testament are the same on how faith comes. David was a man of deep worship. They believe that 78 of the 150 Psalms were written and sang by David. Of course our worship must be sincere and authentic, flowing deep from that of a heart in love with God. The word worship is a very interesting word because in the Hebrew it literally means to fall on your face and to the kiss the feet. To worship means to surrender, to yield, and to give yourself completely over to. It literally means to magnify, to glorify something in your life. Remember the commandment that was given to the descendants of Abraham, thou shalt worship the Lord thy God and him only shalt thou serve!

Exodus 34:14 *For thou shalt worship no other god: for the Lord, whose name is Jealous, is a jealous God:*

How Faith Comes

Worshiping God is not just singing, you worship God in your financial giving, in your obedience, in your attitude and thoughts. The wise men came to worship **Jesus** when he was still a child by giving him gold, frankincense and myrrh. Whatever you are worshiping is that which you exalt above all else and invest in. When you worship something, or somebody, it will end up literally possessing you! Many people are worshiping sports, they are worship hunting and fishing, they are worshiping their problems, or all they ever do is talk about the government, and the wickedness of people. Whatever you are bragging about, constantly talking about, or boasting about is literally that which you are worshiping. When you are telling everybody about your sickness, or your problems you are worshiping at the altar of demons!

When you are exalting sickness and disease, fears, worries, and problems you are not operating in the faith that is in **Christ Jesus**, but you are worshiping at the altar of devils and demons. Remember how the Israelites were bragging to David about Goliath but unbeknownst to them, they were actually involved in idolatry. They were worshiping their enemy, and exalting him.

When we are truly worshiping **Jesus** then we will exalt **Jesus Christ** above all else.

Romans 14:11 For it is written, As I live, saith the Lord, every knee shall bow to me, and every tongue shall confess to God.

Philippians 2:10 That at the name of Jesus every knee should bow, of things in heaven, and things in earth, and things under the earth;

When you and I worship **Jesus**, faith will come flooding into our souls, because whatever you worship is you're God! Let us look at verse 22 where **Jesus** said you worship you know not what, we know what we worship <u>for salvation</u> is of the Jews, for the hour cometh and now is when the true worshipers shall worship God in spirit and in truth. God is looking for people who will worship him, glorify him, and exalt him, magnified him. God is a spirit and we must have the spirit of faith which comes from God. Faith is a spirit and they that worship God must worship Him in spirit and truth.

Remember that faith is when the word of God is quickened by the spirit and it becomes more real to you than the circumstances or the problems that are confronting you.

Jesus never ever asked people what their problem was! When you are operating in faith you will never ask somebody what's wrong, but what is it they want God to do for them.

Matt20:29 And as they departed from Jericho, a great multitude followed him.30 And, behold, two blind men sitting by the way side, when they heard that Jesus passed by, cried out, saying, Have mercy on us, O Lord, thou son of David.31 And the multitude rebuked them, because they should hold their peace: but they cried the more, saying, Have mercy on us, O Lord, thou son of David.32 And Jesus stood still, and called them, and said, What will ye that I shall do unto you?33 They say unto him, Lord, that our eyes may be opened.34 So Jesus had compassion on them, and touched their eyes: and immediately their eyes received sight, and they followed him.

God really wants to manifest himself to us but if we are not true worshipers, if we are not glorifying **Christ**, if we are not exalting **Christ** above the situation, HE cannot fill us with faith! God wants to fill you with faith but you must be willing to worship HIM and only HIM above all else. Many Christians are torment because they will not worship and obey God! Until you become a true worshiper of **Jesus Christ** from the sincerity of your heart (exalting **Jesus** above everything) you will be tormented, because you're worshiping the problem which will draw demonic powers to you like a dung heap draws flies!

Habakkuk 3:17 Although the fig tree shall not blossom, neither shall fruit be in the vines; the labour of the olive shall fail, and the fields shall yield no meat; the flock shall be cut off from the fold, and there shall be no herd in the stalls:18 Yet I will rejoice in the Lord, I will joy in the God of my salvation.

How Faith Comes

God said I'm looking for people who really mean what they say. They are serious about what they're singing, they really want to be holy and totally committed to **Jesus Christ**. David was such a man. When he brought the Ark of the Covenant into Jerusalem he danced with all of his might before the Lord because he was zealous for God.

Worshiping God on a moonlit night in Alaska

I remember as a 19-year-old boy being out on a deserted shore at a lake in Alaska on one of the Aleutian Islands late at night. The moon was shining as I began to sing amazing Grace with all of my heart. I remember tears flowing down my face, and the presence of God overwhelmed me, with joy and love flowing from my heart. My heart was filled with such thankfulness, love and gratitude towards the one who had given his all to rescue me. God inhabits the praises and worship of his people, I was truly worshiping **Jesus Christ** out of the gratitude and love of my heart!

Worship is so very important and I can prove it to you by looking at the opposite side of the coin. Why does the devil want to be worshiped? Because it will produce an invisible substance called unbelief. Yes, even as faith is the substance of things hoped for, so unbelief is the substance of things we do not want manifested in our lives!

Matthew 4:8 Again, the devil taketh him up into an exceeding high mountain, and sheweth him all the kingdoms of the world, and the glory of them;9 And saith unto him, All these things will I give thee, if thou wilt fall down and worship me.10 Then saith Jesus unto him, Get thee hence, Satan: for it is written, Thou shalt worship the Lord thy God, and him only shalt thou serve.

Why would the devil want to be worshiped? Is it just because he has a big ego? **No,** it is because there is a spiritual principle involved in worship. This is the third time that **Jesus** has been tempted by the devil. He's been in the wilderness for 40 days when the devil takes **Jesus** up to and exceedingly

High Mountain and shows him all the kingdoms of the world and the glory of them. He says to **Jesus**: worship me and I will give it all to you. What you worship will possess your heart, your soul, and your mind. You will become a servant of that which you worship whether you want to or not. Notice what **Jesus** said to the enemy: **IT IS WRITTEN**! Basically **Jesus** said to the devil: I have had enough of your silly games, be gone with you. A lot people think the devil left **Jesus** because he had completed three different temptations. **No** it is because basically **Jesus** said I have had enough of you, I submit myself to God, I resisted you, **now go**!

We need to do the same thing with Sickness, disease, financial lack, nicotine and beer, anxiety, wrong attitudes, anything that is against the will of God! We need to fall down on our face and give our whole heart and allegiance to the creator of all things. He's the only one who has the right to be worshiped and exalted above all else. We have no right to worship ourselves, or to worship any preacher, or to worship any program, or the works of our own hands, or any temptation or problem.

We are commanded to worship God and **Jesus Christ** alone; this is what the early church did. This is why they were hated and despised, because all they did was worship **Jesus**! When we worship the King of Kings and Lord of lord's faith will come flooding into our souls! When you and I worship God, faith will come!

Matthew 2:2Saying, Where is he that is born King of the Jews? for we have seen his star in the east, and are come to worship him.

Matthew 2:11And when they were come into the house, they saw the young child with Mary his mother, and fell down, and worshipped him: and when they had opened their treasures, they presented unto him gifts; gold, and frankincense and myrrh.

Many so-called Christians worship everything but Jesus Christ.

They worshiped the worship team, they worshiped their favorite preacher, they worship the blessings, they worship confession, they worship faith, and they worship the Mark of the beast by spending all of their time talking about it. They worship conspiracies, they worship the illuminati, and they worship the government by spending all of their time attacking it. Please do not misunderstand me, I know that they are doing it out of ignorance because I have made the same mistake. People who are sick are full of unbelief and are worshiping demons because all they do is spend all of their money, time and energy on that sickness when **Jesus has already dealt with it by the stripes upon his back**.

Every one of these chapters could literally be turned into a book by itself, I'm simply giving you the condensed version of these teachings in order to aim you in the right direction in the developing and the growing of your faith in **Christ Jesus**. Paul had an amazing Revelation of how faith comes.

Ephesians 5:17 Wherefore be ye not unwise, but understanding what the will of the Lord is.18 And be not drunk with wine, wherein is excess; but be filled with the Spirit;19 Speaking to yourselves in psalms and hymns and spiritual songs, singing and making melody in your heart to the Lord;20 Giving thanks always for all things unto God and the Father in the name of our Lord Jesus Christ;

You might say: Pastor Mike this isn't talk about faith! Oh yes it is, because we are to have a spirit of faith which is in **Christ Jesus**. When you are full of the spirit you are absolutely full of faith. The Holy Ghost wants to overwhelm you, but in order to do that he is looking for faith, trust, reliance, confidence, dependence upon God. He is looking for those who are true worshipers of **Jesus Christ**. There are many other Scriptures that encourage us to worship God in order for us to be filled with faith. I strongly suggest you take the time to search for the Scriptures and begin to apply them to your life. Faith will come when we begin to worship God in spirit, sincerity and truth. When you're exalting God, you're lifting up God, your glorifying God and he will become your all in your all. Faith will flood your soul!

One major thing that we must **stop doing** is glorifying the devil, stop glorifying your problems, stop glorifying your feelings, stop glorifying anything but **Jesus Christ**. We need to worship nobody but **Jesus Christ**. I do not have to bend my knees to the medical world, I don't have to bend my knees to this government, I don't have to bend my knees to depression, or to fear, or to worry, or to any type of sin. I am a worshiper of **Jesus Christ!** That is why the world hated the early church, because they worshiped nobody but **Jesus. As I worship Jesus Christ faith will come!**

The modern-day church is full of idolatry and idolaters just like Israel was full of idolatry when they built altars on every Greenhill, under every tree. I am asking you: Now come the church is so lukewarm; lackadaisical non-committed in America right now and around the world? They are worshiping at the altar of vain amusements, worshiping all their problems, they and bending their knees at the altar of worry, and are worshiping financial lack, or financial abundance.

The Lord spoke to me when I began to do this series, he said to my heart: I want you to **stop worshiping the devil!** I Said Lord what do you mean? He said do not pray anymore about symptoms in your body, do not speak any more about financial lack, do not boast any more about what the government's doing, and about what the politicians are doing, or even what the wicked church is doing! Give the enemy **NO** worship. HE said to me: **AM I not greater** than all these things?

In the book of Revelation if you look up the word worship, it talks about worshiping God from 8 to 10 times, and then it talks about worshiping the beast, the antichrist, and the devil the same amount of times. Why would it talk about worship in the book of Revelation? Because it is the **worshiping of Christ which brings faith**! And then it is the worshiping of the devil which brings unbelief! You and I cannot be double minded and expect to receive anything from God. The devil who is headed to hell wants to be worshiped. But I want to be filled with faith, so I will worship nobody but God. You will be filled with faith as you worship God and **Jesus Christ!**

Colossians 3:16 Let the word of Christ dwell in you richly in all wisdom; teaching and admonishing one another in psalms and hymns and spiritual songs, singing with grace in your hearts to the Lord.

When Jesus Supernaturally Took the Wheel

In May of 1975 I was driving my sister's 1973 red Maverick from Canada to Wisconsin. I had been discharged from the Navy since I had completed my military service. My sister was in the Air Force and was stationed in New Mexico. She asked me to drive her car from New Mexico to Anchorage, Alaska, which was her next tour of duty. I had driven the Alcan Freeway during the onset of winter the previous year, from Anchorage to Seattle is 2,300 miles long. (At that time I was only eighteen years old and not yet saved. I cover that experience in another book.) I was planning to return to Alaska to go out and minister to the Yupik Indians, so I agreed to drive her vehicle all the way to Anchorage.

I experienced heavy rains as I headed up through Canada for the dirt road which would take me to Fairbanks. To my disappointment, I had to stop and turn around because the bridges were all washed out, and they didn't know when they would open the roads that were washed out due to flooding rivers. The thought occurred to me about driving her car back to Wisconsin where my parents lived.

Looking back, I realize that God was in this event. I came out of the mountains of Canada singing and worshipping God in the Spirit as the sun was at its peak. As I worshipped God, the car became filled with the tangible presence of the Lord. I was overwhelmed by His goodness and love. The reality of **Christ**'s love was so strong that I began to cry. The inside of my car filled with a glistening fog. I got so caught up in worshiping the Lord that I raised my hands toward heaven, taking them off the steering wheel. Time seemed to stand still as I was ushered into another realm. Eventually my hands came back to the steering wheel as the fog was dissipating. I noticed the sun, which had been in the middle of the sky, was just now peeking over the horizon and it was beginning to get dark. I did not check the mileage but

I know my car had gone many miles without me steering it. Someone had driven my car while I was caught up in the Spirit!

#11 When You Cry out for Mercy

In the garden there were two trees, the tree of the knowledge of good and evil and the tree of life. I believe the tree of life is symbolic of faith and of trust in God, complete dependence, reliance upon God, looking to God for everything. Both Adam and his wife before they committed sin were living in that realm of faith, but when they committed sin, they entered into another world. You might say it was like the twilight zone, outer limits, like a nightmare and it is called the realm of unbelief. Now when you live in the realm of unbelief the flesh is more real to you than anything that God has said. When you live in the realm of faith (trusting in God and **Jesus Christ**) God is more real to you than anything in the natural. When you live in the realm of unbelief than financial lack, sickness, disease, poverty, pain and sorrow will overwhelm you. The lust of the flesh, the lust of the eyes, and the pride of life will control and direct every step you take.

Sickness and diseases, sin and disobedience are all enemies and adversaries of God, but when you are living in the realm of faith you have victory over all of these areas. In Ephesians Paul the apostle declares that we do not wrestle flesh and blood, but against principalities and powers, rules of darkness and spiritual wickedness in high places. That we must put on the whole armor of God in order to have victory over the demonic world. One of our weapons above all else we are use is the **shield of faith** wherewith we will be able to quench all the fiery darts of the wicked one. In order to do this, we need to have absolute faith in **Jesus Christ**. The just shall live by faith and the just shall walk by faith! In Hebrews 11 it reveals to us that there were over 50 events with many different characters, which included Able, Enoch, Noah, Abraham, Isaac and Jacob, Joseph, Moses, Joshua and Caleb and many more. They overcame by faith, every single one of them overcame by faith, and we must overcome by faith in **Christ Jesus**. Faith is always built and based upon the reality of God and his word.

Over and over **Jesus** told people that their faith **In Him** had made them whole. That is what he was declaring when he said this to blind Bartimaeus, when he said this to the woman with the issue of blood, when he said this to the Canaanite woman. He was saying: your trust in me, your trust in God has made you whole. So what gives us the victory is trusting in God. When man commits sin it is a spirit of unbelief, that brings death, which brings fear, which brings anxiety, which brings sickness, which brings disease, which brings immorality, which brings hate, which brings murder and corruption! A spirit of unbelief will cause you not to trust God, not believing, not depending upon God, not looking to God, and not relying upon God. God is to be our all in all, but when Adam and his wife sinned a spirit of unbelief came into Adam and brought death. It came through their flesh and entered into their soul.

John 10:10The thief cometh not, but for to steal, and to kill, and to destroy: I am come that they might have life, and that they might have it more abundantly.

When the devil comes to steal and kill and destroy, how does he do it? By a spirit of unbelief, the devil has to get our eyes off of God, off of the truth of God's word. Remember that we are commanded to love the Lord our God with all of our heart, with all of our soul, with all of our mind, with all of our strength, and with all of our being! The disciples asked **Jesus** to help increase their faith because they knew they needed faith in order to do the will of God. I need Faith because without faith it is impossible to please God.

#11 Let us now take a look at the **11ᵗʰ Way** in which faith will come!

2 Chronicles 5:1 Thus all the work that Solomon made for the house of the Lord was finished: and Solomon brought in all the things that David his Father had dedicated; and the silver, and the gold, and all the instruments, put he among the treasures of the house of God.............4 And all the elders of Israel came; and the Levites took up the ark.5 And they brought up the ark, and the tabernacle of the congregation, and all the holy vessels that were in the tabernacle, these did the priests and the Levites bring up........................7 And the priests brought in the ark of the covenant of the Lord unto his place, to the oracle of the house, into the most holy place, even under the wings of the cherubims:........................11 And it came to pass, when the priests were come out of the holy place: (for all the priests that were present were sanctified, and did not then wait by course:12 Also the Levites which were the singers, all of them of Asaph, of Heman, of Jeduthun, with their sons and their brethren, being arrayed in white linen, having cymbals and psalteries and harps, stood at the east end of the altar, and with them an hundred and twenty priests sounding with trumpets:)13 It came even to pass, as the trumpeters and singers were as one, to make one sound to be heard in praising and thanking the Lord; and when they lifted up their voice with the trumpets and cymbals and instruments of musick, and praised the Lord, saying, For he is good; **for his mercy endureth for ever**: *that then the house was filled with a cloud, even the house of the Lord;14 So that the priests could not stand to minister by reason of the cloud: for the glory of the Lord had filled the house of God.*

Here in second Chronicles chapter 5:12 there was assigned 120 priests to sound the trumpets. Notice the amazing coincidence that 120 priest were to blow the trumpets, and in the book of Acts it talks about 120 people were in the upper room on the day of Pentecost. So there's 120 priest and they're blowing the trumpets. In verse 13 something amazing happens. As they were saying:

For he is good; for his **mercy** *endureth for ever: that then the house was filled with a cloud, even the house of the Lord.*

Mercy is very important in a believer's life! It is one of the major attributes and aspects of God's nature, his character, his disposition. It literally talks about God's mercy over 260 times in the Old and New Testament. In the wilderness God had Moses make the Ark of the Covenant which was overlaid with gold. On top of the ark was the lid, with angelic beings, cherubim's overlooking the **mercy** seat. **God sits upon the mercy seat**! That was all symbolic of heaven. They would bring the blood of the Passover lamb and sprinkle it upon the **mercy** seat.

Now when **Christ** died and rose again he took his blood to the heavenly **mercy** seat and sprinkled it upon that golden lid! When Aaron brought it in the 10 Commandments and placed it in the Ark of the Covenant, the manna, and Aaron's rod, they placed over the top of it the **mercy** seat. That was where the blood was sprinkled on the **mercy** seat. And then they would begin to cry out for the **mercy** of the Lord which endured forever. Something supernatural would happen when they began to cry out for God's **mercy**! Listen the house was filled with a cloud that's called the Shekinah glory even the house of the Lord. When they proclaimed the **mercy** of the Lord endures forever it could be translated as his loving kindness and compassion, his forgiveness, his goodness and long-suffering is everlasting.

Something Supernatural Happens When You Cry out for God's Mercy!

You and I do not deserve heaven we deserved hell. We all have sinned and come short of the glory of God. Everything that God does for us as an act of his **MERCY**. When you get healed, when you get your prayers answered, when your sins are forgiven, and when any good thing happens to us as believers it is an act of God's **mercy**!

Gods Mercy is the 11th Way that faith will come!

It happens when you and I begin to cry out and apprehend the **mercy** of God. I cannot tell you how many times when I knew in my heart that I was not really operating in faith and the only thing I had faith in was God's **mercy**. That's all I could do was look to our merciful God. He is a forgiving God, an all loving God, an all compassionate God. This wonderful heavenly **Father** is revealed to us through the redemptive work of **Jesus Christ**.

When the people cried out in the Old Testament and declared the **mercy** of the Lord, the Shekinah glory was manifested. I have personally seen this glory cloud numerous times in my life. Now you might see it at times when nobody else will. When you begin to live in the realm of faith you will begin to see things that other people will never see. Why do people fall under the power? People begin falling under the power when the glory cloud comes upon them, that's the Shekinah, that's the presence of God coming upon a person.

3   Chronicles 7: 7 Now when Solomon had made an end of praying, the fire came down from heaven, and consumed the burnt offering and the sacrifices; and the glory of the Lord filled the house.2 And the priests could not enter into the house of the Lord, because the glory of the Lord had filled the Lord's house.3 And when all the children of Israel saw how the fire came down, and the glory of the Lord upon the house, they bowed themselves with their faces to the ground upon the pavement, and worshipped, and praised the Lord, saying, For he is good; for his __mercy endureth for ever.__*4 Then the king and all the people offered sacrifices before the Lord.*

Does this not sound just like on the day of Pentecost? Notice how the children of Israel connected the glory cloud, the Shekinah, the presence of God with his mercy! Let me ask you something: if you would have been in a meeting like this, do you think faith might have come rushing into your heart? Yes, faith would have exploded into every fiber of your being. Your heart would have been brought into a place of trusting and having confidence in God.

Faith Comes as You Cry out for God's Mercy!

When you and I apprehend Gods **mercy**, faith comes rushing in to our heart.

Blood Guts and Broken Bones!

I remember one time when God's mercy came upon me as I was driving a motorcycle through the mountains of Montana. I was a 21-year-old kid headed for Alaska on my motorcycle. It was early in the morning. Just a half an hour earlier I had broke camp, packed up my sleeping bag and pup tent, jumped onto my motorcycle, and was headed into Oregon on a mountain road. My plan was to take the Alcan freeway all the way up to Alaska (which at the time was nothing but a dirt road), but 1st I was going to Oregon to visit some close friends of mine. I was driving along early in the morning praising the Lord, meditating upon the Scriptures. I was coming around a sharp corner, with banks and trees on both sides of the road. Just as I was at the sharpest point of the corner, I saw a flash of movement off to my right. Faster than I could possibly react, a large mule deer, leaped right into me. In my heart I knew instantly that it was too late. I was going to be hit by this leaping deer. At 50 miles per hour, I knew our bodies were going to be tangled together in blood, guts, skin, and hide. Mule deer flesh and human flesh was about to become as one. I saw his underside was only about two feet away from my head.

Now I am telling you that something supernatural happened at that very moment. At the very last possible second, this mule deer was lifted higher up into the air, right over the top of my head and bike. It landed on the other side of the road and continued on its way.

That is what I call the **mercy** of god! I was so overwhelmed by this act of God's **mercy** that without thinking my hands came off the steering bars of that motorcycle. I cannot tell you how long my hands were lifted up in the air praising God, but I was lost in the Holy Ghost, overwhelmed by his love and his **mercy**.

2 Chronicles 20: 20 And they rose early in the morning, and went forth into the wilderness of Tekoa: and as they went forth, Jehoshaphat stood and said, Hear me, O Judah, and ye inhabitants of Jerusalem; Believe in the Lord your God, so shall ye be established; believe his prophets, so shall ye prosper. 21 And when he had consulted with the people, he appointed singers unto the Lord, and that should praise the beauty of holiness, as they went out before the army, and to say, Praise the Lord; for his mercy endureth for ever. 22 And when they began to sing and to praise, the Lord set ambushments against the children of Ammon, Moab, and mount Seir, which were come against Judah; and they were smitten.23 For the children of Ammon and Moab stood up against the inhabitants of mount Seir, utterly to slay and destroy them: and when they had made an end of the inhabitants of Seir, every one helped to destroy another.24 And when Judah came toward the watch tower in the wilderness, they looked unto the multitude, and, behold, they were dead bodies fallen to the earth, and none escaped.25 And when Jehoshaphat and his people came to take away the spoil of them, they found among them in abundance both riches with the dead bodies, and precious jewels, which they stripped off for themselves, more than they could carry away: and they were three days in gathering of the spoil, it was so much.

As they were praising God for his **mercy** and for his loving kindness, his compassion, something supernatural happened. The Lord set ambushments against their enemy. Notice that the children of Israel were in the will of God crying out for his **mercy**. We also need to be crying out to God to have **mercy** on us and this unbelieving generation, this wicked government, and this wicked society.

*Hebrews 4:16 Let us therefore come boldly unto the throne of grace, that we may obtain **mercy**, and find grace to help in time of need.*

Mercy is only apprehended by those who receive God's forgiveness, fear the Lord, and have a forgiving heart. If you don't have **mercy**, you will not receive **mercy**. David was a man filled with **mercy**, Solomon was a man filled with **mercy**. Jehoshaphat when he began to sing about the **mercy** of the lord, God caused the merciless to turn on each. I have seen this happen many times in my life. I have watched people with no **mercy** turn on others that had no **mercy**, thereby trying to destroy each other. It takes faith to have **mercy** on others. When you do not have **mercy** (love covers a multitude of sin) your heart will be filled with bitterness and resentment, selfrighteousness and pride. Faith that is true biblical faith operates by love. **Mercy** is an act of love and as you and I cry out for God's **mercy** and operate in His **mercy,** faith will come rushing into our hearts.

A SAD BUT TRUE STORY!

I had a former pastor one time that lead a rebellion against me in our Christian school and our church. This gentleman had been one of the teachers in our school for a number of years (he had also been a pastor of a local church) and because of a decision I had made he had become extremely angry and upset at me. He was so upset at me that he spoke to all of our school teachers and personnel against me.

This bitterness in his heart spread like a house on fire throughout the whole ministry. Strife, gossip, and rumors about me began to spread like an incurable disease. It became so bad that after the school year, I simply had to shut the school down. I mean it was so vicious that it was impossible to keep going with our school.

James 3:16 For where envying and strife is, there is confusion and every evil work.

During this whole conflict not one time did I ever get angry, bitter or upset with him knowing that I could not afford to be bitter. The next thing that I heard was that this dear brother had been hit with a deadly and incurable disease. I began earnestly praying for him, he had been a good pastor and teacher at one time, but had allowed the seed of bitterness to spring up in him, contaminating many others with him. One day out of the blue I received a phone call from this man's wife. She said her husband would like to speak to me. I had to press the phone tightly against my ear because he was speaking to me with barely a whisper. He asked me to please forgive him for what he had done. He said he knew he was wrong for causing all of the strife which he had caused. With tears rolling down my face I told him that he was forgiven. We spoke for a little bit longer before we both hung up. Late that same evening he passed on to be with the Lord. Praise God for his mercy and his goodness that even when we disobey him, there is still **mercy** and forgiveness available.

How Faith Comes

Hebrews 12:15 Looking diligently lest any man fail of the grace of God; lest any root of bitterness springing up trouble you, and thereby many be defiled;

We have to be careful that a root of bitterness is not allowed in any of us. It is literally a demonic seed of unbelief which rises up against the **mercy** of God that we must operate in for other people, whether they are right or wrong. We're going take a look at four stories in the Gospels how people were healed by **Jesus** because of the fact they cried out for mercy.

Story #1 *Matthew 9:27 And when Jesus departed thence, two blind men followed him, crying, and saying, Thou son of David, have **mercy** on us.28 And when he was come into the house, the blind men came to him: and Jesus saith unto them, Believe ye that I am able to do this? They said unto him, Yea, Lord.*

Stories #2 *Matthew 20:29 And as they departed from Jericho, a great multitude followed him.30 And, behold, two blind men sitting by the way side, when they heard that Jesus passed by, cried out, saying, Have **mercy** on us, O Lord, thou son of David.31 And the multitude rebuked them, because they should hold their peace: but they cried the more, saying, Have **mercy** on us, O Lord, thou son of David.*

Story #3 *Mark 10:46 And they came to Jericho: and as he went out of Jericho with his disciples and a great number of people, blind Bartimaeus, the son of Timaeus, sat by the highway side begging.47 And when he heard that it was Jesus of Nazareth, he began to cry out, and say, Jesus, thou son of David, have **mercy** on me.*

All of these people had one thing in common, and that is that they recognized that if healing was the going to be theirs it was only going to happen because of the mercy of God. They knew in their hearts that **Jesus** was the son of David, the promised Messiah, and that they would have to apprehend their healing by having faith in God's mercy. And as they cried out for mercy, I am totally convinced that faith arose in their hearts.

Story #4 *Matthew 15:22 And, behold, a woman of Canaan came out of the same coasts, and cried unto him, saying, Have mercy on me, O Lord, thou son of David; my daughter is grievously vexed with a devil.23 But he answered her not a word. And his disciples came and besought him, saying, Send her away; for she crieth after us.24 But he answered and said, I am not sent but unto the lost sheep of the house of Israel.25 Then came she and worshipped him, saying, Lord, help me.26 But he answered and said, It is not meet to take the children's bread, and to cast it to dogs.27 And she said, Truth, Lord: yet the dogs eat of the crumbs which fall from their masters' table.28 Then Jesus answered and said unto her, O woman, great is thy faith: be it unto thee even as thou wilt. And her daughter was made whole from that very hour.*

Now here's an amazing story about a woman, who was not even of the descendants of Abraham, Isaac and Jacob. And yet she boldly took a hold of healing by believing in the **mercy** of God.

As she was Crying out for Mercy, Faith Began to Flood Her Soul, Mind and Emotions.

I Cried out for Mercy as My Son Was Dying from Rabies

My son Daniel when he was 16 years old (in 2000) brought home a baby raccoon. He wanted to keep this raccoon as a pet. Immediately people began to inform me that this was illegal in the state of Pennsylvania. That in order to have a raccoon in Pennsylvania you had to purchase one from someone who was licensed by the state to sell them. The reason for this was the high rate of rabies carried among them. But stubbornness rose up in my heart against what they were telling me.

You see I had a raccoon when I was a child. Her mother had been killed on the Highway, and she had left behind a litter of her little ones. I had taken one of the little ones and bottle-fed it, naming her candy. I had a lot of fond memories of this raccoon, so when my son wanted this raccoon, against better judgment, against the law of the land, I said okay. I did not realize that baby raccoons can have the rabies virus lying dormant in them for months before it will be manifested. I knew in my heart at the time that I was wrong to let him keep this raccoon, but like so many when we are out of the will of God we justify ourselves. We do not realize the price that we will have to pay because of our rebellion and disobedience. Daniel named his little raccoon rascal, and he was a rascal, because he was constantly getting into everything. A number of months went by, and one day my son Daniel told me he had a frightening dream. I should've known right then and there that he needed to get rid of this raccoon. He said he had a dream where rascal grew up and became big like a bear, and that it attacked him and devoured him.

Some time went by and my son Daniel began to get sick, running a high fever. One morning he came down telling me that something was majorly wrong with rascal. He said that he was wobbling all over the place, and bumping into stuff. Immediately the alarm bells went off. I asked him where his raccoon was. He informed me that rascal was in his bedroom. Immediately I went upstairs to his room, opening his bedroom door, and their rascal was acting extremely strange. He was bumping into everything, with spittle coming from his mouth. Immediately my heart was filled with great dread. I had grown up around wildlife and farm animals, and I had run into animals with rabies before. No ifs, ands or buts, this raccoon had rabies. I immediately went to Danny asking him if the raccoon had bitten him, or if he had gotten any of rascal saliva in his wounds? He showed me his hands where he had cuts on them, informing me that he had been letting rascal lick these wounds. He had even allowed rascal to lick his mouth. Daniel did not look well, and he was running a high grade fever, and informed me that he felt dizzy. I knew in my heart we were in terrible trouble. I immediately called up the local forest ranger. They put me on the line with one of their personnel that had a lot of expertise in this area. When I informed him of what was going on, he asked me I did not know that it was illegal to take in a wild raccoon. I told him I did know, and that I had chosen to ignore the law.

He said that he would come immediately over to our house to examine this raccoon, and if necessary to take it with him. I had placed rascal in a cage, making sure I did not touch him. When the forest ranger arrived I had the cage sitting in the driveway. He examined the raccoon without touching it. You could tell that he was quite concerned about the condition of this raccoon. He looked at me with deep regret informing me that if he had ever seen an animal with rabies that according to his almost 30 years in wildlife service, this raccoon definitely had rabies. He asked me if there was anyone who had been in contact with this raccoon with any symptoms of sickness. I informed him that for the last couple days my son Daniel had not been feeling well. Matter of fact he was quite sick. When I told him the symptoms that Daniel was experiencing he was obvious shaken and upset. He told me that anybody who had been in contact with this raccoon would have to receive shots, and that from the description of what my son Daniel was going through, and for how long, that it was too late for him! He literally told me he felt from his experience that there was no hope for my son, and he would die from rabies. He loaded the raccoon up in the back of his truck, leaving me standing in my driveway weeping. He said that he would get back to me as soon as they had the test results, and that I should get ready for state officials to descend upon myself, my family and our church.

I cannot express to you at that moment the hopelessness and despair that had struck my heart. Just earlier in the spring our little girl Naomi had passed on to be with the Lord at 4 ½ years old, and now my second son Daniel was dying from rabies. Both of these situations could've been prevented if I would have simply listened to the Spirit of God! Immediately I gathered together my wife, my first son Michael, my third son Steven, and my daughter Stephanie. We all gathered around Daniels bed and began to cry out to God. We wept, cried, and prayed crying out to God. I was repenting and asking God for mercy. Daniel as he was lying on the bed running a high fever and almost delirious informed me that he was dying, and he was barely hanging on to consciousness. He knew in his heart he said that he was dying!

How Faith Comes

After everyone disbursed from his bed with great overwhelming sorrow, I went into our family room where we had a wood stove. I opened up the wood stove which still had a lot of cold ashes from the winter. Handful after handful of ashes I scooped out of the stove pouring it over my head, saturating my body, with weeping and tears of repentance and sorrow running down my face, and then I laid in the ashes. The ashes got into my eyes, mouth and nose and into my lungs, making me quite sick. I did not care, all that mattered was that God would have mercy on us, and spare my son, and all our loved ones from the rabies virus. As I lay on the floor in the ashes, crying out to God with all I had within me, you could hear the house was filled with weeping, crying and praying family members. All night long I wept and prayed, asking God to please have mercy on my stupidity. I prayed that He would remove the rabies virus not only from my son, but everyone else that had been in contact with this raccoon. I also asked God to remove the virus from the raccoon as a sign that he had heard my prayers. I continued in this state of great agony and prayer till early in the morning (about 16 hours) when suddenly the light of heaven shined upon my soul. Great peace that passes understanding overwhelmed me, I got up with victory in my heart and soul.

I went upstairs to check on my son Daniel. When I walked into his bedroom the presence of God was all over him. The fever had broken, and he was resting peacefully. Our whole house was filled with the tangible presence of God. From that minute forward he was completely healed. A couple days later I was contacted by the state informing me that to their amazement they could find nothing wrong with the raccoon. God had supernaturally removed the rabies virus not only from my son, and those in contact with rascal, but from the raccoon itself. Thank God that the Lord's mercy endures forever!

AS WE CRY OUT TO GOD FOR MERCY, FAITH WILL COME!

Dr Michael H Yeager

#12 By Signs, Wonders & Miracles

For us to understand the **12th Way in which faith comes**, let us take a look in the book of Acts chapter 4.

Acts 4:29 And now, Lord, behold their threatenings: and grant unto thy servants, that with all boldness they may speak thy word,30 By stretching forth thine hand to heal; and that signs and wonders may be done by the name of thy holy child Jesus.31 And when they had prayed, the place was shaken where they were assembled together; and they were all filled with the Holy Ghost, and they spake the word of God with boldness.32 And the multitude of them that believed were of one heart and of one soul: neither said any of them that ought of the things which he possessed was his own; but they had all things common.33And with **great power** *gave the apostles witness of the resurrection of the Lord Jesus: and great grace was upon them all.*

God wants our hearts to be filled with faith, trust, confidence, reliance and dependence upon nothing but him. In the book of Galatians Paul says that the man that works miracles among us does it by the hearing of faith. Not only does it take faith to work signs, wonders, and miracles, but it takes faith to crucify the old man, the flesh. Faith in **Jesus Christ** is the victory that always overcomes the world, the flesh and the devil. Right at the beginning of Acts chapter 3 Peter and John were at the gate beautiful where they saw a man who had been lame from his mother's womb.

Acts 3:1 Now Peter and John went up together into the temple at the hour of prayer, being the ninth hour.2 And a certain man lame from his mother's womb was carried, whom they laid daily at the gate of the temple which is called Beautiful, to ask alms of them that entered into the temple.3

Who seeing Peter and John about to go into the temple asked an alms.4 And Peter, fastening his eyes upon him with John, said, Look on us.5 And he gave heed unto them, expecting to receive something of them.6 Then Peter said, Silver and gold have I none; but such as I have give I thee: In the name of Jesus Christ of Nazareth rise up and walk.7 And he took him by the right hand, and lifted him up: and immediately his feet and ankle bones received strength.8 And he leaping up stood, and walked, and entered with them into the temple, walking, and leaping, and praising God.9 And all the people saw him walking and praising God:

Now when God had performed this miracle through Peter and John, there is no denying the reality of what the Lord had done. As a result of this amazing miracle, 5000 men believed on the Lord **Jesus Christ**. If you will do a study on the Scriptures of the New Testament you will discover throughout the book of acts that many people came to **Christ** as a result of seeing the miracles that were performed by the believers. Throughout the rest of this chapter on the **12ᵗʰ Way** that faith comes I will be giving you many examples of how God used miracles to cause faith to a rise in the hearts of the people.

#12 The 12ᵗʰ Way that faith comes is by seeing Signs, Wonders, & Miracles!

Back to acts chapter 4, it reveals to us that when they had prayed the place was shaken where they were assembled together, and they were filled with the Holy Ghost. To be full of the Holy Ghost, you must be full of faith. When your heart is full of unbelief you will be full of fear, worry, anxiety, and bitterness. When You Are Walking, Living, Moving and Operating in Faith you will be possessed with a peace and joy that passes all understanding. Paul very boldly declares that because of the demonstration of the spirit and the power of God, faith came flooding into the lives of the Corinthian people.

1 Corinthians 2:4 And my speech and my preaching was not with enticing words of man's wisdom, but in demonstration of the Spirit and of power:5

How Faith Comes

That your faith should not stand in the wisdom of men, but in the power of God.

Listen to what Paul said in this particular Scripture which is very important! Paul said: *...my speech and my preaching was not with enticing words of man's wisdom, but in demonstration of the Spirit and of power*.

Why Paul? That your heart would not stand in the wisdom of man. It is the demonstration of the spirit and the power of the living God that brought Faith to the Corinthians. If you look into the Old Testament you notice that God had Moses performed many mighty signs and wonders by the spirit of the Lord. We need to understand that without mighty signs and wonders the majority of the people will never get right with God? They will never be free from the bondage of the enemy. That is why America is so dead spiritually. That's why so many people have no hunger for the things of God, because they have not seen the mighty deeds of God. They do not have the Faith that overcomes because they have not seen Mighty Signs, Wonders, and Miracles. **Jesus** in his earthly ministry did many wonderful signs and wonders. He declared that it brought faith, and that if people did not have faith as a result of seeing all of these amazing things, it was because of their wicked hearts.

Matthew 11:20   Then began he to upbraid the cities wherein most of his mighty works were done, because they repented not:21 Woe unto thee, Chorazin! woe unto thee, Bethsaida! for if the mighty works, which were done in you, had been done in Tyre and Sidon, they would have repented long ago in sackcloth and ashes.22 But I say unto you, It shall be more tolerable for Tyre and Sidon at the day of judgment, than for you. 23 And thou, Capernaum, which art exalted unto heaven, shalt be brought down to hell: for if the mighty works, which have been done in thee, had been done in Sodom, it would have remained until this day.24 But I say unto you, That it shall be more tolerable for the land of Sodom in the day of judgment, than for thee.

Remember that when **Christ** was raised from the dead he appeared to Peter and John and then he appeared to the other disciples. Thomas is one of the apostles who was not there, and they could not convince him to believe. He literally stated that he would not believe unless he could put his hand into the side of **Jesus**'s pierced side, and put his finger into his nail pierced hand. It's amazing when **Jesus** appeared what he said to Thomas:

John 20:27 Then saith he to Thomas, Reach hither thy finger, and behold my hands; and reach hither thy hand, and thrust it into my side: and be not faithless, but believing.

Christ so desired for Thomas to have faith, to believe that he was more than willing to have him stick his hand into His wounded side and put his finger into His nail pierced hand. You see God wants us to experience mighty signs, wonders, and miracles performed in the name of **Jesus** that we might have strong faith.

2 Corinthians 12:12 Truly the signs of an apostle were wrought among you in all patience, in signs, and wonders, and mighty deeds.

Let us look now in Romans chapter 15:

Romans 15:18 For I will not dare to speak of any of those things which Christ hath not wrought by me, to make the Gentiles obedient, by word and deed,19 Through mighty signs and wonders, by the power of the Spirit of God; so that from Jerusalem, and round about unto Illyricum, I have fully preached the gospel of Christ.20 Yea, so have I strived to preach the gospel, not where Christ was named, lest I should build upon another man's foundation:

Paul said that their faith needed to be built upon the dynamite explosive power of God, and his word. Most of the modern day church is not built upon this reality. Most churches today are built upon programs, games, fun, entertainment and worldly events. The early church experienced mighty signs, wonders, and miracles, which created in them a faith that could handle the persecution that eventually tested and tried them. The early Saints had enduring faith because they saw the mighty hand of God. I have been a pastor since 1977, and I was a missionary before that, and I can testify that I have seen many believers fall away by the wayside because their faith was not built upon the mighty works of God.

The early believers saw the mighty signs, wonders, and miracles done by the apostles and it created within them a desire to be completely free from the things of this world. Many of them went out and sold everything they had because they did not want the things of this world any more.

James 2:5 Hearken, my beloved brethren, Hath not God chosen the poor of this world rich in faith, and heirs of the kingdom which he hath promised to them that love him?

Acts 4:33 And with great power gave the apostles witness of the resurrection of the Lord Jesus: and great grace was upon them all.34 Neither was there any among them that lacked: for as many as were possessors of lands or houses sold them, and brought the prices of the things that were sold, 35 And laid them down at the apostles' feet: and distribution was made unto every man according as he had need.

You see my friend it takes great faith to want to be free from the things of this world. It is not a vow of poverty, but recognition that nothing matters but **Jesus Christ**. When Paul, Peter, Stephen and the early believers preach the gospel it was in the power of **Christ** with signs, wonders, and miracles. **Jesus Christ** is the same yesterday today and forever, but because most preachers are not walking where they're called of God to walk, they have come up with a doctrine that says God does not do miracles any longer, so most believers are filled with a very weak and anemic, sickly faith that cannot take a hold of God and his word.

Now let us look at this amazing set of Scriptures, where Paul clearly declares that the reason why the Corinthian's were obedient was because of the mighty signs and wonders he did in the name of **Jesus**!

115

Romans 15:17 I have therefore whereof I may glory through Jesus Christ in those things which pertain to God. 18 For I will not dare to speak of any of those things which Christ hath not wrought by me, to **make the Gentiles obedient, by word and deed,** *19 Through mighty signs and wonders, by the power of the Spirit of God; so that from Jerusalem, and round about unto Illyricum, I have fully preached the gospel of Christ.*

Did you hear what Paul said? We are never going to be able to help people the way they need to be helped until we are moving in the power and the spirit of the living God. We are not going to cause people to believe by criticizing them, finding fault with them, by attacking or going on a crusade against this group or that group. This is a Mickey Mouse and Stupid dead end alley! **Stop**: what you and I really need is a deep revelation of what the real the problem is. You see I have discovered the real problem, and it's **me not being full of the Holy Ghost and full of faith**. If I was truly moving in the power of God many unbelievers would believe, and many of the atheists would believe, and many of the immoral would repent and come to **Christ**.

An Unbelieving Man Receives a New Knee Cap! (1980)

One day as I was preaching in a tent in the Huntington fair, a man who looked to be in his mid-thirties was hobbling by the tent really slow on a pair of crutches. He was not even looking in the direction of our tent, but was looking straight ahead, minding his own business. As I looked at him, the Spirit of God quickened the gift of faith inside of me. When God quickens my heart in this way I do not even think what I'm about to do. I simply act upon the quickening and the witness in my heart.

I found myself calling out to this particular man, speaking over the microphone system. Everybody could hear me within a hundred feet, if not further. Probably the whole Huntington Fair could hear us! (Actually the fire department was really upset with us because we were disturbing their bingo games.) I called out to this man but he ignored me. Once again I challenged him to come into the tent so God could heal him. This time he looked my way but kept hobbling along. I called out the third time, encouraging him to come and be healed of his problem.

After the third time, he finally came into the tent. When he came to the front, I asked him if he had faith to believe that God would heal him. He looked at me as if I had lost my mind. He was probably thinking, *you're the one who called me up here, and I don't even know what this is about. Everybody was staring at me, so I had to come!* He did not respond to my question. I told him that I was going to pray for him now and God would heal him! I asked him again if he believed this. Once again he did not respond. Then I laid my hands on him and commanded him to be healed In the name of **Jesus Christ** of Nazareth. After I was done praying, I told him to put down his crutches and start walking without them. He stood there staring at me. Everybody else was also staring at me. This was okay because the gift of faith was at work in my heart.

I reached forward and took away his crutches, and then I threw them on the ground and spun him around. When I'm in this realm I'm not thinking, I'm simply acting. Then I pushed him. He stumbled forward and began to walk toward the back of the tent. He was picking his legs high up in the air, high stepping it. When he got to the edge of the tent he spun back toward me. Tears were streaming from his eyes and down his cheeks. He came back toward me walking perfectly normal with no limp whatsoever!

I gave him the microphone, and asked him to tell everyone what had happened to him. He kept saying, "You don't understand" over and over. Once again, I encouraged him to tell us his story. I had him face the people in that tent and those outside of it who had been watching. He told us that last winter he had been walking on a very icy sidewalk and that he had lost his footing. Slipping and sliding, he fell forward onto the concrete and ice right onto his right kneecap. He fell down so hard on his kneecap that he knew right away that something terrible had happened to it. He could not move his knee whatsoever, and it was extremely painful. He went to the doctor's office and they x-rayed it. The x-rays revealed that his kneecap had literally been shattered and destroyed. In just two more days from now he was scheduled to have a major operation to replace his kneecap.

I encouraged him to go back to his doctor and get it x-rayed again. Sure enough, a couple days later he came back to the tent giving a wonderful testimony. He had gone to his doctor. He said when he walked into the doctor's office they could tell that his knee was normal. The doctor asked him what had happened. He told them about the encounter he had with **Jesus** at our tent meeting. They x-rayed his kneecap and discovered he had a brand-new kneecap! As a result of this tent meeting God raised up a church of over 400 people in Huntington PA. We still desperately need signs, wonders and miracles.

The Only Way Mighty Signs & Wonders Will Happen Is When We Die to Self, and are Completely given Over to God!

John 4:46 So Jesus came again into Cana of Galilee, where he made the water wine. And there was a certain nobleman, whose son was sick at Capernaum.47 When he heard that Jesus was come out of Judaea into Galilee, he went unto him, and besought him that he would come down, and heal his son: for he was at the point of death.48 Then said Jesus unto him, Except ye see signs and wonders, ye will not believe.49 The nobleman saith unto him, Sir, come down ere my child die.50 Jesus saith unto him, Go thy way; thy son liveth. And the man believed the word that Jesus had spoken unto him, and he went his way.51 And as he was now going down, his servants met him, and told him, saying, Thy son liveth.52 Then enquired he of them the hour when he began to amend. And they said unto him, Yesterday at the seventh hour the fever left him.

So now listen to this: *53 So the Father knew that it was at the same hour, in the which Jesus said unto him, Thy son liveth: and himself believed, and his whole house.*

Did you notice that as a result of this miracle of this noble man son, this man and his whole family believed and were saved.

Signs and wonders will produce faith in those that see them.

118

How Faith Comes

Let us look at one more example within the gospel of John where **Jesus** raises Lazarus from the dead. Even though from Genesis all the way to the book of Revelation there is example after example of how God caused faith to come forth in the hearts of people as he manifests mighty signs and wonders.

John 11:24   Martha saith unto him, I know that he shall rise again in the resurrection at the last day.25   Jesus said unto her, I am the resurrection, and the life: he that believeth in me, though he were dead, yet shall he live.26   And whosoever liveth and believeth in me shall never die. Believest thou this?27   She saith unto him, Yea, Lord: I believe that thou art the Christ, the Son of God, which should come into the world.28   And when she had so said, she went her way, and called Mary her sister secretly, saying, The Master is come, and calleth for thee.29   As soon as she heard that, she arose quickly, and came unto him.30   Now Jesus was not yet come into the town, but was in that place where Martha met him.31   The Jews then which were with her in the house, and comforted her, when they saw Mary, that she rose up hastily and went out, followed her, saying, She goeth unto the grave to weep there.32   Then when Mary was come where Jesus was, and saw him, she fell down at his feet, saying unto him, Lord, if thou hadst been here, my brother had not died.33   When Jesus therefore saw her weeping, and the Jews also weeping which came with her, he groaned in the spirit, and was troubled,34   And said, Where have ye laid him? They said unto him, Lord, come and see.35   Jesus wept.36   Then said the Jews, Behold how he loved him!37   And some of them said, Could not this man, which opened the eyes of the blind, have caused that even this man should not have died?38   Jesus therefore again groaning in himself cometh to the grave. It was a cave, and a stone lay upon it.39   Jesus said, Take ye away the stone. Martha, the sister of him that was dead, saith unto him, Lord, by this time he stinketh: for he hath been dead four days.40   Jesus saith unto her, Said I not unto thee, that, if thou wouldest believe, thou shouldest see the glory of God?41   Then they took away the stone from the place where the dead was laid. And Jesus lifted up his eyes, and said, Father, I thank thee that thou hast heard me.42

And I knew that thou hearest me always: but because of the people which stand by I said it, that they may believe that thou hast sent me.43 And when he thus had spoken, he cried with a loud voice, Lazarus, come forth.44 And he that was dead came forth, bound hand and foot with graveclothes: and his face was bound about with a napkin. Jesus saith unto them, Loose him, and let him go.

Not what were the results of this miracle?

John 11:45 Then many of the Jews which came to Mary, and had seen the things which Jesus did, believed on him.

The 12th Way that faith comes is by seeing Signs, Wonders, & Miracles

CHAPTER FIVE

#13 Remembering what God has done!

To understand the **13th Way** in which faith can come we must once again go in to the old covenant. David is such a central figure when it comes to walking by faith. Yes we could use many other historical biblical figures, but what David said and did is such a clear example of how to walk by faith, and how faith comes. We will once again look at first Samuel 17:

1 Samuel 17:33   And Saul said to David, Thou art not able to go against this Philistine to fight with him: for thou art but a youth, and he a man of war from his youth.34 And David said unto Saul, Thy servant kept his Father's sheep, and there came a lion, and a bear, and took a lamb out of the flock:35 And I went out after him, and smote him, and delivered it out of his mouth: and when he arose against me, I caught him by his beard, and smote him, and slew him.36 Thy servant slew both the lion and the bear: and this uncircumcised Philistine shall be as one of them, seeing he hath defied the armies of the living God.37   David said moreover, The LORD that delivered me out of the paw of the lion, and out of the paw of the bear, he will deliver me out of the hand of this Philistine. And Saul said unto David, Go, and the LORD be with thee.

Now it is obvious that David was a man of faith. And that we must apprehend faith the same way that the saints of the old covenant did even as we must in the new. It is the same faith by which we understand that the worlds were framed by the word of God, and that faith is the substance of things hoped. Faith is literally a spiritual invisible substance just like electricity is a substance, just like nuclear power is a substance. Faith is an invisible force that God used to create and to hold everything together by his word. We need to have this faith by which David used to overcome Goliath.

In Verse 33 King Saul said to David: thou art not able to go against this Philistine to fight with him for thou art but a youth, and he a man of war from his youth. And David said unto Saul: **(now listen to what he says because this declaration is how faith comes)**

Thy servant kept his Father's sheep, and there came a lion, and a bear, and took a lamb out of the flock:35 And I went out after him, and smote him, and delivered it out of his mouth: and when he arose against me, I caught him by his beard, and smote him, and slew him. And this uncircumcised Philistine shall be as one of them seeing that he has defied the armies of the living God.

#13 The **13th Way** in which faith will come is by reflecting, remembering the victory that God has given to his people, to you and me. Now some might call this our testimonies, but we're going to take this much deeper. David is remembering what God has done for him, the victories that he has experienced because of his walk with God. You need to know that faith comes when you remember what God has done for you. Did you know that God told Moses to write a book of remembrance?

Exodus 17:14 And the Lord said unto Moses, Write this for a memorial in a book, and rehearse it in the ears of Joshua:

This is how faith will come. Why do you think we have such exquisite details of the life of **Jesus Christ**? The four Gospels are a book of remembrance. We are to remember what God has done for us! Consistently God had the children of Israel to build monuments in order to remember what he had done for them.

Joshua 4:7 Then ye shall answer them, That the waters of Jordan were cut off before the ark of the covenant of the Lord; when it passed over

How Faith Comes

Jordan, the waters of Jordan were cut off: and these stones shall be for a memorial unto the children of Israel forever.

You look up the words remember, remembrance, memorial, Monument, and you will be amazed at how many times God required them to build things, to do certain things, say things, and write certain events down in order that they would remember from generation to generation.

For over 30 years I have lived in Gettysburg Pennsylvania. One thing you'll discover when you get to Gettysburg is that it is a town filled with statues and monuments to the Civil war. This is to remind us Americans of the lives that were lost for the freedom of the slaves and to keep our nation under one flag. There are many quotes dealing with his particular subject, here is one of them:

"Those who don't know history are doomed to repeat it."
Edmund Burke

Another way for us to remember the past, which is important at times, is to visit a graveyard. The very first items you notice when you enter into a graveyard are the Gravestones! The gravestones are there to remind us of our loved ones. Sometimes when I visit the graveyard where our little girl Naomi was buried (that is her body) I am overwhelmed with emotions that come from the memory of her. Granted there are memories we must subdue and overcome, but then there are other memories we must take a hold of in order for faith to come.

Paul said: *this one thing I do forgetting those things that are behind, and reaching forth unto those things which are before me.*

Those things which we must not meditate upon are the things the devil has done or that we have done against the will of God. Do not allow yourself to be constantly remembering and thinking upon your shortcomings. The enemy will use this to bring defeat into your life. If you have repented in your heart from that which was wrong, then you need to move on. Remember what God has done, and share it with others, then faith will come rushing into your heart as your emotions are overwhelmed with God's goodness and mercy. The Lord spoke to me a number of years ago and he said this: **tell my people that their testimonies are eternal!** I asked the Lord, how is this possible? He spoke to my heart saying: my word is eternal, and it is my word that is at work in them.

Revelation 12:11 and they overcame him by the blood of the Lamb, and by the word of their testimony; and they loved not their lives unto the death.

Have you ever asked yourself why do so many people hate true believers? It is because they remind them that there is a God in heaven! And the day will come when they will stand before him, and give an account of their lives.

The Bible Is a Book of Remembrance!

Why did God give us this Bible? It is in order to cause us to reflect upon who God is, what he has done, and what he has made available to us.

If you read the book of Psalms you will discover that David was constantly speaking about calling to remembrance the things that God had done for him.

*Psalm 20:7 Some trust in chariots, and some in horses: but we will remember the name of the Lord our God.

*Psalm 22:27 All the ends of the world shall remember and turn unto the Lord: and all the kindreds of the nations shall worship before thee.

*Psalm 45:17 I will make thy name to be remembered in all generations: therefore shall the people praise thee for ever and ever.

*Psalm 63:6 When I remember thee upon my bed, and meditate on thee in the night watches.

*Psalm 77:11 I will remember the works of the Lord: surely I will remember thy wonders of old.

How Faith Comes

Psalm 78:35 And they remembered that God was their rock, and the high God their redeemer.

Psalm 105:5 Remember his marvellous works that he hath done; his wonders, and the judgments of his mouth;

Psalm 119:52 I remembered thy judgments of old, O Lord; and have comforted myself.

Psalm 119:55 I have remembered thy name, O Lord, in the night, and have kept thy law.

Psalm 143:5 I remember the days of old; I meditate on all thy works; I muse on the work of thy hands.

I encourage you to begin to write down every answer to prayer, every miracle, and every time God has been good to you, every time God protected you, and provided for you! This has been a routine of mine since I gave my heart to **Christ** in 1975. Every time I begin to reflect and remember all that God has done for me, faith begins to flood my soul. Remember how God has blessed you because that's what the devil absolutely does not want you to remember. God was constantly encouraging the children of Israel to remember and to remind themselves of all the wonderful marvelous things he had done for them.

1 Chronicles 16:11 Seek the Lord and his strength, seek his face continually.12 Remember his marvellous works that he hath done, his wonders, and the judgments of his mouth;13 O ye seed of Israel his servant, ye children of Jacob, his chosen ones.

If you are having difficulty in trusting God, simply remember what God has done for you in the past. If you do not have a lot of experiences in God, then simply look at what he has done for others whether it be in the Bible or somebody else's personal testimony. Why you might ask? Because God is not a respecter of people, what he has done for one, he will do for others! If time would permit we could look in the book of Leviticus and we would discover that all of the customs, feast days, Sabbath days, holy days, symbolism, even the construction of the tabernacle in the wilderness was in order for the children of Israel to remember who God is. When God gave to Moses the Passover Lamb it was about remembering what God had done for them with a look into the future of the coming of **Christ**. The Scripture even declares in the book of Job that God sends the heavy snow and rain that men may stop and consider him. God designed it for us to stop and remember the one who made all things.

Even the priestly robes were designed with 12 different stones as a reminder of God's will for the children of Israel. Since 1978 I have been wearing a wedding ring to remind me that I have a covenant with my precious wife Kathleen, and when other people see that ring on my finger they know that I have a covenant, and I belong to another.

1Corinthians 11:23   For I have received of the Lord that which also I delivered unto you, That the Lord Jesus the same night in which he was betrayed took bread:24   And when he had given thanks, he brake it, and said, Take, eat: this is my body, which is broken for you: this do in remembrance of me.25   After the same manner also he took the cup, when he had supped, saying, This cup is the new testament in my blood: this do ye, as oft as ye drink it, in remembrance of me.26   For as often as ye eat this bread, and drink this cup, ye do shew the Lord's death till he come.

The apostle Paul emphasized to the Corinthian church that they must call to remembrance what **Christ** had done for them by the partaking of communion. By partaking of communion we are declaring the death and the resurrection of **Jesus**. What **Christ** has done for us is extremely important to our faith, and its development. At every opportunity when I speak at different gatherings I encourage all of the believers to write a book of their **own stories** of what **Christ** has done for **them**. My wife and I wrote a book called "Living in the Realm of the Miraculous" based upon 127 true experiences that we have had with the Lord. Actually at this moment I am in the midst of writing the second book with the same title #2 with approximately 130 more stories. As I read through my own personal experiences, faith begins to rise in my heart, and begins to flood my soul. I cannot encourage you enough to make **your own book of remembrance** of what God has done for you in all areas of your life. Not only is it important for you to remember what God has done for you, but as others read your stories, including your children and grandchildren, faith will begin to rise in their hearts to believe God.

We need to fully understand that the devil does not like it when we reflect upon and remember what God has done for us, because that is when faith will come. Let us go back once again and look at this particular Scripture about communion. Remember what the unleavened bread symbolizes. It is a declaration of the sinless and holy life that **Jesus Christ** lived when he walked the earth. The bread is symbolic of his physical body which was broken for us. It is speaking about the sacrifice that was paid for our redemption. The bread is broken in half because **Christ** was broke for us and for our freedom. We are to remember the sufferings that **Jesus** went through for his church, you and I. Remember the stripes upon his back, 39 lashes for our healing. Remember the thorns upon his head that declares our freedom from mental, emotional anguish. Remember the holes in his hands and feet, remember all of the abuse, pain and suffering that he bore for our redemption. Remind yourself of the price that **Christ** paid for us to be saved. By partaking of communion I remind myself of the awesome amazing sacrifice that **Jesus** paid.

I can honestly say that from the time I saw by the Scriptures the price that **Christ** paid for me, I have never doubted his love. He declared at that last supper that the cup of wine was symbolic of his blood. It is this blood that cleanses and redeems us, transforms us, and causes us to overcome the world the flesh and the devil. He boldly declared this cup is the New Testament in my blood that is shed for you. As you drink this cup of grape juice do it remembrance of me, **Jesus** said. As we stand around the communion table, with in our heart and mind we should be saying: **Lord thank you for shedding your blood**. I remember you shed your blood for my redemption, because without the shedding of your blood there is no remission of sins. Lord I thank you for your blood and you told me that I am to drink this cup which is a declaration that you have blotted out my sins. I'm supposed to drink it in remembrance, to remind myself of what you have accomplished.

All of the parables were given to us to create within our mind and heart images of remembrance. **Jesus** said that the kingdom of God is like a mustard seed planted into the soil, even though is the least of all seeds: but when it is grown, it is the greatest among herbs, and becomes a tree, so that the birds of the air come and lodge in the branches thereof. There are parables dealing with building your house upon a rock, the servants given the pounds, the 10 virgins, and so many more. These are all designed for you to reflect and remember in order that faith may rise in your heart. And when faith comes it brings peace and joy, life and strength, rest and tranquility. These are all manifestations that faith is at work in a person's heart. Paul declared in the book of Timothy that God has not given us a spirit of fear, but of power, love and a sound mind.

The kingdom of God is not meet and drink, but righteousness, peace and joy in the Holy Ghost!

The Apostle Peter emphasized the importance of calling to remembrance all of what God has done for us. In second Peter he begins to share with the Saints that he is about to depart, and that they must not forget, but call to remembrance all that **Christ** said and did.

3Peter 1:14 Knowing that shortly I must put off this my tabernacle, even as our Lord Jesus Christ hath shewed me.15Moreover I will endeavour that ye may be able after my decease to have these things always in <u>***remembrance.***</u>***16 For we have not followed cunningly devised fables, when we made known unto you the power and coming of our Lord Jesus Christ, but were eyewitnesses of his majesty.17 For he received from God the Father honour and glory, when there came such a voice to him from the excellent glory, This is my beloved Son, in whom I am well pleased.18 And this voice which came from heaven we heard, when we were with him in the holy mount.19 We have also a more sure word of prophecy; whereunto ye do well that ye take heed, as unto a light that shineth in a dark place, until the day dawn, and the day star arise in your hearts:***

Remember that **Jesus Christ** is the same yesterday, today and forever! He declares that I am the Lord and I change not! Read the Scriptures and discovered all that God has done for those who have lived before us.

Constantly remind yourself of all the wonderful miracles, signs and wonders, and faith will rise up within your heart.

Incredible Testimony of being Engulfed in a Consuming Fire! (2011)

Back in 1980 I began to memorize and meditate on Scriptures declaring that fire cannot consume me.

Isaiah 43:2, "When thou passest through the waters, I will be with thee; and through the rivers, they shall not overflow thee: when thou walkest through the fire, thou shalt not be burned ; neither shall the flame kindle upon thee."

I meditated on the scriptures because I kept burning myself with our woodstove. Through the years, I have maintained these scriptures in my heart. In the summer of 2011, I had an amazing experience when God used these scriptures to come to my rescue, otherwise I would have been burned to death. This particular morning, I woke up lost in the Holy Ghost. I mean, my mind and my heart was so caught up in God, I was almost drunk in the spirit. I was so heavenly minded at the time that you could even say I was not really much earthly good. In this condition I decided it was a good day to burn the large pile of brush that we had on our property.

This very large brush pile which was way over my head, and needed to be burned. It was a very, very hot day. I am sure it was over 90° outside! I took a 2-gallon plastic gas container to this pile of brush with the full intention of lighting the brush on fire. When I took the cap off this container, the container was so hot you could see the visible fumes of the gasoline in the air. I had with me one of those long stemmed lighters that you can pick up at any hardware store.

I stepped into this pile of very dry brush which was higher than my head by four or five feet. I took the gas container and began to spread gasoline over the pile by splashing it out of the container all over the brush and wood pile. The liquid gasoline was up to the edge of my feet. At the time I was not really thinking about what I was doing, I was actually meditating on the word. My son Daniel saw me put the gas container in my left hand. The fumes were visible as they were radiating out of the container. I took the lighter in my right hand and reached down to light the gas. My son Daniel saw what I was about to do and yelled at the top of his lungs, but I only heard him partly because I was so lost in the spirit. I pulled the trigger of the long stemmed lighter and instantly there was an explosion of fire and I was totally engulfed in the flames. I was completely surrounded with fire. My son Daniel said that he could not see me because the fire had swallowed me up.

I remember being in the flames of this fire and it seemed as if there was this shimmering invisible force field around me, and the heat and the flames could not penetrate this invisible force field. I remember standing being surrounded completely by fire thinking WOW, this is Awesome. And immediately at the same time something clicked in my head: you need to get out of this fire!

Immediately, I began to backtrack away from the fire walking backwards. When I was out of the fire, I looked down at my body and my clothes and not a flame had kindled upon me. The gas container in my left hand alone should have exploded, because of the fumes that were coming out of it.

Once again God had miraculously delivered me from my stupidity. My son Daniel can attest to this story for he saw the whole thing. We rejoiced in God for His great mercy! Of course, my son Daniel was extremely upset with me and was in a state of shock and amazement because he saw me engulfed in the fire. He thought surely I was a dead man!

#14 Instant Obedience to Gods Voice!

1 Samuel 11:14   Then said Samuel to the people, Come, and let us go to Gilgal, and renew the kingdom there.15   And all the people went to Gilgal; and there they made Saul king before the LORD in Gilgal; and there they sacrificed sacrifices of peace offerings before the LORD; and there Saul and all the men of Israel rejoiced greatly.

In this chapter we are dealing with the **14ᵗʰ Way** that faith will come. Because faith and its characteristics are the same in the Old and the New Testament we will be looking at Samuel and how faith was developed in his life. Of course every human being is born with faith in his heart just like every human being is born with a brain, muscles, and other natural necessary parts. Even as the brain and the muscles can be trained and developed it is also true with faith. In Chapter 11 verse 14 we see that the prophet Samuel gathers all the people to come together. Literally millions of people were gathered together will in one place. So the impact of what is about to happen through the prophet Samuel is amazing. We can learn a lot by this historical gathering and what Samuel did in order to cause faith to come forth in the hearts of God's people.

1 Samuel 12:14   If ye will fear the LORD, and serve him, and obey his voice, and not rebel against the commandment of the LORD, then shall both ye and also the king that reigneth over you continue following the LORD your God:15But if ye will not obey the voice of the LORD, but rebel against the commandment of the LORD, then shall the hand of the LORD be against you, as it was against your fathers…….18   So Samuel called unto the LORD; and the LORD sent thunder and rain that day: and all the people greatly feared the LORD and Samuel.

If you would study this historical account, you'll discover that Samuel was very upset because they wanted a king other than God himself. God is really quite upset with the Israelites because he wanted to be their one and only king. Understand God wants to be your king and he wants you to want him to be your king and Lord. **Jesus** said:

why do you call me Lord, Lord and do not the things I say?

This was not the will of God, but because the people wanted a king, God gave them a king other than himself. If you really look at our lives you will discover that there are a lot of things that God will grant us, even though it is against his will, but even in these numerous situations he will continue to try to work with us where we are. We need to take particular notice to Samuel declaring that the people must walk in the fear of the Lord. The fear that Samuel was speaking about is not a satanic fear, but a revelation of who God really is. We are talking about an overwhelming awesome mind-boggling heart clenching reality of God.

Psalm 119:120 My flesh trembleth for fear of thee; and I am afraid of thy judgments.

Luke 12:5 But I will forewarn you whom ye shall fear: Fear him, which after he hath killed hath power to cast into hell; yea, I say unto you, Fear him.

The book of Psalms says that the beginning of wisdom is the fear of the Lord, and the fear of the Lord is to hate evil and to depart from evil.

You cannot have strong, living, vibrant, active, and great faith where the fear of God does not exist.

You and I must choose the fear of the Lord, and to serve him. Now the word serve in Hebrew would mean to be his slave. If you will choose the fear of the Lord and to be God's servant, to obey his voice, your nation will be blessed, God told the Israelites through Samuel. Please remember that God is the same yesterday, today and forever. Samuel also warned them that if they did not obey the voice of the Lord, but rebelled against his commandments, then the hand of the Lord would be against them.

How Faith Comes

1 Samuel 12:16   Now therefore stand and see this great thing, which the LORD will do before your eyes: 17 Is it not wheat harvest to day? I will call unto the LORD, and he shall send thunder and rain; that ye may perceive and see that your wickedness is great, which ye have done in the sight of the LORD, in asking you a king:18   So Samuel called unto the LORD; and the LORD sent thunder and rain that day: and all the people greatly feared the LORD and Samuel.

If only there were prophets like Samuel alive in this generation, how quickly the eyes of the people would be opened to the reality of who God really is. Many ministers have turned God into nothing but a celestial Santa Claus that wants to come down the chimney of your life in order to give you whatever your flesh desires. This modern day celestial Santa Claus does not even have a list of who has been naughty or nice. They declare that God really doesn't care any longer what you do because of what the blood of his son **Jesus** did for us when he died upon Calvary. This is a modern-day gospel being propagated by false prophets who say peace, peace but then sudden destruction!

Now let us look at the results of God sending thunder and rain on what I believe was a perfectly beautiful clear and sunshiny day.

1 Samuel 12:19   And all the people said unto Samuel, Pray for thy servants unto the LORD thy God, that we die not: for we have added unto all our sins this evil, to ask us a king.:20   And Samuel said unto the people, Fear not: ye have done all this wickedness: yet turn not aside from following the LORD, but serve the LORD with all your heart:21   And turn ye not aside: for then should ye go after vain things, which cannot profit nor deliver; for they are vain.

Let us get to the matter at hand. How did Samuel become a man who was used of God in such a mighty way?

1 Samuel 3:1   And the child Samuel ministered unto the LORD before Eli. And the word of the LORD was precious in those days; there was no open vision.

Notice in this verse that it says that he ministered unto the Lord. That means as he was taking care of the responsibilities of the temple, even as a young man he was doing it as onto God. We have discussed this in Chapter 8 of How Faith Comes: **They that wait upon the Lord**. Now there is something that drastically happens from verse one to verse 19 in the life of Samuel.

1 Samuel 3:19   And Samuel grew, and the LORD was with him, and did let none of his words fall to the ground.

God wants you and me to have faith in him, to trust him, to rely upon him. Would you believe me if I told you that we could live in a place to where whatever you said would come to pass? The apostle Paul was preaching one day to a king and there was a sorcerer who was trying to stop him from listening. Paul spoke to this sorcerer and said you're a deceiver and perverter of the truth, may you go blind from this day forward! That very instant the man went blind. Peter said to Ananias you're a dead man, and then he said to his wife you're a dead woman, and they both fell down dead. The Scripture says that not one of the words that Moses spoke fell to the ground.

In first Samuel chapter 3 it says that the child Samuel was laid down to sleep. If you study this in the Hebrew it actually says he was sleeping in the sanctuary where he was close to God. Number **one he was serving the Lord**. Number two he was **sleeping in the sanctuary**, when out of the blue God began to call out to him. The Scripture says: ***draw night to God and he will draw nigh to you***! God began to call out Samuel! **Jesus** said: behold I stand at the door and knock, if you will open this door, I will come in and sup with you, and you with me.

Brothers and sisters God wants to come and heal you, to deliver you, to set you free, to reveal himself to you, he wants you to hear his audible voice!

I Heard Gods Audible Voice, and I Fell to My Knees!

I have never sought to hear the audible voice of God and yet I have heard it on numerous occasions. I remember one specific time when I heard his audible voice back on a cold winter day, December the 5th, 1983. Right after my wife gave birth to Daniel, we had some good friends come and stay with us. They were our spiritual parents to some extent. Mary was helping my wife clean the house and care for Michael who was about 2 years old. I basically stayed out of their way. While they were cleaning the kitchen, I was upstairs in my prayer room spending time with the Lord and meditating on God's Word. When I finished, I got up and started to come down the stairs. As I was coming down the stairs I heard the audible voice of God.

This is what He said to me, and I quote, **"Go on TV!"** That's what I heard. The audible voice of God was so real, that I instantly fell to my knees. I said, "Lord, the church does not have the money to put me on TV!" We had just started the church about 5 months previously. They could not even afford to pay me the salary that we agreed upon. Then the Lord began to communicate with me in His still quiet voice. He spoke to my heart and said: ***"The church will not pay for your TV time. You will believe and trust Me for it"*** I said, ***Yes, Lord!*** (Please notice my instant obedience and declaration that I would obey when I heard his audible voice).

#14 This is the **14th Way that faith comes!** The Lord then quickened to my heart that the first TV station I would be on would be Channel 25 out of Hagerstown, Maryland which was about 45 miles from us. The Spirit literally informed me that I would have a program on Sunday Mornings at 6:30 a.m. Once again, I told the Lord **I would obey Him.** How God speaks to me audibly is that in every situation I have heard just a couple words that are very blunt and specific, and then he would begin to speak to my heart in greater detail.

Dr Michael H Yeager

My wife is always very supportive of me. (Or maybe I should say she never tries to stop me!) She is a real trooper. In fact, she is so much of a trooper that she was up and at work within twenty minutes of giving birth to Daniel.

After the Lord had finished speaking to me, I went downstairs to share this with her. When I told her this, she became very upset with me. I believe part of the reason is because financially we were already in need of some miracles. We did not even have money for fuel oil to heat our house. We probably only had enough fuel oil for one more day. She was so upset with me that she went and told Mary. (Mary, by the way is an aggressive pioneer woman. Mary and her husband Paul have done many wonderful works in other countries). She is a mother of the faith. I'm sure it did not help that my wife was distraught and had just given birth to Daniel.)

When I entered into the kitchen, Mary cornered me. She tried to speak some sense into me, or you might say she basically skinned me alive! Of course, I didn't blame Mary or my wife, but I had heard from God! Later that day as I was praying, a brother who had been saved and filled with the Holy Ghost in our church, Andy, knocked at our front door. He was self-employed and he had been cleaning up people's properties. He asked me how Kathee and I were doing, and how was our newborn son? He then informed me that he had two fifty-five gallon barrels of fuel oil on the back of this truck and wanted to know if I knew anyone that needed heating oil. I said, "Yes, Andy, we do!" He backed his truck up, and put the fuel into our fuel tank. You might ask: how do we know that you heard the audible voice of God? Because everything the Lord spoke to me on that day came to pass exactly as the Lord had spoken to me. Let us go back and gleam from first Samuel the 14th Way that faith comes.

1 Samuel 3:2 And it came to pass at that time, when Eli was laid down in his place, and his eyes began to wax dim, that he could not see; 3 And ere the lamp of God went out in the temple of the LORD, where the ark of God was, and Samuel was laid down to sleep:4 That the LORD called Samuel: and he answered, Here am I: 5 And he ran unto Eli, and said, Here am I;

136

for thou calledst me. And he said, I called not; lie down again. And he went and lay down.

Did you notice that Samuel is actually hearing the audible voice of God? To Samuel it was audible and real, but probably if anyone else had been in that room with him they most likely would not have heard it. You see my friend God is the one who created our five senses. If he so desires he can cause us to hear something audibly that nobody else can, or to see something that nobody else can (like Elijah when he saw the horses and the chariots of fire) or to cause us to smell something that no one else can, or to feel something that no one else is feeling at that time! He can cause us to know things that nobody else will know but us and him.

1 Samuel 3:8   And the LORD called Samuel again the third time. And he arose and went to Eli, and said, Here am I; for thou didst call me. And Eli perceived that the LORD had called the child.

We are now about to take you into a deeper realm were most people who call themselves Christians have never walked. This realm can only be accessed by those who have been willing to do the written word of God. We discussed this in Chapter 9 in How Faith Comes. Samuel without realizing it has come to a place where God could audibly speak to him, which was going to take him into a much deeper realm of faith.

As you study this particular set of Scriptures you'll discover that Samuel was **submitted to authority with a positive godly attitude**. Even though Eli was disobedient to God, grossly overweight, did not make his sons obey him, or respect the temple, yet Samuel had great respect for him, did not find fault with him and completely submitted to him according to the will of God. He also had a great love for the upkeep of God's temple. If you were to find Samuel in the evening he would be ministering to the Lord, and sleeping in the sanctuary. This attitude, his faithfulness and his hunger for God is what opened the door for the Lord to manifest himself in such a wonderful way.

This is a Realm of Faith Where God Can Now Reveal Himself to YOU in a Super Natural Way! God begins to manifest himself to **crucified flesh**. Yes, **crucified flesh** is completely different than flesh that has not yet been brought under the authority and the Lordship of **Jesus Christ**. **Crucified**

137

flesh is holy ground, where the very presence and fire of God will burn. It is like the sacrifices of the old covenant that was declared holy because all the natural blood had been drained out. These sacrificed animals had been placed upon the altar as a sacrifice to God. **Crucified flesh** is where God himself will manifest his spirit and his presence. Un-crucified flesh is where devils and demons can manifest themselves because they are operating out of Gods will. Samuel had come to the place to where his heart, his mind, his purpose in living was all directed towards God.

CRUCIFIED FLESH IS A SWEET FRAGRANCE UNTO THE LORD!!! GOD WILL MANIFEST HIMSELF THERE!

1 Samuel 3:6 And the LORD called yet again, Samuel. And Samuel arose and went to Eli, and said, Here am I; for thou didst call me. And he answered, I called not, my son; lie down again. 7 Now Samuel did not yet know the LORD, neither was the word of the LORD yet revealed unto him. …………..9 Therefore Eli said unto Samuel, Go, lie down: and it shall be, if he call thee, that thou shalt say, Speak, LORD; for thy servant heareth. So Samuel went and lay down in his place.10 And the LORD came, and stood, and called as at other times, Samuel, Samuel. Then Samuel answered, Speak; for thy servant heareth.

Did you notice the amazing statement that God had called for Samuel at other times? Samuel simply had not been in a place where he could hear the audible voice of God. This is so true today in many believers' lives, they are not living in a place where God can speak to them audibly. Oh if only we would come to that place where Samuel came, having a heart eagerly willing and wanting to serve the Lord.

Now something simply amazing takes place as Samuel responds with *speak for thy servant heareth*!

*1 Samuel 3:10 And the **LORD came, and stood**, and called as at other times, Samuel, Samuel. Then Samuel answered, Speak; for thy servant heareth.*

How Faith Comes

Samuel is about to enter into an amazing world where all things are possible because he is responding to the audible voice of God. This is the **14th Way in which faith will come** flooding into your soul when you instantly respond in obedience to the **Quickend, or Audible, or Revealed Word of God**.

God gives to Samuel a very unpopular message of coming judgment because of Eli's disobedience and sloppy spiritual attitude. Samuel as a young man, I am sure did not want to deliver such a message. Even though Eli was a man who was not walking with God the way he should, he still knew the ways of the Lord. He encouraged Samuel to tell him all that God had said no matter what the consequences were.

1 Samuel 3:16 Then Eli called Samuel, and said, Samuel, my son. And he answered, Here am I.:17 And he said, What is the thing that the LORD hath said unto thee? I pray thee hide it not from me: God do so to thee, and more also, if thou hide anything from me of all the things that he said unto thee.18 And Samuel told him every whit, and hid nothing from him. And he said, it is the LORD: let him do what seemeth him good.19 And Samuel grew, and the LORD was with him, and did let none of his words fall to the ground.

Please notice the progression of Samuel spiritual growth in faith. He hid nothing from Eli, but told him all that God had said. Because he was not afraid of the faces of man, but obedient to the voice of the Lord, faith began to skyrocket in his heart. It takes great faith to obey God in delivering the truth in love no matter what people might do or say against you.

FAITH IS NOT GIVEN FOR US TO TELL GOD WHAT TO DO, BUT FOR US TO HEAR AND TO OBEY GOD IN WHAT HE TELLS US TO DO!

If you study the Scriptures will discover that the prophets of old and those of the new, heard the voice of God, and simply did what they were told to do. Every time that you respond to the voice of God, and see the results, your faith will increase and grow. Elijah prayed that it might not rain, because he heard God tell him to do this. Elijah prayed that fire would come down from heaven, because he heard God say to do that. Jeremiah simply did what the Lord told him to do. Noah simply did what he heard the Lord told him to do. Moses simply obeyed the voice of the Lord. This is why faith has been given to us, to obey and to do what God tells us to do. Not the hearers of the word will be blessed, but the doers!

1 Kings 19:11 and he said, Go forth, and stand upon the mount before the LORD. And, behold, the LORD passed by, and a great and strong wind rent the mountains, and brake in pieces the rocks before the LORD; but the LORD was not in the wind: and after the wind an earthquake; but the LORD was not in the earthquake:12 And after the earthquake a fire; but the LORD was not in the fire: and after the fire a still small voice.:13 And it was so, when Elijah heard it, that he wrapped his face in his mantle, and went out, and stood in the entering in of the cave. And, behold, there came a voice unto him, and said, What doest thou here, Elijah?

God says Listen to My Still Small Voice which will say: Don't Watch That, Don't Read That, Don't Say That, and Don't Do That. As You Obey HIS Voice All of a Sudden you are walking into the realm of the Supernatural with a Face-To-Face Encounter with God!

As we finish this chapter we will take a look at the most important person that we could ever look at, and that is **Jesus Christ**. We could've looked at this whole chapter and every chapter with **Jesus** as our main example. In order to give us a broader perspective dealing with the natural human hearts, we have used men and women who have lived and walked with God in the Old Testament. What **Jesus** has to say is so profound that his words alone should reveal this **14th Way** in which faith comes.

By hearing and instantly obeying from the heart the voice of God!

John 5:19   Then answered Jesus and said unto them, Verily, verily, I say unto you, The Son can do <u>nothing of himself</u>, but what <u>he seeth</u> <u>the Father do</u>: for what things <u>soever he doeth, these also doeth the</u> <u>Son likewise</u>.:20 For the Father loveth the Son, and sheweth him all things that himself doeth: and he will shew him greater works than these, that ye may marvel.

John 5:24 Verily, verily, I say unto you, He that heareth my word, and believeth on him that sent me, hath everlasting life, and shall not come into condemnation; but is passed from death unto life.:25 Verily, verily, I say unto you, The hour is coming, and now is, when the dead shall hear the voice of the Son of God: and they that hear shall live.

John 8:26 I have many things to say and to judge of you: but he that sent me is true; and I speak to the world those things which I have heard of him:28 Then said Jesus unto them, When ye have lifted up the Son of man, then shall ye know that I am he, and that I do nothing of myself; but as my <u>Father hath taught me, I speak these things.</u>

John 8:38 I <u>speak that which I have seen with my Father:</u> and ye do that which ye have seen with your Father.

Please notice the constant emphasis that **Jesus** made on hearing from the **Father**, and doing exactly what he was told to do. Faith cannot but help to grow in this kind of atmosphere, and it is this kind of faith that pleases God alone. Let us now step into this 14th way in which faith comes.

Psalms 25:9 The meek will he guide in judgment: and the meek will he teach his way.

Psalms 32:8 I will instruct thee and teach thee in the way which thou shalt go: I will guide thee with mine eye: 9 Be ye not as the horse, or as the mule, which have no understanding: whose mouth must be held in with bit and bridle, lest they come near unto thee.

Gods Audible Voice Said TO Me: YOU'RE A DEAD MAN! (1981)

I was driving into Mount Union, Pennsylvania with my wife to do some grocery shopping. I was driving a sport Ford Granada with a 302 Engine. The urge came to me to put the pedal to the metal and let it roar. The Lord had already delivered me from speeding years ago, but at that moment it was as if a devil took hold of me. I willingly gave in to this urge as I mashed down the gas pedal and began to increase my speed. Yes, I knew better, but I caved and gave into temptation. My wife looked over at me just shaking her head. (Someone else was watching our newborn son Michael so he was not with us.)

I ended up accelerating to over 80 miles per hour. Kathleen was praying out loud that if we had an accident, she would not be hurt because of my stupidity, and then she began to pray faster in the spirit. I was coming around the corner on Route 747 right before you enter into Mount Union when I heard the audible voice of God say to me, **"You are a Dead Man!"** Instantly the **fear of the Lord** hit me like a **sledgehammer**.

The **fear of God** went right to the very marrow of my bones. I saw a stop sign ahead of me to the left and to the right. **At that very moment, I slammed on the brakes of my car, instantly slowing down**. A flash of white zipped past my left. I mean right then and there I saw a totally white, souped-up Dodge charger come speeding through the stop sign from the left. He ran the stop sign without stopping or slowing up in the least. I mean he really had the pedal to the metal. I'm convinced he must've been going over 80 miles an hour. If I would not have slammed on my brakes **exactly** when I heard the audible voice of God, his car would have slammed right into my driver's side door. There is no doubt in my mind or my heart that I would have been instantly killed. Thank God for his long-suffering and mercy.

1 Peter 5:8 Be sober, be vigilant; because your adversary the devil, as a roaring lion, walketh about, seeking whom he may devour:9 Whom resist steadfast in the faith, knowing that the same afflictions are accomplished in your brethren that are in the world. 1 Peter 5:8-9 (KJV)

#15 Acknowledging Every Good Work!

I cannot over emphasize the absolute complete necessity of faith. God has absolute confidence and faith in himself. He cannot deny himself.

2 Timothy 2:13 If we believe not, yet he abideth faithful: he cannot deny himself.

The apostle Paul said: I have fought a good fight, I have kept the faith! It will be a fight of faith for you to love God, follow God, obey God, serve God, surrender to God, submit to God and to give Him everything. It is a good fight because a good fight is a fight that you win. When you look at two men who are fighting over who is going to be the next heavyweight boxing champion of the world, both of these men will be bloodied, bruised and beat up. Even the champion of this fight will be in this condition. Why do believers think that when you fight the fight of faith that everything is going to be just hunk-adore, peaches and cream, and cotton candy? Let us now look at another Scripture for this chapter.

Philemon 1:4   I thank my God, making mention of thee always in my prayers,:5 Hearing of thy love and faith, which thou hast toward the Lord Jesus, and toward all saints;6 That the communication of thy faith may <u>*become effectual by the acknowledging of every good thing*</u> *which is in you in Christ Jesus.7 For we have great joy and consolation in thy love, because the bowels of the saints are refreshed by thee, brother.*

The apostle Paul said that he had heard of their love and faith which they had in the Lord **Jesus Christ**. Then he says something quite amazing because he says that the communication or participation of their faith will become effectual by the acknowledging, sharing or declaring of every good thing which is in us because of **Christ Jesus**. Actually the King James is probably one of the closest correct translations of this particular set of Scriptures. The apostle Paul said by the spirit of God that the communication of our faith will cause our faith to grow by the speaking, declaring and acknowledging of every good thing which is in you in **Christ Jesus**. The word acknowledgment means when you admit or declare something that is true and correct! So when somebody says something to you that is obvious, you acknowledge it with a rock solid agreement. So when you agree with what God has said about you, then your faith will begin to increase in your heart. Let me give you some simple biblical examples.

1 John 4:4 Ye are of God, little children, and have overcome them: because greater is he that is in you, than he that is in the world.

1 John 5:4 For whatsoever is born of God overcometh the world: and this is the victory that overcometh the world, even our faith.

Romans 8:31 What shall we then say to these things? If God be for us, who can be against us?

Romans 8:37 Nay, in all these things we are more than conquerors through him that loved us.

Hebrews 13:5 Let your conversation be without covetousness; and be content with such things as ye have: for he hath said, I will never leave thee, nor forsake thee.

Philippians 4:13 I can do all things through Christ which strengtheneth me.

When you begin to agree with verbally, out loud with what God has declared about you in his word it will bring faith. The word communication means to participate, to partake of, and to become one with. There are certain things that God declares about you and me that is absolute truth. Then there are divine truths that God wants you and I to become, but we are not there yet. There are many examples that I could use, but let me use one in particular. Many so-called believers are declaring they are righteous in

Christ by faith, but yet they are living like the devil. They think that faith is just a confession when it actually must be apprehended and worked out by faith in **Christ Jesus**. Another example is that God declares:

1 Peter 1:15 But as he which hath called you is holy, so be ye holy in all manner of conversation;16 Because it is written, Be ye holy; for I am holy.

You can declare your holy all you want, but until it is manifested in your heart and your life you are deceiving nobody but yourself. That's where the Scripture would apply in the book of James 1:22

James 1:22 But be ye doers of the word, and not hearers only, deceiving your own selves.23 For if any be a hearer of the word, and not a doer, he is like unto a man beholding his natural face in a glass:24 For he beholdeth himself, and goeth his way, and straightway forgetteth what manner of man he was.25 But whoso looketh into the perfect law of liberty, and continueth therein, he being not a forgetful hearer, but a doer of the work, this man shall be blessed in his deed.

Did you notice in verse 25 it says a ***doer of the work***? In Philippians it says that we must work out our own salvation with fear and trembling. Now we know **Christ** lives in us by faith, and people love to make good confessions about themselves which is wonderful, but there is a difference between telling the truth and lying to yourself.
You can walk around and declare you're full of the fruit of the spirit all day long when there's no truth to it. What are the nine fruits of the Spirit in Galatians 5? Love, joy, peace, long-suffering, gentleness, goodness, faith, meekness, and self-control. You can claim that these are operating in your life when they really are not.

We really need a spirit of discernment when it comes to the declaring what is true in us now, and those things which we still need to work out. For almost 40 years and I've heard a lot of phony baloney, hot air teaching because people are not rightly discerning the word of truth. If you are telling people that you are righteous then they better see the evidence of that righteousness. Yes the Scripture does declare that we are made righteous through **Jesus Christ,** but it is because of his divine nature and his word at work in us, as we are being doers of the word.

2 Corinthians 5:21 For he hath made him to be sin for us, who knew no sin; that **we might be made the righteousness of God in him.**

Romans 6:18Being then made free from sin, ye became the servants of righteousness.

Romans 6:22 But now being made free from sin, and become servants to God, ye have your fruit unto holiness, and the end everlasting life.

Jesus made an amazing statement in the gospel of John.

John 1:12 *But as many as received him, to them gave he power to* **become** *the sons of God, even to them that believe on his name:*

Did you notice **Jesus** said to become, how do we do that? We must do it with the faith that produces action and obedience that we have been ordained to walk in. We really are dealing here with two different issues.

#1 The Acknowledgment of every good thing that is in us by Christ Jesus!

#2 The divine elements which God desires to be manifested and matured in us!

You can proclaim all you want you are full of faith, but that does not make it so. Now we can say God will never leave us nor forsake us, or greater is he that is in me then he that's in the world, or God supplies all of my needs according to his riches in glory, or if God before me who can be against me.

Proclaiming that you're righteous in **Jesus Christ** even when you are committing adultery, stealing, lying being ugly and nasty in your attitude and character is nothing but a lie. That is not faith but it is the spirit of deception at work in you.

The communication of your faith is when you acknowledge every good thing, every good thing that **Christ** has accomplished for you. I knowledge by his stripes I am healed! I say to myself **by his stripes I am healed.** And I then begin to thank him and praise him for it even though I do not feel it or see it. Your brain is always working, you're always thinking, most likely muttering to yourself. And what is it that you are thinking and speaking? We need to think and speak that which **Christ** has accomplished for us.

#15 The 15th Way that faith comes is by the acknowledging of every good thing that God has done for you through Jesus Christ.

Jesus said rejoice because your names are written down in heaven, so Lord I rejoiced that my name is written in heaven. You and I have never seen our name in heaven, but **Jesus** said it so I knowledge it. I acknowledge I am, I have, and can do what God says I am, can do, and have. Here is a wonderful revealing of this truth discovered in the book of Jeremiah.

Jeremiah 1:4 Then the word of the LORD came unto me, saying,5 Before I formed thee in the belly I knew thee; and before thou camest forth out of the womb I sanctified thee, and I ordained thee a prophet unto the nations.6 Then said I, Ah, Lord GOD! behold, I cannot speak: for I am a child.7 But the LORD said unto me, Say not, I am a child: for thou shalt go to all that I shall send thee, and whatsoever I command thee thou shalt speak.8 Be not afraid of their faces: for I am with thee to deliver thee, saith the LORD.9 Then the LORD put forth his hand, and touched my mouth. And the LORD said unto me, Behold, I have put my words in thy mouth.10 See, I have this day set thee over the nations and over the kingdoms, to root out, and to pull down, and to destroy, and to throw down, to build, and to plant.

147

God had a wonderful plan for Jeremiah. I believe that God has a plan for every person that was ever born, but most do not believe or accept it. *"many are called; few are chosen "*

God said that he would have all men to repent and to come to the knowledge of the truth, and yet people do not embrace God's plan for their lives! This is the difference between the sheep and goats. Most of what they call Christianity today is nothing but little clicks and clubs were people are just trying to impress one another.

After this experience that Jeremiah had with God his life was never the same. From that moment forward he never argued with what the Lord had spoken to him. Jeremiah said exactly what he had heard God say to him: I am a prophet, and I am sent to the nations in order to warn them of coming judgment. He had to be saying this to himself in order for faith to continue to operate in his life to fulfill this difficult task that the Lord had given to him. If you and I are going to fulfill the will of God for our lives we are going to have to begin to talk to ourselves in the same way. You need to declare in the name of **Jesus Christ**: I will love God, I will serve God, I will follow God, and I will go all the way for **Jesus**, because greater is he that is in me then he that is in the world.

Another example is when and Angel came to Mary the mother of **Christ** and said blessed art thou among women. God has chosen you to be the mother of the Savior of the world. The Holy Ghost will come upon you, therefore that which you conceive will be of the Holy Spirit and you will give birth to the son of God, even though you have never known a man. She said let it be done to me even according to your word.

Luke 1:38 And Mary said, Behold the handmaid of the Lord; be it unto me according to thy word. And the angel departed from her.

Faith will come as you acknowledge and declare what God has said about you and for you to yourself.

148

How Faith Comes

Whatever you do, do not repeat what fleshly people say about you! They are not the foundation that you build your life upon. Praise God we build your life upon **Jesus Christ** and him alone. When you hear the voice of God {there needs to be evidence in your life that you hear his voice} you need to immediately say what he says about you, what you're going to do, and where you're going, and act upon it!

Here is one illustration of hearing the voice of God Very Clearly.
(1983)

As I was in prayer one day, the Lord quickened to my heart to build a church that would seat eight hundred people. At the time, the size of our congregation was only about seventy people, plus we had no money. I knew the members of our congregation pretty well, and as far as I could tell, none of them were wealthy. When the Lord quickened my heart, I immediately acted upon on what he spoke to me. I went to the land that we owned which was nothing but an empty cow field. I began to walk that field declaring by the word of the Lord we would have a church upon this property that would sit 800 people. I did this day after day speaking to myself declaring what God had said to me.

Of course then I had to act upon this declaration by doing the obvious. We checked with local construction companies to put up this building. Just to put up the exterior steel building and pour the concrete floor would cost us more than $800,000. I knew in my heart that this was not the way to go. There was a man in our congregation who represented Wedge Core a steel building company from South Dakota. We began to coordinate with them for the purchase of the steel we needed. They provided us with all the blueprints that were necessary for the foundation. I located an architectural company in Hanover, Pennsylvania that was willing to work with us. I drew up a rough, simple schematic of what we were looking for, and with this drawing they were able to provide for us the simplest blueprint possible which would be approved by the state of Pennsylvania. We went through the proper process to get the right building permits from local, county, and state authorities. We had everything in hand to start the project. We had done everything we could do. Daily I was continuing to speak to myself in agreement with what God Had Quicken to my heart. This maintained and caused faith to continue to operate within me.

Now what? We had no money. As I was in prayer, the Spirit of God quickened my heart to simply step out in faith and do it. There was a man in our church who owned a backhoe. I approached Richard about what I wanted to do and he said, "Let's do it." We went out to the property and staked out where the footers and foundation were going to be. Then he brought his son Carol up from Maryland to dig these footers. We ended up with a 100 x 150-foot ditch. We prayed every step of the way. As the Spirit of the Lord would quicken me, I would order the building materials.

On the day we were to lay the blocks that the metal building would sit on, it was pouring down rain. The men of the congregation wanted to cancel the Saturday work party. I told them that God was going to make it possible for us to lay the blocks on that day. As we were on the building site, we cried out to the Lord and immediately the rain stopped and the sun came out! By the end of that day 500 feet of block had been laid.

My Life on the Line

The company that was providing the steel for our building called from South Dakota, telling us that the steel building was almost ready to be shipped. They said they could ship it by cash on delivery. When the building arrived I would have to give them approximately $49,000. At the time, we only had $1,000 in our building account, with no other means of finances. The representative from the steel company also informed us they could store the building for about $1,200 a month, or they could ship it out within six to eight weeks.

As I was listening to the man over the phone, I heard the Spirit of the Lord say to me, *Tell them to send it!* I became very still before the Lord, because I wanted to make sure that I heard him correctly. The Spirit spoke to me again, *Tell them to send it*! I told the gentlemen from the steel company to go ahead and send the building! He told me that would be fine and they

would prepare it to be sent. On the other hand, he also informed me that we better be aware that if the building got there and I did not have the money, that I would be breaking interstate laws (I believe he said there were five of them) and that I would be going to jail, as I was the one who gave the approval for the building to come! I got very quiet before the Lord and asked Him,
What I should do? The Spirit once again reconfirmed, and quickened to my heart, to have them send it. Once again I told the representative to go ahead and send it. He gave me a warning again.

The gift of faith was operating in my heart, and I knew that it was done. After I got off the phone, a desire came into my heart to give away the $1,000 in our building account. I was not trying to bribe God to do something for us. The $1,000 we had was not going to do a thing for us, so why not give it away out of faith? We took that thousand dollars and divided it up into ten different checks, sending it to ten different ministries. That Sunday, I went before the congregation and told them this story. I told them the steel was coming and if they wanted to, they could get involved. I also told them we had invested $1,000 into ten other ministries. I did inform them that if I was missing God in this regards, I was going to have a prison ministry. I had put my life on the line.

Amazingly, I had no fear or anxiety whatsoever during the six weeks leading up to the steel arriving. Without a shadow of a doubt, I knew the money would be there. I kept thanking God to myself and declaring that the money was there. The finances began to trickle in. To this day, I do not remember where it all came from. I did not beg, plead, or call anybody for money. I received a phone call approximately six weeks later from the representative of the steel company. They told me that they were loading this steel up on their big trucks, and was I ready to receive it. At that point we were still $15,000.00 short of the finances we needed. I told them to go ahead and send it. Within three days the truck pulled onto our property.

I went and met the truck driver at the construction site. He handed me the paperwork. There were certain documents which I had to fill out. I started filling out the paperwork, knowing that I was still $15,000 short of the

$49,000 I had to pay them in just a few short moments. As I was signing the papers, one of the men from our church pulled into the parking lot. He drove his car right up to me with his window rolled down. There was something in his right hand. He handed a check to me for $15,000! Thank you **Jesus**!

One day as we were busy putting the steel sheeting on the roof of our new facility with a handful of volunteers, a violent wind storm blew in. It was coming over the top of the Allegheny Mountains, which are just two miles west from us. We could see very dark blue and purple clouds swirling violently and racing toward us. Lightning was striking everywhere in those clouds as echoes of thunder rolled across the valley. This was a fast moving thunderstorm system. If that storm was to hit us with its fierce winds, we would be in big trouble. I was on the top of the building with all of our volunteers. It seemed like all of us had stopped working at the same time. There were about fifteen of us there that day.

As I was looking at this storm, the Spirit of the Lord quickened me. Faith rose up in my heart. Every supernatural work of God is from His Spirit. I told them all to stretch forth their hands toward the storm. I pointed my hand with the rest of the men towards the storm. I declared, "In the name of **Jesus Christ** of Nazareth I rebuke this storm. I command it to split in half and go around us in the name of **Jesus Christ** right now!" Whatever God quickened to my heart is what I spoke at that moment

When I knew it was done inside of me, I turned my back to the storm and went back to work. It seemed as if this same faith also came upon the other men. As far as I know, we all turned our back to the storm and did not look back. Why? It was because we knew in our hearts that this storm had to obey. I kept on working with the men until I saw flashing and movement to my left and to my right. I stood up and looked, and this violent lightning storm was on the north and south side of us. The storm was behind us and in front of us. It had literally obeyed us. It had split right down the middle, and had gone around us. When it reached the east side of us, it joined itself back together and went on its way. We just kept on with constructing our new facility that day.

How Faith Comes

Within five months of breaking ground we had our dedication service. This first phase of construction was 15,000 square feet. The next year we added 7,500 more square feet for our Christian school. The day the steel came in for that particular edition we were still $5,000 short. Once again a man from the church drove up and handed me a check for $5,000. At the time of this book being written, we have close to 40,000 square feet of building. To God be the glory!

Isaiah 54:17No weapon that is formed against thee shall prosper; and every tongue that shall rise against thee in judgment thou shalt condemn. This is the heritage of the servants of the Lord, and their righteousness is of me, saith the Lord.

If we had the time in this space we could talk about many different men of God in the Bible. For instance listen to what God said to Abraham in Genesis.

Genesis 17:3   And Abram fell on his face: and God talked with him, saying,:4 As for me, behold, my covenant is with thee, and thou shalt be a Father of many nations.:5 Neither shall thy name any more be called Abram, but <u>thy name shall be Abraham</u>; for a Father of many nations have I made thee.:6 And I will make thee exceeding fruitful, and I will make nations of thee, and kings shall come out of thee.

We could take a look at what God told Abraham about Sarah.

Genesis 17:15   And God said unto Abraham, As for Sarai thy wife, thou shalt not call her name Sarai, but <u>Sarah shall her name be.</u>

He has just told Abram to declare that he was Abraham which means **Father** of many nations. From that moment forward Abraham began to declare this to himself, and to others. Then God had Sarai change her name to Sarah. Because she was going to be a mother of many nations. As far as God was concerned it was done. But Abraham and Sarah had to get it into their hearts. For faith to come and grow within our hearts, a faith that will overcome the world, the flesh and the devil, we must begin to say what God says about us to ourselves!

IF YOU DO NOT HAVE A FAITH THAT CRUCIFIES YOUR FLESH THEN YOU DO NOT HAVE A FAITH THAT WILL SAVE YOUR SOUL!!!!

1 John 4:4 Ye are of God, little children, and have overcome them: because greater is he that is in you, than he that is in the world.

We could talk about God telling Joshua to march around the city of Jericho one time every day, and seven times on the seventh day. That when the children of Israel obeyed this direction God himself would cause the walls of Jericho to fall flat. If we could have been there on those seven days I believe we would have heard the children of Israel talking about what was going to happen on the seventh day when they had completed their God-given task. Faith always requires you to do something! People who are teaching that you do not have to do anything are extremely deceived, and never will really have many wonderful results!

FAITH WITHOUT WORKS IS DEAD!

1 John 3:1   Behold, what manner of love the Father hath bestowed upon us, that we should be called the sons of God: therefore the world knoweth us not, because it knew him not.:2   Beloved, now are we the sons of God, and it doth not yet appear what we shall be: but we know that, when he shall appear, we shall be like him; for we shall see him as he is.

Galatians 5:6 For in Jesus Christ neither circumcision availeth anything, nor uncircumcision; but faith which worketh by love.

Joel 3:10............: let the weak say, I am strong. 1 Peter 2:24 Who his own self bare our sins in his own body on the tree, that we, being dead to sins, should live unto righteousness: by whose stripes ye were healed.

CHAPTER SIX

#16 Eating and Drinking Jesus Christ

The Bible says in the last days that there is going to be a famine in the land. In my opinion this famine has already been manifested and it is a famine of faith. Many believers really do not understand God. They do not know how to trust God, or to look to God because there has been a lack of those in leadership who move in the realm of faith. Much of the modern church leaders are successful not because of faith in **Christ**, but simply because they are worldly wise. Using natural practical worldly wisdom to grow their local churches, and yet the Scripture declares that ***the just shall live by faith.***

MOST OF THOSE WE HAVE CALLED SUCCESSFUL PASTORS ARE SIMPLY WORLDLY WISE MAN. TRUE SUCCESS IS WHEN WE SEE THE IMAGE & CHARACTER OF CHRIST BEING FORMED IN PEOPLE!

Proverbs 3:5-6 Trust in the Lord with all thine heart; and lean not unto thine own understanding. In all thy ways acknowledge him, and he shall direct thy paths.

If you read Hebrews 11 there is actually 50 events in this particular chapter. We call this chapter the faith Hall of Fame. We need to really take a good look at these men and women and the conditions that they were experiencing. How they responded to all of these trials, tribulations and test. They overcame by faith in God. It is a faith that works by love, and when you are walking in this realm of faith you will not worry, you will not be fearful, you will not be angry, you will not be frustrated, you will not be upset, you will not be self-centered, you will not be self-serving and self-seeking, you will not be self-pleasing! True biblical faith takes a hold of the divine nature of **Christ** and will not let go. When **Jesus** said that faith had made a person whole, what he was saying is: your confidence in me, your confidence in **Christ** has made you whole. So it's your faith in **Christ Jesus** that makes all things possible. As we go through every one of the ways that faith comes it will seem that there is some repetition here, but there really is not, because each one of these ways are unique in its application and emphasis. Let us now look at the **16ᵗʰ Way** in which faith will come!

John 6:1 After these things Jesus went over the sea of Galilee, which is the sea of Tiberias.² And a great multitude followed him, because they saw his miracles which he did on them that were diseased.³ And Jesus went up into a mountain, and there he sat with his disciples.⁴ And the passover, a feast of the Jews, was nigh'

The **Passover** is indeed the most important festival, feast day, tradition and ceremony of the Jewish people. In order to better comprehend exactly what the **Passover** is we would have to step back into history and take a look in the book of Exodus when God had sent Moses to deliver the Israelites from the hands of Pharaoh.

God sent Moses to the Israelites in order to bring deliverance and freedom because they have been in captivity for 400 years. Of course Moses is a typology of **Jesus Christ** who came to set us free from the slavery of sin by or through the means of us having faith in **Christ**. God told Pharaoh through Moses to let his people go. We all know the story how Pharaoh refused to obey God. The Lord had Moses to bring plague after plague in order to free the people from the hands of Pharaoh. None of these plagues convinced Pharaoh to lose God's people. There was to be one last judgment, and It was the **Passover lamb**. This would be the final blow to hit Egypt which would release the children of God, by and through the **Passover** God would change the world. From this moment forward nothing would ever be the same. As you and I receive revelation on the **Passover**, and what it means to us, our lives will never be the same. The **Passover** in the Bible is talked about specifically **73 times**. It talks about the **lamb** or the **Passover lamb one hundred times.**

Exodus 12:12 And the Lord spake unto Moses and Aaron in the land of Egypt saying,2 This month shall be unto you the beginning of months: it shall be the first month of the year to you.3 Speak ye unto all the congregation of Israel, saying, In the tenth day of this month they shall take to them every man a lamb, according to the house of their fathers, a lamb for an house:4 And if the household be too little for the lamb, let him and his neighbour next unto his house take it according to the number of the souls; every man according to his eating shall make your count for the lamb.5 Your lamb shall be without blemish, a male of the first year: ye shall take it out from the sheep, or from the goats:6 And ye shall keep it up until the fourteenth day of the same month: and the whole assembly of the congregation of Israel shall kill it in the evening.7 And they shall take of the blood, and strike it on the two side posts and on the upper door post of the houses, wherein they shall eat it.8 And they shall eat the flesh in that night, roast with fire, and unleavened bread; and with bitter herbs they shall eat it.9 Eat not of it raw, nor sodden at all with water, but roast with fire; his head with his legs, and with the purtenance thereof.10 And ye shall let nothing of it remain until the morning; and that which remaineth of it until the morning ye shall burn with fire.11 And thus shall ye eat it; with your loins girded, your shoes on your feet, and your staff in your hand; and ye shall eat it in haste: it is the Lord's passover.

Did you notice that God told Moses that everyone should go and get themselves a lamb without spot or blemish? The Lord told Moses that if you obey me in the keeping of this celebration it will finally set you free from the control of the enemy! If we as believers would do likewise, with the revelation of **Christ** our **Passover lamb**, we would truly be set free. What is the **16th Way** in which faith will come?

#16 By Eating & Drinking Jesus Christ

Hebrews 11:28
Through faith he kept the passover, and the sprinkling of blood, lest he that destroyed the firstborn should touch them.

Faith comes when you partake of the **Passover** with a sincere heart of love and devotion. Of course this **Passover lamb** is **Jesus Christ**, the only begotten of God. John the Baptist had a revelation of **Jesus Christ**. When he was baptizing at the river Jordan and John saw **Jesus** walking towards him, he said: **Behold the Lamb of God Which Takes Away the Sins of the World!**

Now there were conditions that had to be met in order for the people to have a right to partake of the **Passover lamb**, and to protect them from the death Angel which was going to pass through the land. Everyone must be dressed ready to leave, the blood had to be applied to the door post and the lintel which is symbolic of our thought life and the works of the flesh. All of the men had to be physical circumcised.

In order to do the **Passover** justice, we would have to look at every spiritual truths and lesson that is wrapped up in the **Passover** which in itself would become a book. Suffice it to say that as we partake of the bread and the grape juice as **Jesus** commanded us, recognizing by faith that it is his body and his blood which he gave for our salvation, faith will begin to rise in our hearts for our deliverance. In the Garden of Gethsemane **Jesus** said to the Father: if at all possible let this cup pass from me, but not my will be done, let your will be done. The cup he was speaking about was the cup of cursing. In the old covenant it talks about the curse placed upon sinful flesh. **Jesus Christ** became a curse for us that we might be made free from the curse of the law.

⁴⁷ All the congregation of Israel shall keep it.

Everyone that names the name of **Christ** is required to keep the **Passover**. I'm not referring to the one that was observed in Exodus, but the one that **Christ** declares today.

1Corinthians11: For I have received of the Lord that which also I delivered unto you, that the Lord Jesus the same night in which he was betrayed took bread:24 And when he had given thanks, he brake it, and said, Take, eat: this is my body, which is broken for you: this do in remembrance of me.25

After the same manner also he took the cup, when he had supped, saying, this cup is the new testament in my blood: this do ye, as oft as ye drink it, in remembrance of me.26 For as often as ye eat this bread, and drink this cup, ye do shew the Lord's death till he come.27 Wherefore whosoever shall eat this bread, and drink this cup of the Lord, unworthily, shall be guilty of the body and blood of the Lord.28 But let a man examine himself, and so let him eat of that bread, and drink of that cup.29 For he that eateth and drinketh unworthily, eateth and drinketh damnation to himself, not discerning the Lord's body.30 For this cause many are weak and sickly among you, and many sleep.31 For if we would judge ourselves, we should not be judged.

Back in February 2012 I had an amazing visitation. In the dream I saw the Lamb of God slain. This dream was very precise and intent, but space will not permit me to share it all with you, so let me just share a portion of it.

The Lamb of God! An amazing dream I had!

As I looked into the heavens to my amazement there was the Lamb of God. His wool was glistening white as snow. He was lying upon His side as if He had been slain. His backside was away from me, His underside toward me. Out from His rib, it seemed to be His third rib, from his side flowed a stream of bright shimmering living, quickening blood. Directly in front of His body there had formed a pool of this living blood. I knew there was no bottom to this pool of blood. It is hard to explain what I sensed in my heart as I looked upon His, the Lamb of God's precious living blood. Overwhelming love rose up within my heart for him. His amazing love possessed my heart, my soul, my mind, and my emotions. I was filled with gratitude beyond description for what he **Jesus Christ** the Lamb of God had accomplished for me and others.

As I was looking upon this pool of precious blood, I felt something manifest itself in my right hand. I looked down, and there in my right hand was a branch, a ROD. (This was the specific word that came to my mind) This was not just any ordinary Rod. It was absolutely straight, and it was made of Olive Wood, seemingly seven feet tall. (These are things I just knew to be true in this dream)

Immediately I knew what I was to do with this Rod in my right hand. I lifted this Rod towards the pool of blood in the heavens. To my amazement it seemed to be just the right length to reach up into the heavens. This blood was in the heavens, and yet this seven-foot Rod was able to reach the precious blood of **Jesus**.

I put the end of the Rod right into this pool of living blood. The blood immediately flowed to the end of the Rod. This living blood wrapped itself around the end of the Rod as if it was in absolute oneness with the Rod. Then with my right hand I pulled the Rod back towards me. Once the Rod was back into my Realm (I do not know how else to explain it). I directed the end of the Rod towards my mouth. It looked as if the blood was going to fall off from the end of the Rod, but not a drop fell to the ground.

I opened my mouth wide, and stuck the end of the Rod with the Living Blood into my mouth. I drank all of the blood which had been on the Rod. The very moment that I drank the blood, it was as if an incredible Power exploded inside of me, knocking me flat on my back like a dead man. It slammed me violently to the ground. I cannot properly express how drastic and violent the power of God hit me. **There is power in the blood of the Lamb.**

Revelation 12:11
And they overcame him by the blood of the Lamb, and by the word of their testimony; and they loved not their lives unto the death.

Sense I saw **Jesus Christ** as my lamb over 40 years ago I have never questioned his love for me, or humanity, and yet in order for God to deliver us there are conditions that must be met.

⁴⁸ And when a stranger shall sojourn with thee, and will keep the Passover to the LORD, let all his males be circumcised, and then let him come near and keep it; and he shall be as one that is born in the land: for no uncircumcised person shall eat thereof.

There must be a circumcision of our heart. *1st Corinthians 11:30* says that many believers are sickly and dying because they are not rightly discerning the Lord's body. They are partaking of the covenant meal by eating the unleavened bread which is symbolic of the flesh of **Christ**, and are drinking the grape juice which is symbolic of the blood of **Jesus Christ,** but they have not been circumcised in the flesh of their hearts.

Romans 2:29 But he is a Jew, which is one inwardly; and circumcision is that of the heart, in the spirit, and not in the letter; whose praise is not of men, but of God.

Now here's some amazing facts about partaking of the **Lamb**. **1st** it needed to be cooked in bitter herbs. It was not cooked in honey and brown sugar or with wonderful tasting spices. It was bitter because what **Christ** went through for us was extremely bitter and painful. If they followed exactly what Moses had told them to do, it would not have been a very tasteful and enjoyable meal. What **Jesus Christ** went through for us should in our hearts be excruciating and painful, and yet wonderfully beautiful because it is through the **Passover lamb Jesus Christ** we have been made set free.

The **2nd** aspect of the Passover lamb is that all of it had to be devoured. You had no right to pick and choose the best parts. I have ministered in other nations were every part of the animal whether it be a fish, a chicken or a pig is used. They eat the eyeballs, the brains, the intestines, the feet, every part of the animal is used. We must eat all of the **Lamb** and not just a part of it. And yes I did eat what was ever put before me. Preachers who declare that they are called only to preach certain parts of the gospel are deceived. If I only preached what I consider the best parts of the truth, then those who I minister to will not know the whole truth which is designed to set the listeners free from the world, the flesh, and the devil.

Romans 15:19 ....I have fully preached the gospel of Christ.

Acts 20:20 And how I kept back nothing that was profitable unto you, but have shewed you, and have taught you publicly, and from house to house,

Romans 2:28 For he is not a Jew, which is one outwardly; neither is that circumcision, which is outward in the flesh: 29 But he is a Jew, which is one inwardly; and circumcision is that of the heart, in the spirit, and not in the letter; whose praise is not of men, but of God.

The 3rd aspect is that all the males had to be circumcised. In the New Testament we are required to circumcise the foreskin of our hearts, and we have to circumcise our own flesh. I cannot circumcise your flesh or anyone else's. You have got to circumcise yourself with the word of God and obedience to his word. I cannot circumcise the heart of my wife. I cannot circumcise the heart of my sons, my daughters, of the parishioners of the church I pastor. If you do not circumcise your heart when you eat the **Passover Lamb,** it brings judgment to you. When you eat his flesh and drink his blood it going to bring faith or it will bring judgment.

Colossians 2:10 And ye are complete in him, which is the head of all principality and power:11 In whom also ye are circumcised with the circumcision made without hands, in putting off the body of the sins of the flesh by the circumcision of Christ:

God commands us to crucify the flesh by putting to death the deeds, actions, thoughts or attitudes that are against the will of God. The Spirit of faith will rise up and take authority over your flesh. Without faith you cannot circumcise your flesh. It takes faith to circumcise, to crucify the old man. It does not take any faith for me to jump on somebody else and their flesh. It Takes faith to handle people tenderly, gently, softly and meekly. The Scripture says: *in meekness instructing those that oppose themselves if per adventure they will repent to the acknowledging of the truth.*

Remember when the Shepherd boy David faced Goliath the Philistine, he said, who is this uncircumcised Philistine that he should defy the armies of the living God? The whole covenant is based on the foundation of circumcising your heart.

How Faith Comes

Jesus Christ overcame the devil as the **Passover lamb**. 26 times it talks about the **Lamb of God** in the book of Revelation.

Revelation 5:12 Saying with a loud voice, Worthy is the Lamb that was slain to receive power, and riches, and wisdom, and strength, and honour, and glory, and blessing.

The **Lamb of God** has defeated the devil, and now God requires us to eat the flesh and drink the blood of the **Lamb of God**!

John 6:47 Verily, verily, I say unto you, He that believeth on me hath everlasting life.48 I am that bread of life.49 Your fathers did eat manna in the wilderness, and are dead.50 This is the bread which cometh down from heaven, that a man may eat thereof, and not die.51 I am the living bread which came down from heaven: if any man eat of this bread, he shall live for ever: and the bread that I will give is my flesh, which I will give for the life of the world....[55] For my flesh is meat indeed, and my blood is drink indeed.[56] He that eateth my flesh, and drinketh my blood, dwelleth in me, and I in him.[57] As the living Father hath sent me, and I live by the Father: so he that eateth me, even he shall live by me.

Jesus said whosoever eaters my flesh and drinks my blood has eternal life, and I will raise him up at the last day, for my flesh my flesh is meat indeed and my blood is drink indeed. He explains what he means to us in verse 63.

John 6:63 It is the spirit that quickeneth; the flesh profiteth nothing: the words that I speak unto you, they are spirit, and they are life.

You will notice that many ministers today no longer preach **Jesus Christ** and him alone. It is as we meditate, think upon, sing about, read about **Jesus Christ** and who he is, and what he has accomplished, that in a sense we are eating and drinking him. There is no deeper revelation than **Jesus Christ**. He is the glory of the **Father**, manifested in the flesh, seen of men. He said:

163

When you see me you have seen the **Father**. So we are going to eat, drink, sleep, read, think, sing, speak, and meditate upon nothing but **Jesus**.

#16th way that faith comes is by eating and drinking Jesus Christ!

#17 Abiding & Dwelling in Jesus Christ!

In order for us to get a good grasp of the **17ᵗʰ Way** that faith comes we must look at Psalms 91. As we have intimacy with **Christ** we will come into oneness with **Jesus Christ**. Now we can never over emphasize the need to apprehend and the development of our faith in **Christ**. The growing, developing and increasing of our faith is extremely important to our success in the fulfilling of the will of God in all that we do on the earth. Everything that we have, everything that we partake of in **Christ** has to be done by faith. All things were created by God, by faith. God created all things by having faith in himself! Believers are those who do not trust in themselves, but we trust and faith in God.

Psalm 37:5 Commit thy way unto the Lord; trust also in him; and he shall bring it to pass.

Jesus said at the very end of the ages right before he came back would be there any faith left on the earth? The faith that we are talking about is a faith that apprehends the character, the nature, the mind, the heart, and the will of God. A faith that takes a hold of **Jesus Christ** and brings the believer into a place of victory over sin, the world, the flesh, and the devil. Faith is just like the physical muscles in your body. You know a lot of people are out of shape physically in America. It is not because we they have any less muscles then what previous generations had. We have the exact same muscles that our parents or grandparents, or are great-great-grandparents had. Most people are simply out of shape because they are not exercising their natural muscles. They are not eating the proper type of foods. The natural world is symbolic of what's going on in the spiritual. People spiritually are not exercising their faith, and they are not eating the proper spiritual foods.

1 Timothy 4:8 For bodily exercise profiteth little: but godliness is profitable unto all things, having promise of the life that now is, and of that which is to come.

People are not exercising physically, or eating properly because for some reason they do not think it is important to do so. This is causing major health problems in our nation. The same thing can be said of our faith spiritually. People are not doing what it takes to develop strong faith in **Christ**. They are also partaking of those things which are very destructive to their faith. Faith in **Jesus Christ** is so vitally important to our victory, our success, our overcoming the enemy and everything he throws at us.

Ephesians 6:16 Above all, taking the shield of faith, wherewith ye shall be able to quench all the fiery darts of the wicked.

We need to see people begin to rise up in faith and go after the will of God. When faith is in operation it will cause you to pray, gathered together with the Saints, meditate upon God's word, deny your flesh, share your faith with others, and take care of the needy. We have lost our faith in **Christ** in America, and yet there is still great hope because our faith can still be restored in **Christ**. Let us now look at Psalms 91.

Psalm 91:1 He that **dwelleth** *in the secret place of the most High shall* **abide** *under the shadow of the Almighty.2 I will say of the Lord, He is my* **refuge** *and my* **fortress***: my God; in him will I* **trust**.......*3 Surely he shall deliver thee from the snare of the fowler, and from the noisome pestilence.4 He shall cover thee with his feathers, and under his wings shalt thou trust: his truth shall be thy shield and buckler.5 Thou shalt not be afraid for the terror by night; nor for the arrow that flieth by day;6 Nor for the pestilence that walketh in darkness; nor for the destruction that wasteth at noonday.7 A thousand shall fall at thy side, and ten thousand at thy right hand; but it shall not come nigh thee.8 Only with thine eyes shalt thou behold and see the reward of the wicked.9 Because thou hast made the Lord, which is my refuge, even the most High, thy* **habitation***;10 There shall no evil befall thee, neither shall any plague come nigh thy dwelling.11 For he shall give* *his angels charge over thee, to keep thee in all thy ways. 12 They shall bear thee up in their hands, lest thou dash thy foot against a stone. 13 Thou shalt tread upon the lion and adder: the young lion and the dragon shalt thou trample under feet. 14 Because he hath set his* **love** *upon me, therefore will I deliver him: I will set him on high, because he hath* **known my name.** *15 He shall call upon me, and I will answer him: I will be with him in trouble; I will deliver him, and honour him. 16 With long life will I satisfy him, and shew him my salvation.*

Notice that all of Psalms 91 is built and established upon the 1st and 2 verses of this Psalms. All of the other following promises are based upon this relationship that we have with **Christ**. The psalmist declares that we shall not be afraid because God is with us. This is a man who is **dwelling** and **abiding** in **Christ**.

#17 by dwelling and abiding in Christ!

This might sound like number 16 when I said that we must eat and drink **Jesus**, but believe me when I say that it is not exactly the same. Many of these points are like the facets on a beautiful and expensive diamond. Yes, it is the same diamond, but it has many facets. God desires us to have faith, and he has provided for us many different ways to acquire it. All of these blessings, provisions, protections will be activated in our life as we are **dwelling** and **abiding** in **Jesus**.

2 Timothy 1:7 For God hath not given us the spirit of fear; but of power, and of love, and of a sound mind.

There is no fear of what men will do to you, or of sickness, or disease, or poverty, or financial lack, or plagues, or afflictions. There is no fear, there is no worry, and there is no torment when we are walking in the realm of faith. You will have peace that passes all understanding, joy unspeakable and full of glory. When somebody is sick in the natural we can put our hands on their fore head and see if they are running a fever. The doctor can have you open your mouth, and he will look at the tonsils or your tongue. Symptoms in your physical body will reveal your sickness by certain manifestations.

This is also true when it comes to divine faith. If you are truly operating in faith than the divine attributes of **Christ** will be manifested. The 9 fruits of the spirit will be evident. You will be living a holy separated and consecrated life for God. If you are not, then it is evidence that you need to step back into that realm of faith.

1 John 5:4 For whatsoever is born of God overcometh the world: and this is the victory that overcometh the world, even our faith.

I am not implying that we look at somebody in a critical way, but in order that we can help them if at all possible to get them into the realm of faith.

Psalm 91:1 He that dwelleth in the secret place of the most High shall abide under the shadow of the Almighty.2 I will say of the Lord, He is my refuge and my fortress: my God; in him will I trust.

I mean you're right at home in **Jesus Christ**. You are **living** and **dwelling** in him, you're **abiding** in him. This is a place of such wonderful and deep intimacy. Your fellowship is sweet beyond description. You're not only eating the Passover lamb, but you are in fellowship with him. Your mind is constantly stayed upon him.

Isaiah 26:3 Thou wilt keep him in perfect peace, whose mind is stayed on thee: because he trusteth in thee.

Christ has become your **habitation** and **dwelling** place. You are **dwelling** in **Christ** and he is **dwelling** in you.

Revelation 3:20 Behold, I stand at the door, and knock: if any man hear my voice, and open the door, I will come in to him, and will sup with him, and he with me.

The table is set before you in the presence of your enemies. God has given his angels charge over you to keep you in all of your ways, and they shall bear you up in their hands lest you should dash your foot against a stone. Now you are able to tread upon the lion and the snake.

How Faith Comes

Jesus said: behold, I give unto you (they that dwell and abide in **Christ**) power to tread on snakes and scorpions and over all the power the enemy. Nothing, yes he said nothing shall be able to harm you. This is such a wonderful place of victorious faith in **Christ Jesus**. I believe this is what Paul declared when he spoke these amazing words in the book of Colossians.

Colossians 3:4 When Christ, who is our life, shall appear, then shall ye also appear with him in glory.

Abiding and **dwelling** is based upon our deep love for God. Notice verse 14 God said because he has set his love upon me, therefore… etc. No one is exactly sure who wrote Psalms 91, but if you look at Psalms 90 it is revealed to us that it was from Moses.

Psalm 90:1 Lord, thou hast been our dwelling place in all generations.

Moses is talking about dwelling in God. In Psalms 91 God says: because you have set your love upon me, therefore will I deliver him, because he has known my name. God is a rewarder of them that diligently seek him. We must believe that God is hearing our prayers. David the Shepherd said: *though I walk through the valley of the shadow of death, I will fear no evil, for thou art with me, thy rod and thy staff they comfort me.* He also declared many are the afflictions of the righteous but the Lord delivers them out of them all.

If you will go through Psalms 91 very slowly, highlighting every time it refers to the person who is **dwelling** and **abiding** in God, you'll discover in 16 versus, this person is mentioned **40** times. And then it refers to God where God speaks of himself as the Most High, the Almighty, the Lord, refuge and fortress, God in him will I trust over **25** times! Now why would it emphasize us more than God? The reason why is because God is waiting for us to seek him.

2 Chronicles 16:9 For the eyes of the Lord run to and fro throughout the whole earth, to shew himself strong in the behalf of them whose heart is perfect toward him.

God wants to show himself strong on our behalf, but we must **dwell** and **abide** in him. It is simply amazing to me how the Old Testament saints had such deep understanding and revelation of these truths. They literally saw God as their all and all.

Psalm 27:1 The Lord is my light and my salvation; whom shall I fear? the Lord is the strength of my life; of whom shall I be afraid?

All of the book of Psalms it's very personal and intimate. Many of these Psalms were written by David. He said: I will not fear even if war should rise up against me, in this I will be confident that God will deliver me. David was literally speaking about life and death struggles on the battlefield where he was in jeopardy of losing his life at any moment from sword, spear and arrows, but because he dwelt in God, he had total confidence in his safety and victory.

To me this is amazing faith that can only come by **dwelling** and **abiding** in **Christ**. In the mist of all these battles with dangerous enemies notice what he said: *this one thing I desired of the Lord that I may dwell in the house of the Lord all the days of my life, to behold the beauty of the Lord, and to inquire in his temple*.

Remember when they brought the Ark of the Covenant to Jerusalem, David danced before the Lord with all of his might. King David so desperately wanted to build the temple, and yet God did not allow him to because he had shed so much blood. So his son Solomon built the temple that David wanted to build. Solomon really did not have to do that much when it came to the blueprints or preparations because David had already done it all. David had gathered much of the building materials which were necessary in the construction of this temple. He had gathered much of the wood, the gold, the silver, large stones that were necessary. David had been doing it because it was in his heart to be in the presence of God.

How Faith Comes

Whenever God's presence is real in your life you will prosper. So if you are **dwelling** and **abiding** in **Christ**, and his word is **dwelling** and **abiding** you, God will not withhold anything from you.

Psalm 84:11 For the Lord God is a sun and shield: the Lord will give grace and glory: no good thing will he withhold from them that walk uprightly.

Believers need to understand that their faith in **Christ** will never grow until they become aggressive in their fellowship with him. I meet a lot of Christians who are living in the twilight zone. They are out there in the outer limits of entertainment. They are sitting in front of their TV sets and watching soap operas, or there sitting in front of the TV set shouting with Bill O'Reilly: yeah that's right, yeah that's right yeah, that's right.

This is the reason why we are not having a move of God. We are not **dwelling** and **abiding** in **Jesus Christ**. It would be almost like you trying to cook your Thanksgiving turkey with the oven set at 150 °. And then shoving the turkey into the oven for only 30 minutes and then pulling it out. There is no way that turkey is going to be cooked all the way through. You might say: Pastor I would never be that stupid, but you know that's exactly what we do when we only come to church Sunday mornings. We are not **abiding** and **dwelling** in **Christ** the way we need to in order to be transformed and changed. Faith will come if we will **dwell** and **abide** in **Christ**.

When **Christ** was in his earthly ministry moving in the Holy Ghost, his disciples lived with **him** for 3 and half years. They walked with him, slept at his side, ate when he ate, moved when he moved. They heard him speaking the parables and the teachings that he proclaimed from his heavenly **Father** 24 hours a day, 7 days a week. They saw and experienced everything he did. And then after the resurrection he appeared to them for another 40 days, continuing to do what he had done before his betrayal, death and resurrection. Why you might ask is this so important? Because he was bringing them into a place of victorious, unwavering confidence and faith in him. And according to the Gospels he spent more time with Peter, James and John, because he was cultivating and developing them to be leaders in the church, to be over the other disciples.

Psalm 24: 1 The earth is the Lord's, and the fulness thereof; the world, and they that dwell therein.2 For he hath founded it upon the seas, and established it upon the floods.3 Who shall ascend into the hill of the Lord? or who shall stand in his holy place?4 He that hath clean hands, and a pure heart; who hath not lifted up his soul unto vanity, nor sworn deceitfully.5 He shall receive the blessing from the Lord, and righteousness from the God of his salvation.6 This is the generation of them that seek him, that seek thy face, O Jacob. Selah.7 Lift up your heads, O ye gates; and be ye lift up, ye everlasting doors; and the King of glory shall come in.8 Who is this King of glory? The Lord strong and mighty, the Lord mighty in battle.9 Lift up your heads, O ye gates; even lift them up, ye everlasting doors; and the King of glory shall come in.10 Who is this King of glory? The Lord of hosts, he is the King of glory. Selah.

I want you to notice the King of glory is going to come in and **dwell** and **abide** in us. In verse 3: **who shall ascend into the hill of the Lord, and who shall stand in his holy place?** If you study the word **WHO** it is used in the Bible over **500** times. It's a very interesting study because many times God is talking about **who** it is that will be blessed! In the wisdom books of Job, Psalms, and Proverbs the word **who** is used over **150** times.

3 Who shall ascend into the hill of the Lord? or who shall stand in his holy place? 4 He that hath clean hands, and a pure heart; who hath not lifted up his soul unto vanity, nor sworn deceitfully.5 He shall receive the blessing from the Lord, and righteousness from the God of his salvation.6 This is the generation of them that seek him, that seek thy face, O Jacob.

The Scriptures are very clear and precise about those **who dwell** and **abide** in **Christ** will be extremely blessed. Now blessings do not always translate into material possessions. Only the carnal mind thinks along those lines.

How Faith Comes

James 2:5 Hearken, my beloved brethren, Hath not God chosen the poor of this world rich in faith, and heirs of the kingdom which he hath promised to them that love him?

You can **abide** and **dwell** in **Christ** by keeping him at the center of your conversation. For instance I like to go for hikes with my family, I like looking up into the blue sky, looking at the green trees, being surrounded by nature, all the time my heart and my mind is upon **Christ**, who created and made all of this amazing world.

You and I need desperately to get alone with God. We need to get into our prayer closet. I get alone with God many times through the day, I just get alone with God whether it be in my office, sometimes in our front room when everyone else is asleep. More times than I can count I have crawled out of bed between 3 o'clock and 5 o'clock in the morning just to get alone with God.

Let us finish this chapter by looking in the gospel of John chapter 15. This is a major way in which faith comes, when you and I are **abiding** and **dwell** in **Jesus Christ**. When you set your heart upon **Jesus** some amazing things will begin to happen in your heart and in your life.

John 15: 1 I am the true vine, and my Father is the husbandman. 2 Every branch in me that beareth not fruit he taketh away: and every branch that beareth fruit, he purgeth it, that it may bring forth more fruit. 3 Now ye are clean through the word which I have spoken unto you. 4 Abide in me, and I in you. As the branch cannot bear fruit of itself, except it abide in the vine; no more can ye, except ye abide in me. 5 I am the vine, ye are the branches: He that abideth in me, and I in him, the same bringeth forth much fruit: for without me ye can do nothing. 6 If a man abide not in me, he is cast forth as a branch, and is withered; and men gather them, and cast them into the fire, and they are burned. 7 If ye abide in me, and my words abide in you, ye shall ask what ye will, and it shall be done unto you.8 Herein is my Father glorified, that ye bear much fruit; so shall ye be my disciples.

In verse 1 **Christ** is trying to get us ready to become one with him and his **Father**. I am the true vine, I am the vine like you find on a grapevine. Grapes seem to be a very important part of the lives of the Israelites. Remember what they carried out of the Promised Land in numbers chapter 13, it was a large cluster of grapes. **Jesus** declared I am the true vine, and my **Father**'s the husbandmen! He is the cultivator, caretaker, the one who prunes and fertilizes in order that the branches might produce much fruit. He is talking about the fruit of the spirit, love, joy, peace, long-suffering, gentleness, goodness, faith, meekness, self-control. These are only apprehended by faith as we **abide** in **Christ**. God also declares that every branch in me that bears not bear fruit he will take it away. He says if you are going to bear fruit then you must let me be everything to you, you're all in all. Think about me, dwell on me, and love me, for in me you will discover all that you need. The branch cannot bear fruit of itself, even so without me, **Jesus** says you can do nothing. **Jesus** declared that if you keep his commandments you shall remain and abide in his love.

The 17th Way in which faith comes Is by Abiding and Dwelling in Jesus Christ!

WHEN GOD SHOWED UP! (1981)

We were preparing to leave the church that we had been pastoring for two years. Because the church was bringing in new candidates for examination, they did not need me to preach the Word to them any longer.

As a result, I was able to spend many hours praying, meditating on Scriptures and talking to the Lord. I would walk the mountain that Was right behind our parsonage for hours on end every day just fellowship with God. A sense of great expectancy grew within my heart. The air was charged with

His tangible presence. This continued for a number of weeks. At the time, I did not realize that I was about to step into a deeper realm of the Spirit.

My wife and I were scheduled to minister at a number of meetings, and I had been invited previously to minister at the Mifflin Full Gospel Businessmen's meeting located in Belleville, Pennsylvania. We arrived right before the meeting was to start. As I sat at a table with my wife, I remember that I felt no particular quickening of the Spirit of God on the inside whatsoever. One of the members of the organization came over and asked me if I would like to pray with some of the members before the beginning of the meeting. I consented to do so.

They were standing in a circle holding each other's hands. I simply stepped into this circle and took the hand of the man on my right and left. The men began to pray, and I prayed very softly, agreeing with them. During this time of prayer, I did not perceive in my heart that I should pray aloud. When we were done praying, the man on my right, an older

gentleman, stared at me. He said, "What in the world was that?"

I said to him, **"What do you mean?"**

He said it was like a streak of lightning came out of your hand, and up my arm, through my face. You could tell that something really radical had taken place. I told him that I had not felt anything.

That was the beginning of an unusual night. This same gentleman came to me at the end of the service, crying. He asked me to look into his eyes. I still remember to this day, his eyes were clear and glistening. He said to me, "My eyes were covered in cataracts. The minute you touched me, the cataracts literally melted right off of my eyeballs!" Thank you **Jesus**!

Right up to the minute before I opened my mouth I had not felt a single thing spiritually. However, the minute I began to talk, the rivers began to flow. I do not remember what I said, but I do know I was speaking under a strong influence of the Holy Ghost. I flowed right into the gifts of the Spirit after the teaching of the Word. A very precise word of knowledge began to operate. I remember looking out over the people and beginning to call

175

specific people out. Many of the women and men appeared to be Mennonite or Amish.

I began to point to specific people, and call them to come forward. As they came, I would tell them what it was that was going on in their bodies. When they would get within ten feet of me, they did not fall forward or backwards, but they would simply float to the floor like fresh falling snow. I never have seen anything like it! It was like they just simply, and very gently went down. As far as I know, all of them were instantly healed. I do not remember laying hands on anyone that night. The **Father**, **Son**, and **Holy Ghost** were in the house.

#18 God Given Visitations, Visions & Dreams

If you truly study the New Testament you will discover that there is only 2 realities, the realm of the spirit, and the realm of the flesh. To be spiritually minded will bring life and peace, but when you operate in the carnal mind, the natural, that which is ruled by the physical it brings nothing but death. There is an old saying: *you're so heavenly minded that you are no earthly good*, but this statement is absolutely false. When you're walking in the realm of the spirit (which is the realm of faith) you are not flaky, but you are operating in the law of the spirit of life in **Christ Jesus**. When you have entered into the realm of the spirit by faith, everything about you is quickened by the Holy Ghost. Your natural capacities are enhanced beyond that of a normal person. Here is an example: I dropped out of school at 15 years old, was born with a speech impediment, with hearing problems, and with lung problems. I remember being in the hospital in an oxygen tent barely breathing as a young boy. By the time that I was 17 years old I was drinking heavily, doing drugs, running with the bad group of guys.

On my 19th birthday as I was committing suicide, getting ready to slice my wrist with a large survival knife, the fear of God fell upon me. I fell to my knees and cried out to **Jesus Christ**, and was gloriously born again. I grabbed my little green military Bible and began to devour Matthew, Mark, Luke and John. As I believed what I read I literally entered into another realm and all of a sudden all of these mental and physical disabilities were gone as I laid claim to Gods wonderful promise.

Jesus Christ boldly proclaiming to those who looked to him for their healings that their faith had made them whole. What faith was he speaking about? The faith that they were placing in **Jesus Christ**. Their confidence, trust, dependence, belief, and reliance was upon nobody but **Jesus Christ**. When man committed sin he literally became the slave of his flesh and the fleshly desires which had been sown into him by the enemy through his act of disobedience to God. At one time Adam ruled and reigned supreme by the spirit of God. But now his flesh had taken control because it had been invaded by the spirit of disobedience.

Ephesians 2:2 Wherein in time past ye walked according to the course of this world, according to the prince of the power of the air, the spirit that now worketh in the children of disobedience:

Christ Jesus came to take us back into that place where we were created to walk, to move, and to have our being which is only discovered and found in **Christ**. This is only accomplished by faith in **Jesus Christ**, the one who has paid the ultimate price for our salvation and deliverance.

We are not wrestling against flesh and blood, but against principalities, against powers, against the rulers of the darkness of this world, against spiritual wickedness in high places. The place of victory over these demonic powers is only found by faith in **Jesus Christ**. Faith will take you from the flesh into the spirit. Now we are dealing with the **18th Way** in which faith will come, increase, mature and grow.

Habakkuk 2:1 I will stand upon my watch, and set me upon the tower, and will watch to see what he will say unto me, and what I shall answer when I am reproved. 2 And the Lord answered me, and said, Write the vision, and make it plain upon tables, that he may run that readeth it.3 For the vision is yet for an appointed time, but at the end it shall speak, and not lie: though it tarry, wait for it; because it will surely come, it will not tarry.4 Behold, his soul which is lifted up is not upright in him: but the just shall live by his faith.

If we went back to chapter 1 in the book of Habakkuk we would discover that it is talking about the deeds of the wicked. And then it makes an amazing statement in chapter 2 verse 4 that the just shall live by his **own** faith, yes your own faith in God. (This faith is of and by **Jesus Christ**) **Jesus** constantly emphasize the faith of the individual person in HIM. Yes, we can join our faith together in agreement and see mighty things happen. ***One can put a thousand to flight God says, and two can put 10,000 to flight.*** I might not be able to lift up 200 pounds by myself, but if I can get a couple other people to join me, it will be simple. So yes we can join our faith together in order to get tremendous results, and yet we need to have our own faith.

Romans 14:22 Hast thou faith? have it to thyself before God.

We are using Habakkuk chapter 2 as a launching pad into this **18ᵗʰ Way** in which faith comes. Habakkuk was bringing before God the reality of the wickedness of his generation. He recognized that faith had died in the hearts of most of God's people. He proclaims that he is like a watchman on top of the wall looking down upon the masses and recognizing their terrible and desperate condition. And he is saying, Lord what are you going to do about this. How does God respond? If you will believe this, it has the potential of changing your life. The
answer to Habakkuk's problem is a vision, a dream, a divine revelation.

#18 Faith Comes When God Gives You a Vision!

If you go from the book of Genesis to the book of Revelation, and count how many times the Lord gave a dream, a vision a prophetic blueprint to God's people, you would be simply amazed. I have painstakingly gone through the Scriptures to discover all the times that God gave dreams, visions and angelic visitations to his people. I have personally discovered over 500 times that God revealed himself to his people by dreams, visions, and angelic visitations. Actually the whole Bible is a super natural revelation of who God is and what his will is for humanity.

Many times in my life God has given to me visions and dreams. Most of them were pertaining to specific directions and how to handle a situation. By dreams and visions he also has warned me about coming disaster and destruction. At times I did not listen to these prophetic visitations, and it brought destruction to my life. The Lord is having me write a book at this time about the 20 ways that God leads and guides us. I hope to have that available before the end of 2014. Did you notice that in Habakkuk chapter 2 he tells the person who reads the vision to now run? Within this divine vision or dream there is embedded a supernatural endowment of faith. When God

179

gave to Noah a vision of the coming destruction, there was within that vision or dream the plans for the building of the ark. Faith rose up, the faith that was imparted through this visitation to build that ark made of gopher wood.

When I speak about visions and dreams within this category I am also including angelic visitations. There is within these elements an endowment of supernatural faith. It's just like with electricity that it is the volts that carry the amps. The volts by themselves do not have the capacity to kill you, or cause the equipment to work. It is the amps that help produce the results that are necessary to run the electrical appliances. Within this category of visions and dreams I'm including impressions, perceptions, and divine given mental images. You might ask: how come many of those within the body of **Christ** are not having these visitations? Here's the simple answer: **they are not believing God for them.** I believe God to reveal himself to me supernaturally. Do not misunderstand, I am not seeking a visitation, I'm simply believing and expecting God to give them to me. Why would I need these? Because this is how God communicates and reveals himself to his people. This is a major way in which faith will come into your heart and into your life. All the saints of old had dreams and visions given to them by God whether it be Abraham, Jacob, Isaac, Joseph, Moses. In the new covenant we discover many visitations. If you read the 4 Gospels you would discover that it is implied that **Jesus Christ** had many such experiences. The apostle Paul himself had many such experiences.

2   Corinthians 12:1 It is not expedient for me doubtless to glory. I will come to visions and revelations of the Lord.2 I knew a man in Christ above fourteen years ago, (whether in the body, I cannot tell; or whether out of the body, I cannot tell: God knoweth;) such an one caught up to the third heaven.3 And I knew such a man, (whether in the body, or out of the body, I cannot tell: God knoweth;)4 How that he was caught up into paradise, and heard unspeakable words, which it is not lawful for a man to utter.

AN OPEN VISION THAT CHANGED MY LIFE!

God strongly dealt with my heart that I was not spending enough time in his word. I informed our church staff that I would begin to give myself to long hours of prayer and the Word. I began with the book of Ephesians, starting with the very 1st chapter. I did not want to only memorize it, but I wanted to get it into my heart. This took me close to three weeks and countless hours to memorize.

Then the next mountain I climbed was the book of Galatians. As I was memorizing scriptures and chapters of the Bible, I would get tremendous headaches. But I kept working at it because I knew that without pain, there is no gain.

When I had conquered the book of Galatians, I moved to the book of Philippians. As I was into the second chapter of the book of Philippians, something supernatural and amazing took place. I had what the Bible calls an **open vision**. This happens when you are wide awake and everything disappears except what God is showing you literally with your human eyes. There in front of me was a never ending body of water. It was deep blue with not one ripple upon it, stretching as far as my natural eyes could see in every direction. The room I was in was gone and there was nothing but this gigantic blue never ending body of water. I lifted my head to look into a light blue cloudless sky, I saw a large, crystal-clear rain drop come falling down in slow motion from the heavens. I watched in utter amazement as it slowly came tumbling down towards this body of water. When it hit the surface of this body of water, it caused ripples to flow forth.

These ripples, as they flowed forth from the center of where the drop had hit, began to grow in size and intensity. Then all of a sudden, the vision was over. I stood there in amazement, not understanding what had just happened.

I knew this experience was from God, but I did not know what its significance was?

I knew in my heart that God eventually would show me what it meant. You see, when the Lord gives me a supernatural visitation like this, I do not lean to the understanding of my natural mind. I just simply give it to the Lord, knowing that in His Time, He will show me what He meant, or what He was saying.

I picked up my Bible to get back to memorizing scriptures. I immediately noticed that there was a change in my natural mental capacity. It seemed like as if my brain was absorbing the Word of God like a sponge absorbs water. Within one hour I memorized a whole chapter, as if it was nothing. To my amazement, my brain had the capacity now to remember very quickly. Where it took me days to memorize a chapter before, now I could memorize a chapter in an hour. I continued to memorize books of the Bible until there were nine books inside of me. This is not including thousands of other scriptures that I continued to memorize dealing with certain subjects.

I could have memorized the whole New Testament had I not allowed the activities of ministry to overwhelm me and keep me preoccupied. The enemy is trying constantly to distract us in order to keep us out of that realm of faith were all things are possible.

Now faith does not only come when you have a vision, dream, or divine visitation, but it can come when you read and hear about those who have had these visitations. A good example of this is when **Jesus** declared that we need to go and preach this gospel to every creature which is under heaven. This was a divine commission, visitation that **Christ** had from his **Father**. And yet as he shared this vision, purpose, and divine commission with his disciples, faith rose up in their hearts for them to run with this vision.

Joseph is a tremendous example of the divine visitation by dreams and visions. Within this visitation there was imparted into Joseph and unwavering faith to believe God to see to come to pass that which he had spoken to his heart. When he shared these dreams with his family, because it was not their revelation, therefore they did not have the understanding, and rose up against him. Unbeknownst to them this was a part of God's plan in order to get the seed of Abraham into the land of Egypt. Joseph went through tremendous suffering, and yet as we read the Scriptures it does not seem like he ever wavered. Within in his visitations there was the seed of faith, which rose up and overcame the world, the flesh, and the devil. By faith he overcame the test and the temptations that were thrown at him. These visitations kept his heart flying straight and clear like an arrow right into the middle of God's will! Supernatural visitations and visions are extremely important in the development of our faith in **Christ**. I am not exalting visitations because it is simply a tool that God uses to mold and shape us into his likeness and into his image. At the same time please realize there are many people who experience visitations that are not of God. Your experiences should never contradict the character and the nature of **Christ**, or the written word which has been provided to us by the Bible.

I Saw Blood upon the Cross

I experienced a supernatural visitation when I was about seven years old. One cold winter night I had to get up to go to the restroom, so I went into our little bathroom. After I finished, I washed my hands and turned off the lights. I noticed that the moon was reflecting off the bathroom mirror. So I turned around and looked at this window. This light was coming through the perforated, frosted-glass. As I looked out this glass window at the snow covered ground, all of a sudden I saw three crosses. The two outer crosses seemed to be set back from the much-larger middle cross. My eyes were supernaturally drawn to this larger middle cross. As I looked at it through the perforated frosted colored window, there appeared to be blood running down from it. At that moment my heart was smitten to its very core. A very great overwhelming sorrow engulfed my heart as I was looking at this cross. At that moment I began to weep uncontrollably, with tears flowing down my cheeks like a miniature stream. That experience radically changed my personality and attitude for a season. I became helpful, kind, and caring. This wonderful transformation lasted for a brief time before I became the same spoiled and self-centered child that I was before.

As I look back over my life I realize that without divine visitations I would've never got born again. The majority of those spoken of in Hebrews chapter 11 had divine visitations, visions, and dreams. If Saul of Tarsus would not have been visited by **Christ** on the road to Damascus would he have ever become the apostle Paul? Throughout his whole ministry Paul kept referring to this experience he had. He told King Agrippa that he was not disobedient to this heavenly vision. It was literally the foundation upon which he went forth preaching **Jesus Christ**.

I have had many amazing visitations from the Lord. The majority of those things which God has allowed me to accomplish is because I have had divine visitations from heaven. Whether it be the large facility that God allowed us to build when we had no money, or the uplink C band system, TV network, writing of books, evangelizing other nations. Almost all of these came to pass because of visitation, which created faith within my heart to accomplish that which in the natural I could never have accomplish. You can read about many of these experiences in our books:

" Living in the Realm of the Miraculous 1, 2 & 3"

In the book of Joel it is revealed to us that God was going to pour out his Spirit upon all flesh in the last days. Notice the emphasis that the Holy Ghost gave to dreams and visions. The will of God can never be accomplished without divine visitations. Remember we are involved in a supernatural warfare; in which it takes supernatural weapons to defeat the demonic world. As we get closer to the end of the ages I believe there will be an increase of these divine visitations. God will be manifesting himself to his bride by visions, dreams, and angelic encounters. Do not seek for a visitation, but simply begin to expect it to happen in whatever situation you find yourself in.

Joel 2:28 And it shall come to pass afterward, that I will pour out my spirit upon all flesh; and your sons and your daughters shall prophesy, your old men shall dream dreams, your young men shall see visions:

How Faith Comes

The Apostle Peter reaffirmed the book of Joel in the 1ˢᵗ sermon he preached after he was baptized in the Holy Ghost. And then he declared that visions, dreams, and prophecies would continue to the end of the ages. God revealing himself to us in this way is such a threat to the devil that he has done everything he can to influence the modern day church that God no longer works in these ways. Why would the enemy try to convince so many within the body of **Christ** this is not for today? It is because of the fact that faith will rise up in the hearts of those who experience these visitations. And by Faith we overcome every work of the devil.

Acts 2:38 Then Peter said unto them, Repent, and be baptized every one of you in the name of Jesus Christ for the remission of sins, and ye shall receive the gift of the Holy Ghost.39 For the promise is unto you, and to your children, and to all that are afar off, even as many as the Lord our God shall call.40 And with many other words did he testify and exhort, saying, Save yourselves from this untoward generation.

Acts 2:15 For these are not drunken, as ye suppose, seeing it is but the third hour of the day.16 But this is that which was spoken by the prophet Joel;17 And it shall come to pass in the last days, saith God, I will pour out of my Spirit upon all flesh: and your sons and your daughters shall prophesy, and your young men shall see visions, and your old men shall dream dreams:18 And on my servants and on my handmaidens I will pour out in those days of my Spirit; and they shall prophesy:

As we finish up this chapter let me encourage you to try the spirits. Many false religions and doctrines have been started because people had visitations that were not of the Lord. Every time I have an experience the 1ˢᵗ thing I do is go to the Scriptures to verify that everything I just saw, felt or experienced was in line with the
Scriptures. Remember the enemy can appear to us as an angel of light. Through the years I have run into many people that have had experiences which were obviously not of God. But these experiences went so deep inside of them, that they could not see the truth that what they experienced was a lie from the devil.

2 Timothy 3:15 And that from a child thou hast known the holy scriptures, which are able to make thee wise unto salvation through faith which is in Christ Jesus.16 All scripture is given by inspiration of God, and is profitable for doctrine, for reproof, for correction, for instruction in righteousness:17 That the man of God may be perfect, thoroughly furnished unto all good works.

CHAPTER SEVEN

#19 The Indwelling of Jesus Christ!

To understand the 19th Way in which faith comes we will be looking in the book of Galatians chapter 2. We have been teaching and ministering on the reality of faith. **Jesus** told his disciples that the laborers are few, but the harvest is great. This is one of the main reasons that we need to have great faith in order that we will go into the harvest field and reap the harvest. It was never God's will that we would go into the harvest field without being equipped supernaturally to deal with the enemy. Signs, wonders and miracles will follow them that believe. **Jesus** said: *freely you have received, freely give. Heal the sick, cleanse the lepers, raise the dead, and cast out devils*! **Jesus** boldly declared that in his name you and I shall *tread upon snakes and scorpions and over all the power of the enemy, and nothing shall by any means come to harm us. Without faith it is impossible to please God.* When **Christ** was baptized in the river Jordan by John the Baptist, he came up out of the water and the Holy Ghost came upon him bodily in the form of a Dove. There came a thundering voice from heaven saying *this is my beloved son in whom I am well pleased.* When our hearts are full of faith, the Holy Ghost will move upon us mightily. Faith is the divine supernatural weapon that God has provided for us to defeat every work of the devil and the demonic world.

We are now going to be sharing with you an astounding way, a mind-boggling way in which faith comes to us as born-again believers. Let us take a look at what Paul said in Galatians chapter 2 verse 20!

Galatians 2:20 I am crucified with Christ: nevertheless I live; yet not I, but Christ liveth in me: and the life which I now live in the flesh I live by the faith of the Son of God, who loved me, and gave himself for me.

Notice in this Scripture Paul said *I am crucified*. You and I can come to the place where our flesh is completely crucified. Do not think that I am saying that you will never again struggle with the flesh because the enemy is always trying to creep back into our lives like weeds in a garden. You have to constantly be pulling the weeds out of a natural garden, even so is it with our hearts. But we do not have to wait for these weeds to become deeply rooted and strong. When they are still small and seemingly insignificant, and tender you can pluck them out with your little fingers. The apostle Paul declared: *I am crucified with Christ, nevertheless I live, yet not I but it is Christ that lives within me.* Paul had this amazing revelation that **Christ** lived in him. Not just the fact that **Christ** was with him, for him, or helping him, but that **Christ** actually lived in him.

Colossians 1:27 To whom God would make known what is the riches of the glory of this mystery among the Gentiles; which is Christ in you, the hope of glory:

This same **Jesus Christ** who overcame the world, the flesh, the devil, healed the sick, raise the dead, cast out demons, cleansed the lepers, who walked upon the sea of Galilee, turned water into wine, fed the multitudes with just 2 fish and 5 loaves of bread, now lives in us! When the believer truly has this revelation he'll never take credit for anything that he may accomplish, but will give all of the credit and glory to God. We are talking about the great mystery that Paul proclaimed in the book of Ephesians chapter 5.

Ephesians 5:31 For this cause shall a man leave his Father and mother, and shall be joined unto his wife, and they two shall be one flesh.32 This is a great mystery: but I speak concerning Christ and the church.

There is a oneness that we need to experience with **Christ**. I love my lovely bride Kathleen and we have been married for over 36 years. I cannot imagine my life without her. We are there for each other without exception. Of course we have not attained a complete oneness because there are strongholds in each of our lives that prevent us from having the type of intimacy that God truly plans for us to enjoy. It is the same with us and **Christ**, there are strongholds within our mind, emotions, desires, attitudes, and thought life that must be dealt with in order for this amazing oneness to take place. There is no hindrance whatsoever in Christ himself. Within this chapter I will share with you the **19ᵗʰ Way** in which faith will arise within your heart.

#19 by The Indwelling reality of Christ!

I am crucified with **Christ**, and yet Paul said that this **Christ** lived within him, and this is an absolute amazing truth. Right now we are to live by the faith of the son of God! Notice it does not say faith in **Christ**, but the faith of **Christ**. It is **Christ** and his faith at work inside of me. This is what I believe that Paul proclaimed in Ephesians chapter 3 when he said:

Ephesians 3:.20 Now unto him that is able to do exceeding abundantly above all that we ask or think, according to the power that worketh in us,21 Unto him be glory in the church by Christ Jesus throughout all ages, world without end. Amen.

This is the great mystery which I believe he was referring to in Ephesians 5. Let me try to explain it this way. When I was a little boy we used to visit my dad's mom and dad. In their kitchen they had one of these old hand pumps that they would use to pump water directly out of their well into the kitchen. But in order to get the water to come up from the depths of the earth they had to prime that pump with water. We would take about a gallon of water and dump it into this hand pump. Then we would begin to pump it very fast up and down. I still remember feeling the suction and the pressure as it created a vacuum by which to pull the water right up out of the earth into my grandma's kitchen sink. I believe that is how our natural faith works. We begin to draw close to God, and then all of a sudden he comes rushing in upon us.

James 4:8 Draw nigh to God, and he will draw nigh to you. Cleanse your hands, ye sinners; and purify your hearts, ye double minded.

We must use this God-given faith that we received when we were conceived in our mother's womb. We take this little bit of faith like that of a gallon of water and begin to use it to believe on **Christ**. We confess with our mouths and believe in our heart that God has raised **Jesus** from the dead and declare that he is Lord of our lives. At that moment **Christ** himself comes rushing into our heart and into our life like the water being pulled up through that pump, and with his entrance comes his nature, character, his life and his faith. Yes, the same faith that he used to overcome every temptation, every sickness and disease, every affliction, every trial, and every work of the devil. It's the same faith that raised **Christ** from the dead that is now dwelling in us.

May the Lord help me to explain this even in a greater sense! Let's say for instance that you owed somebody $1 million. Let's say this debt was going to cause you to end up in prison for a very long time, plus causing you to lose everything you possessed. It looked like you were gone for sure, when out of the blue a man you did not know shows up, and for no other reason then the fact that he had great compassion on you, he pays your debt. Let's say the people that you originally owed the money to still keep trying to come back to collect the debt that is already been paid by this most generous man. What would you do? You would laugh at them out right! It is literally because of what this person has done for you that you are now set free.

You're not basing your freedom upon what you were able to accomplish but simply upon the fact of what this person had done for you. It is the same reality when it comes to **Christ** in all of his amazing provisions, blessings, and promises that he has made available to us by the new covenant in his own precious blood. And yet he not only paid the price for our salvation, but he himself has stepped into us, bringing with himself his divine nature and his faith. Did you hear that? It is **his faith** now at work in us.

How Faith Comes

Galatians 2:20 I am crucified with Christ: nevertheless I live; yet not I, but Christ liveth in me: and the life which I now live in the flesh I live by the faith of the Son of God, who loved me, and gave himself for me.

Read that scripture to yourself, and listen to what Paul said by the spirit of God. *I live by the faith of the Son of God*! Paul said he lives by the faith of the son of God. It is now **Jesus Christ** who lives in you, and it is the faith of **Jesus Christ** that is waiting to be manifested in us. Let me give you another example.

Let us say that you were going to the airport to pick up an extremely wealthy man. Let's say the car you are driving is in truth a piece of junk, but it is sufficient to get you there. Just for a minute imagine that this car represents your faith and my faith. You pick up this very wealthy man in your vehicle, but unbeknownst to you this very wealthy man loves to give and lives to give. The minute you pick him up he notices your poverty stricken condition. He decides out of the liberality of his heart that he wants to help you. As you leave the airport he directs you a Mercedes-Benz car lot. He goes in for a little bit to discuss something with the owner. Then he comes back to your vehicle and within his hand he is holding the keys to the most expensive car you have ever seen. He gives you those keys and informs you that now this vehicle is yours in order to take him that is the wealthy man wherever he needs to go. This is exactly what **Christ** has done for us, you and me.

John 15:8 Herein is my Father glorified, that ye bear much fruit; so shall ye be my disciples.

This same spirit of faith that was operating in **Jesus Christ** to fulfill the will of the **Father**, is now in us because **Christ** is in us. The faith I am speaking about is so far beyond the faith that we began with that there is no words that we can describe what we can now accomplish with this faith that is of **Christ Jesus**.

Romans 5:2 By whom also we have access by faith into this grace wherein we stand, and rejoice in hope of the glory of God.

We need to realize that it takes faith in **Christ** to operate in the faith that is of **Christ**. Let me give you another illustration. I had a neighbor who had an old Ford galaxy 500. Whenever I seen this lady driving her car I always thought that it was a large gutless vehicle. She was always just poking along, going below the speed limit. She reminds me of a lot of Christians who do not understand what is under their hood. One day I really needed to get somewhere, but my vehicle was not available. I went to this ladies house asking her if possibly I could use her old galaxy 500 Ford? She said it would be okay, to go right ahead, and she gave me the keys. I started the engine, and I put it in reverse. I pushed down a little bit too hard on the gas pedal thinking that it was a gutless engine, the engine kicked in with a roar. My tires began to spin shooting dirt and gravel everywhere. I could hardly believe what just happened. This engine had a lot of horse power and get up and go. As I pulled out on the highway I decided to open it up to see what it had. I put the pedal to the metal, and the thrust of that car shoved me back into the driver seat. I had been deceived by watching my neighbor lady driving her vehicle, not realizing what was under the hood. I am convinced that's the way most Christian believers are living their lives. They have no comprehension of the faith that is waiting to explode inside of them if they would but believe that it is **Christ** himself that lives in them.

How do we explain the unlimited ability that we have in the faith of **Christ**? I guess you could say it would be like having a gallon of water within you before **Christ** came into your heart. This gallon of water can be symbolic of our faith, but now that **Christ** has come within us, it would be like taking all of the water that is on earth, and pouring it into your heart all at once. This explanation might seem to be an exaggeration, but if anything it doesn't come anywhere near to the potential of the faith of **Christ** within us. Hebrews chapter 1 declares that **Christ** holds all things together with his word by faith.

Hebrews 1:3 Who being the brightness of his glory, and the express image of his person, and upholding all things by the word of his power, when he had by himself purged our sins, sat down on the right hand of the Majesty on high: 11:3 Through faith we understand that the worlds were framed by the word of God, so that things which are seen were not made of things which do appear.

You might say that it is like an unlimited spending debit card that the Heavenly **Father** gave to his son, but now the son has given it to us. **Philippians 3:5** tells us that we need to have the mind of **Christ**. Now we know that everything we received from God must be by faith in **Christ**. We could take this set of Scriptures though and simply change the word mind to the word *let this* **Faith** *be in you*, and still be accurate in our declaration.

Philippians 2:5 Let this <u>FATH</u> be in you, which was also in Christ Jesus:6 Who, being in the form of God, thought it not robbery to be equal with God:7 But made himself of no reputation, and took upon him the form of a servant, and was made in the likeness of men:8 And being found in fashion as a man, he humbled himself, and became obedient unto death, even the death of the cross.

This **Jesus Christ** who has been exalted above all else, now lives in the heart of every born-again believer. **Christ** and his faith is amazing beyond understanding. This is what Paul meant when he declared in a book of Colossians that they preached this **Jesus Christ**.

Colossians 1:27 To whom God would make known what is the riches of the glory of this mystery among the Gentiles; which is Christ in you, the hope of glory:

It is **Christ** in us the hope of glory whom we are preaching, for he is the answer and the solution to every problem, circumstance and situation. **Christ** was born in the likeness of sinful flesh. He was tempted and tested and tried in every way that we are, and yet never once did he sin. All of the sins of the world and sicknesses were placed upon him, and yet he never stepped out of the will of God. That amazing triumphant faith which **Christ** had and has is now in us! Can you grasp a hold of this reality? The faith of **Christ** is in us.

We can overcome anything the world or the devil throws at us by this faith, the faith of **Jesus Christ**. When the day of Pentecost came **Jesus** had a group of people that he had breathed his spirit and his faith into.

John 20:22 And when he had said this, he breathed on them, and saith unto them, Receive ye the Spirit:

    Christ Jesus is a quickening spirit, where Adam was simply a living soul. All of them that gathered on the day of Pentecost were born again men and women, with **Christ** living inside of them. **[The Holy Ghost comes rushing in where ever there is faith]**. These men and women were full of the faith of **Christ,** which opened the door wide for the empowerment and the fire of the Holy Ghost. This is mysterious and wonderful. You see it is **Christ** in me speaking to the **Christ** which is in heaven. Now how can **Christ** be in me, and everybody else, and in heaven all at the same time? Well, it works like this: **HE IS GOD! And he is om·ni·pres·ent.** It is now his spirit within us that cries out Abba **Father.** From my innermost being his voice cries out: **Father** your will be done on earth as it is in heaven.

19th Way that faith comes is by Christ in you the hope of glory. It is the faith of Christ in you and me!

    The purpose of the Holy Ghost is revealed to us in John chapter's 14, 15, and 16. He comes to lead us into the reality of who **Christ** is, and that he lives within us. We rise up and begin to take the faith of **Christ** by faith to crucify our carnal contaminated sinful and wicked flesh. In the mist of this struggle the Holy Ghost reveals to us that we have an unlimited banking account. But if you are not operating in the faith of **Christ** you will miss use and misappropriate all of the blessings that God has given to us. Next thing you know you'll be foolishly spending what God has given to you on vain amusements and foolish Mickey Mouse junk. Your flesh will want a $40,000 toilet seat, or $120,000 boat. You begin to think you have a right to have a 10,000 square-foot, $3 million mansion. When you are walking in the faith which is of **Christ**, all of these things will be insignificant to you. It's the same faith that overcame the devil in the wilderness when he said it is written. Remember **Jesus** chose not to use faith in order to have a nice bed to sleep in every night. He even told one man who wanted to follow him that he needed to be ready to lay his head upon a rock, because **Christ** had nowhere to lay his head but on a rock. Could he have believed God for a goose down pillow? Yes, a million times yes, but the faith that was in his heart would not allow him to miss use the authority and the ability that God the **Father** had granted him in his earthly mission. We are talking about a faith that only desires to do those things that are pleasing to the Heavenly **Father**. This is the kind of faith that **Christ** brings with him when he comes into our lives.

James 2:5 Hearken, my beloved brethren, Hath not God chosen the poor of this world rich in faith, and heirs of the kingdom which he hath promised to them that love him?

John 5:19 Then answered Jesus and said unto them, Verily, verily, I say unto you, The Son can do nothing of himself, but what he seeth the Father do: for what things soever he doeth, these also doeth the Son likewise.

As Paul was encouraging the Galatians to go back to the faith which they once had known, he makes an amazing statement.

Galatians 2:16 Knowing that a man is not justified by the works of the law, but by the faith of Jesus Christ, even we have believed in Jesus Christ, that we might be justified by the faith of Christ, and not by the works of the law: for by the works of the law shall no flesh be justified.

Did you notice that? We believe in **Jesus Christ**, that we might be justified by the faith of **Christ**. How does that work? It is the one gallon of water priming the pump to bring forth the never ending water of the faith of **Christ**. We believe in **Jesus Christ** in order to cause the faith of **Christ** to be manifested in us. Oh how I pray that the Holy Spirit is quickening this reality to you right now. It will end all of your fleshly struggles and anxiousness.

1 *Galatians 3:22 But the scripture hath concluded all under sin, that the promise by faith of Jesus Christ might be given to them that believe.*

This is the wonderful promise that was given to Abraham and his descendant's. That the faith of their Messiah, their **Christ**, and their Savior would be manifested in their flesh. That it is no longer we that live, but **Christ** that lives within us. This is why we will be casting our crowns at his feet and declaring boldly, we are unprofitable servants, we have simply done that which was required for us to do.

Romans 3:22 Even the righteousness of God which is by the faith of Jesus Christ unto all and upon all them that believe: for there is no difference:

It is the faith of **Jesus Christ** at work in us which causes us to live holy and righteous lives.

Hebrews 12:2 Looking unto Jesus the author and finisher of our faith;

The Greater One Now Lives within Us! His name is **Jesus Christ**, and it is his faith at work in us! Will you dare to believe this truth? Will you dare to walk in this reality? It is time, that we rise up to our rightful positions in **Jesus Christ**!

1 John 4:4 Ye are of God, little children, and have overcome them: because greater is he that is in you, than he that is in the world.

It Was the Faith of Christ at Work in Me!

My wife and I had just pulled in from a very long night ministering at a full gospel businessmen's meeting. The old boat of a car we were driving was on its last leg. When we pulled up to Kathleen's grandma's house, the old engine could not handle any more, being red hot it froze up on the spot. We were so happy God had gotten us home. We were sitting there in this car rejoicing that we had made it home when the faith of **Christ** rose up in my heart. When I told Kathee that we need a pickup truck, she looked at me funny. I explained that our motor home/old school bus is what we used to haul our tents and equipment around with, but we still needed a pickup truck in order to haul equipment that could not fit in a bus. She looked at me and basically said okay! I took my wife's hand and said I would pray and she could agree with me. Out of my heart came these words "Lord, we would like to have a black Ford pickup truck. Lord, we need this pickup truck to have a 302 engine, and Lord, we need it to be an automatic. We also need this pickup truck to have a cap on its back so whenever we haul anything in the back, the stuff won't get wet."

When we finished praying, we began to praise God for the truck. (Remember prayer, supplication, with thanksgiving.) "Now thank you, Lord, for that black Ford pickup truck!" The next morning, we got up early to get ready to go to the tent meeting we were to be at. It was the church in Huntington, Pennsylvania, which had been a part of the tent revival we had conducted at the Huntington Fair. We were working directly with the pastor, who was a friend of ours, to evangelizing their local community. They had grown so fast that the little building which they had been meeting in could no longer hold them. At that time, they were using our largest tent for their meetings. It would seat over 500 people. Of course, we had no way to get to this meeting. Kathleen's grandma knew our needs, so she called up one of her neighbors to see if we could use their car. Thank God! They agreed to let us use it. This car was almost brand-new.

We arrived at the tent gathering right before it began. I'm sure that everybody thought that God had blessed us with a new car. We did not tell anybody at the meeting that we had to borrow this car because our vehicle was shot. I think people are too quick to tell other people what they need. I love to keep my mouth shut and watch God work.

At the end of the service, when everybody was leaving, a young couple walked up to us. The husband said that during the service he had looked over at us and had a feeling inside of him that they should give us a vehicle that they owned. He had shared this with his wife and she also had a witness. He told me they felt strange coming to me because they saw that we had a very nice car. I did not tell them this was not our car. I simply told them to obey God. I asked them when we could come and see this vehicle they felt led to give us. They informed us that they did not live very far from this meeting, and we could follow them to look at this vehicle. I did not ask him what kind of vehicle it was. We said that we could follow them right then and there and take a peek.

After a number of miles, we pulled up in front of a farmhouse. There was no other vehicle sitting anywhere in sight. They told us the vehicle was behind the house next to their barn. We walked around the house and there next to the barn was a black Ford pickup truck, with a 302 engine, automatic, and with a cap. It was exactly what we had prayed and asked God for, not even eight hours previously. Within two to three days, we were driving around in our black Ford pickup, with a 302 engine, automatic, and a cap on the back, and we did not have to pay a single dime for it! I believe this was the faith of **Christ** at work in me.

#20 by Praying in the Holy Ghost!

We are looking at the **20th Way** in which faith will come. This truth can be discovered in the book of Jude verse 20.

Jude 20 But ye, beloved, building up yourselves on your most holy faith, praying in the Holy Ghost,

If you will study this Scripture in other translations it declares that we must fortify, strengthen, establish our most holy faith! How do we do this? By praying in the Holy Ghost. I do not believe this is only speaking about praying in the gift of tongues which you received when you received the baptism in the Holy Ghost, but it is also speaking about the Holy Ghost leading you in your prayer time. The spirit of the Lord himself will put the words in your mouth that need to be spoken.

2 Samuel 23:2 The Spirit of the Lord spake by me, and his word was in my tongue. Psalm 45:1......my tongue is the pen of a ready writer.

When you build yourself up in your most holy faith, this spiritual response is that it will take a hold of the holiness of God, it takes a hold of the will of God, and it takes a hold of the character and the divine nature of God. There is a teaching that I have done which reveals 10 biblical benefits that take place when you pray in tongues! Out of the 10 gifts of the Holy Ghost revealed within the Scriptures, tongues is one of the simplest that **Christ** has given to the church. This tongues that I'm referring to is not the same diversity tongues that needs to be interpreted. It is your own personal prayer language that the Holy Ghost will give you to communicate to God.

Romans 8:26 Likewise the Spirit also helpeth our infirmities: for we know not what we should pray for as we ought: but the Spirit itself maketh intercession for us with groanings which cannot be uttered.

The exercising of this God-given language opens the door wide for the manifestation of the other 9 gifts of the spirit. It takes faith to believe that God is speaking through you in this super natural language which sometimes sounds like baby talk. I asked the Lord one time why would he give his people a language that sounded ridiculous? He spoke to my heart and said I do it to humble my people. You must be as a child to enter into the kingdom of heaven.

Ephesians 6:18 Praying always with all prayer and supplication in the Spirit,

Let me share an amazing story about how I was baptized in the Holy Ghost, and the difference it made in my life.

How God Supernaturally Healed Me of Being Tongue-Tied!

After I gave my heart to **Christ** a divine hunger and thirst for the Word of God began to possess me. I practically devoured Matthew, Mark, Luke, and John. **Jesus** became my hero in every sense of the word, in every area of my thoughts and daily living. He became my soul reason for getting up every day and going to work, eating, sleeping, and living. I discovered that everything I did was based on a desire of wanting to please Him.

One day I was reading my Bible and discovered where **Jesus** said that it was necessary for him to leave. That because when he would go back to the **Father**, he would send the promise of the Holy Ghost to make us a witness. Furthermore, I learned it was His will for me to be filled to overflowing with the Holy Ghost and that the Holy Ghost would empower and equip me to be a witness an ambassador for God. The Holy Ghost would also lead me and guide me into all truth.

With all of my heart I desperately wanted to reach the lost for **Jesus Christ** in order for they could also experience the same love and freedom that I was now walking in. I searched the Scriptures to confirm this experience. In the book of Joel, in the old covenant, the four Gospels and especially in the book of acts I discovered the will of God when it comes to this baptism. I perceived in my heart that I needed to receive this baptism the same way that I had received salvation. I had to look to **Christ** and trust by faith that he would give to me this baptism of the Spirit. It declared in the book of acts that after they were baptized in the Holy Ghost they all began to speak in a heavenly language. I had not been around what we would call Pentecostal people, so I had never heard anybody else speak in this heavenly language, but that did not really matter to me, because it was within the Scriptures.

Acts 2:39 For the promise is unto you, and to your children, and to all that are afar off, even as many as the Lord our God shall call.

I remember getting on my knees next to my bunk bed where I cried out and asked God to fill me with the Holy Ghost so I could be a witness. As I was crying out to God something began to happen on the inside of me. It literally felt like hot buckets of oil was beginning to be poured into me. Something then began to rise up out of my innermost being. Before I knew what I was doing, a new language came bubbling out of my mouth which I had never heard before, or been taught to speak. I began to speak in a heavenly tongue.

Now up to this time I had a terrible speech impediment. You see I had been born tongue-tied. Yes, they had operated on me, and I had gone to speech therapy, and yet most people could not understand what I was saying. I could not even pronounce my own last name YEAGER properly. My tongue simply refused to move in a way in which I could pronounce my Rs.

After I was done praying in this new language, I discovered to my absolute surprise that my speech impediment was instantly and completely gone! From that time on, I have never stopped preaching **Jesus Christ**. For almost 40 years I have proclaimed the truth of **Jesus Christ** to as many as I can.

For the First Time She Could Understand Me

About 4 months after I gave my heart to **Christ** I went back to my hometown, Mukwonago, Wisconsin, I immediately went to see one of my best friends to share with him my conversion experience. Actually, it was his sister I had been dating for the last three years. I wrote her a letter telling her what happened to me, and how God had gloriously set me free from drugs, alcohol, and all of my worldly living. This caused her to cut me off completely, as if I had lost my mind. Praise God! I had lost my mind by receiving the mind of **Christ**. My friend's mother was listening while I was speaking to her son, and out of nowhere she said, **"Mike, what happened to you?"** I told her how I had been delivered from drugs and immorality because I gave my heart to **Jesus**. She said, "No, that's not what I'm talking about. After many years of knowing you, this is actually the **1st time I can fully understand what you are saying**."

You see, my speech was so garbled that it was very difficult for people to truly understand exactly what I was saying. Those who know me now would not have recognized the old me. Before I was baptized in the Holy Ghost you would not have been able to understand most of I said. I'm still trying to make up for the 1st nineteen years when I could not speak properly.

BY PRAYING IN TONGUES, IN THE SPIRIT OUR FAITH IS BUILT, FORTIFIED AND ESTABLISHED!

#21 by Seed Time and Harvest

Let us now look at the 21st Way that faith will come. It is discovered in the Gospel of Luke chapter 17.

Luke 17: 5 And the apostles said unto the Lord, Increase our faith.6 And the Lord said, If ye had faith as a grain of mustard seed, ye might say unto this sycamine tree, Be thou plucked up by the root, and be thou planted in the sea; and it should obey you.

In the Gospel of Luke chapter's 15, 16, the 14th, and the 1st 3 verses of chapter 17 **Christ** is proclaiming to his disciples what is absolutely expected and required of them. As a response to his declarations they cry out: **Lord increase our faith**! All of these chapters are dealing with our relationships with other people. **Jesus** gives to them specific ways in which they are to treat and respond to people in a loving, forgiving and compassionate way. This will take great faith in **Christ** to walk in his divine nature that we may have mercy upon others even as God has had mercy upon us.

I have had the privilege of Pastoring since 1977. I can honestly tell you that the greatest challenge in being a pastor is people. Back in approximately 1999 I was just so tired of dealing with the nick pickiness, criticism, faultfinding, gossiping and complaining of people that I shut everything down. We had 21 staff, a Bible college, K-12 school, large broadcasting ministry, and a food pantry, clothing ministry. Plus many other things that were taking place that are not worth mentioning. I guess I just did not have enough faith to keep dealing with people. Years later the Lord was able to reprove me. The Scripture he gave me is self-explanatory.

Proverbs 14:4 Where no oxen are, the crib is clean: but much increase is by the strength of the ox.

203

For another words if there are no cattle in the stalls, there will be no manure to clean up. Now that may sound wonderful, but it's devastating for a farmer. It's the same with people, in the sense if you have no people, you basically will have no problems. But then what is the purpose? **Any time a man who is a Christian says that he wants to move to the mountains, and get away from everybody, you know he's not operating in faith.** It takes faith to keep loving, forgiving, blessing and helping people. It takes faith to keep in the will of God when it comes to ministry. It truly takes faith to pastor people in a way that is pleasing to God, especially in this day and hour.

OUR SPIRITUAL LEADERS CAN ONLY TAKE US WHERE THEY LIVE!

Here are some facts from Focus on the Family, and Fuller Seminary! **#1** Fifteen hundred pastors leave the ministry each month due to moral failure, spiritual burnout, or contention in their churches. **#2** Fifty percent of pastors' marriages will end in divorce. **#3** Eighty percent of pastors feel unqualified and discouraged in their role as pastor. **#4** Fifty percent of pastors are so discouraged that they would leave the ministry if they could, but have no other way of making a living. **#5** Eighty percent of seminary and Bible school graduates who enter the ministry will leave the ministry within the first five years.

In Luke 17:6 **Jesus** declares that faith will come as you and I plant seed. This is seed time and harvest. It's the way that God designed it from Genesis to now. As you plant the seed of faith, water it and nourish it, it will grow.

Genesis 8:22 While the earth remaineth, seedtime and harvest, and cold and heat, and summer and winter, and day and night shall not cease.

It also talks about this in the book of **Matthew Chapter 13**, in the book of **Mark chapter 4**, and in the book of **Luke chapter 13**. Another way to look at this is by what **Christ** declared in Luke chapter 19!

Luke 19:12 He said therefore, A certain nobleman went into a far country to receive for himself a kingdom, and to return.13 And he called his ten servants, and delivered them ten pounds, and said unto them, Occupy till I come.....15 And it came to pass, that when he was returned, having received the kingdom, then he commanded these servants to be called unto him, to whom he had given the money, that he might know how much every man had gained by trading.

There can only be an increase when you take that which you have and you begin to invest it in to the will of God. The old saying is if you don't use it you lose it. **Jesus** even declared that the servant lost the pound that he had been given because he did not use it. It was taken from him and given to the one who did use it. If you do not use the faith that **Christ** has already given you, investing it into that which is the will of the **Father**, then you will lose it. We have opportunities every day to use our faith against the powers of darkness, and for the kingdom of light. We help people, minister to the hurting, Speak words of encouragement to the hurting.

Luke 6:38 Give, and it shall be given unto you; good measure, pressed down, and shaken together, and running over, shall men give into your bosom. For with the same measure that ye mete withal it shall be measured to you again.

This Scripture is pertaining to how you treat others, and yet as you give by faith in **Christ**, it will be given back to you good measure, pressed down, shaken together, and running over. **Christ** declared that out of our bellies would flow rivers of living water. You must take the faith you have, no matter how insignificant and small it may seem, and begin to put it to work. Paul declared in a book of Galatians chapter 5 that if you sow to the spirit, you shall of the Spirit reap life everlasting.

#21 Faith Will Come by Seedtime and Harvest!

It takes faith to give when you know in your heart that God is calling you to dig deeper, and give more. Many times in my marriage my wife and I

205

have given all that we had to fulfill God's will. He has always provided our needs exceedingly abundantly above all that we could ever ask or think.

2 Corinthians 9:6 But this I say, He which soweth sparingly shall reap also sparingly; and he which soweth bountifully shall reap also bountifully. 7 Every man according as he purposeth in his heart, so let him give; not grudgingly, or of necessity: for God loveth a cheerful giver.

The essence of living is giving. It defines who God truly is, for he is the giver of every good gift. God so loved the world that he gave his best, his only begotten son. As a result of his giving by faith it has brought forth children as the stars of the heaven, and the sands of the seashore. And if you truly are giving by faith there will be within your heart a wonderful joy, a cheerfulness if you will. For where there is faith in operation, there is peace, joy and righteousness manifested.

Romans 14:17 For the kingdom of God is not meat and drink; but righteousness, and peace, and joy in the Holy Ghost.

Proverbs 3:9 Honour the Lord with thy substance, and with the firstfruits of all thine increase: 10 So shall thy barns be filled with plenty, and thy presses shall burst out with new wine.

When you stop giving to the work of God, whether it be finances, time or resources, you are on a path of death and destruction. If you only give when times are good, or you feel like it, then you are simply moving in the flesh. It takes faith to give the little bit you have like the woman who gave the two widows mites.

Luke 21:2 And he saw also a certain poor widow casting in thither two mites. 3 And he said, Of a truth I say unto you, that this poor widow hath cast in more than they all: 4 For all these have of their abundance cast in unto the offerings of God: but she of her penury hath cast in all the living that she had.

If your faith is truly going to grow to a place that apprehends the impossible, you are going to have to sow the seed of faith. There is no way around this reality. Faith always gives. These are the words of our Lord **Jesus**:

Acts 20:35 I have shewed you all things, how that so labouring ye ought to support the weak, and to remember the words of the Lord Jesus, how he said, It is more blessed to give than to receive.

Jesus Christ operated in such a realm of faith that the Bible declares that he laid aside his deity, gave up his heavenly position and the splendors of heaven, became a servant, suffered, took our sins, died a terrible death for us, and rose again. That is an amazing and incredible faith. This is where the spirit of God is trying to take us.

God Asked Me: Will you die for me?

I heard the voice of God asking me: are you willing to die for me? It was as I was getting ready to leave for the Philippines. I had been to the Philippines on numerous occasions. I had been going into an area of the Philippines where the NPA was extremely active. NPA is the abbreviation for the new People's Army, which are part of a communist movement. At that time they were very active and they were extremely brutal and dangerous. Godly men which I have worked with in the Philippines had been murdered by them. I heard the Lord continue to say to me: if I can use your spilt blood like a seed planted into the ground to bring about a wonderful harvest, are you willing to die? When I heard the Lord say this to me, I took it very seriously. With deep sorrow in my heart and tears rolling down my face, I said yes Lord!

It was not that I was not willing to die for **Christ**, because I had been in many dangerous situations since I had been born again in 1975. I have had numerous encounters with people threatening and trying to kill me. A gang I used to run with out of Chicago tried twice. Some Yupik Indians in Alaska had tried to kill me. A demon possessed woman had stabbed me multiple times in the face and yet the knife could not penetrate my skin. A radical

Muslim kept on wanting to shoot me, as he yelled and screamed in my face, with his finger ready to pull the trigger which would have sent me off into eternity, but the Holy Ghost restrained him.

Yes, I was more than willing to die, but in truth I did not want to. I had a lovely wife, 3 sons and a beautiful little girl. But I said yes Lord, if this is your will! I still remember that morning as I was getting ready to drive myself to the BWI Airport to catch a plane to the Philippines. I hugged my precious wife very tight and my four beautiful children as if it was like the last time I would ever hold them or hug them again on this side of heaven. As I looked at my little girl Stephanie she was sucking on her 2 fingers and I had lovingly nicknamed her two fingers Stephanie. My 2nd son Daniel I had nicknamed him the watermelon kid because he loved watermelon so much. I hugged my oldest son goodbye who we had nicknamed Mick which is short for Michael. my 3rd son Steven could never give enough hugs even to this day.

As I backed out of my driveway leaving my family standing on the front porch tears were rolling down my face. I said Lord you died for me, you gave everything for me, so the least I can do is to be willing to give up everything you've given me, if I can be a seed of revival for others to be born again. As I was driving towards the airport on the main highway I was weeping so hard that I could barely see where I was going. I was thanking God for the years that he had given me with my lovely wife Kathleen. I was thanking God for my 3 sons and my daughter. I was thanking God for all the opportunities he had given to me to minister the word and help others. I was also reflecting upon the fact of how many times I should been dead like many of my former buddies who were now dead. I thought back on the times before I was born again when I had overdosed, drank way too much booze, played chicken with oncoming trains, driving on the other side of the road headed right towards others. When I had been in a gunfight with a crazy man. Oh how many times God had spared me, and yet most of my worldly friends were now dead.

All of those times when God spared my life, he could've allowed me to die and go to hell. But God had rescued me, and now it was my turn to die for him, how could I say no? I remember landing in the Philippines. I was completely free from fear. In my heart of hearts I was already a martyr for **Christ**.

208

How Faith Comes

Now to my wonderful amazement and my great surprise God spoke to my heart while I was over there in the communist infested area. He said: son you're not going to die! I said what Lord? He spoke to me again: you're not going to die! I remember crying with joy, I said why Lord? He said I needed to have you prove your love for me. He said I needed to have you to know that I was number 1 in your life. Even as Abraham offered up Isaac, and I gave him back, so in a sense you have offered up your wife and your children, and I give them back to you.

That has been approximately 23 years ago. I'm still going to areas at times that are extremely dangerous, but I have no fear, because I know that God is with me. What if he ever asked me to offer up my life again as a seed with the shedding of my blood? All I can say is that if it ever happens again, by God's grace I'll say, yes Lord! You gave your life for me, it's the least I can do.

Dr Michael H Yeager

CHAPTER EIGHT

#22 by the Prophetic Word!

Let us take a look at the **22nd way** in which faith will come. It is found in 1st Timothy chapter 4 verse 4.

1 Timothy 4:4Neglect not the gift that is in thee, which was given thee by prophecy ………...

The apostle Paul makes an amazing statement to Timothy. He tells timothy not to neglect what was given to him by prophecy. From Genesis to the book of Revelation we see God speaking through man prophetic words. I realize that most people think that prophetic words are given to us in order to foretell the future, but I do not believe this is the main purpose of prophecy. In the book of Genesis chapter 1 the Scripture declares 11 times, **and God said!** This is hard for us to understand in the natural, but all that God ever created was by his audible spoken word. God has spoken everything of the physical and spiritual world into existence. Now we are to have the same spirit of faith. It literally says in the book of Revelation that prophecy is the spirit of **Christ**.

Revelation 19:10... for the testimony of Jesus is the spirit of prophecy.

Within the prophetic word that is inspired by the spirit of God is a seed of faith. When God speaks to us or through us by prophecy, the faith that is necessary to bring to pass that which is spoken, is within that prophetic word. Listen to what he says to Timothy in this Scripture.

1 Timothy 1:18 This charge I commit unto thee, son Timothy, according to the prophecies which went before on thee, that thou by them mightest war a good warfare;

He told Timothy that by these prophetic words you have been equipped to war a good warfare. As I have shared each one of these ways in which faith comes, every one of them really deserves a much more intense examination, but time simply would not permit us to do this. Let's just look at a couple more Scriptures that reveals the impact and the power that prophecy carries within it.

2 Peter 1:21 For the prophecy came not in old time by the will of man: but holy men of God spake as they were moved by the Holy Ghost.

2 Peter 1:19 We have also a more sure word of prophecy; whereunto ye do well that ye take heed, as unto a light that shineth in a dark place, until the day dawn, and the day star arise in your hearts:

Revelation 1:3 Blessed is he that readeth, and they that hear the words of this prophecy, and keep those things which are written therein: for the time is at hand.

When someone speaks over your life by the Holy Ghost with a prophetic word it will cause faith to rise up in your heart in a wonderful and powerful way. As you study from Genesis to Revelation you'll discover whenever God spoke prophetically over a person, the next thing that transpired was that person or those people were stepping in to that prophetic declaration. Faith was wrapped within that prophetic word. It is like the seed in the middle of a peach, or plum or maybe an avocado. Faith comes with the prophetic word. In Ezekiel's vision chapter 37 God revealed to the prophet a valley full of dead dry bones.

A mighty army which was now dead and gone forever, or was it? God began to have Ezekiel prophesy over those dead bones. And it came to pass as he prophesied the bones once again became a mighty army. And then he told him to prophesy that life would come back into this dead Army.

Ezekiel 37:9 Then said he unto me, Prophesy unto the wind, prophesy, son of man, and say to the wind, Thus saith the Lord God; Come from the four winds, O breath, and breathe upon these slain, that they may live.

212

How Faith Comes

The prophet Joel prophesied that in the last days our sons and daughters would prophesy. Prophetic words will cause faith to once again become alive in God's people. The prophetic word literally has with in it the capacity to transform us and change us into different people. Samuel the Prophet prophesied over Saul when he was not yet a king. He told him the spirit of the Lord would come upon him, and that he would begin to prophesy, and become a different man.

1 Samuel 10:6 And the Spirit of the Lord will come upon thee, and thou shalt prophesy with them, and shalt be turned into another man.

It happened exactly the way that Samuel the Prophet said. As the spirit of God prophesies to you and through you, and you embrace it (the prophetic word must line up with the Scriptures) and believe it you will be transformed, and those who receive it will be transformed. Let the faith that is in the divinely inspired prophetic word rise up within you, and take you into the realm were all things are possible.

He told me you're prophetic word Saved Me $45,000

One day as I was ministering in the church I pastor, the spirit of prophecy began to flow through me mightily. I was calling out numerous different people, and speaking prophetically over their lives. When I do this by the spirit of God, it always brings tremendous results. Many times broken hearts are healed, habits and addictions are broken, sicknesses and diseases are vanquished, words of knowledge and wisdom are mixed within that which I am speaking giving direction and help to the needy. I remember calling out one particular brother prophesying to him about his finances. Many times when I am moving in the spirit, I will make statements or give prophetic words to people and not fully comprehend or remember what I said. This is probably for the best, that way I cannot take any glory for myself. Sometime later this particular brother came back to me and made an amazing statement, he declared, Pastor Mike you saved me $45,000. It kind of surprised me that he made this statement. I said to him, what exactly are you talking about?

He told me: you prophesied over me, telling me that I needed to trade in my 401(k) s, because they were going to become worthless if I did not. When he heard these prophetic words coming from my lips, faith rose up in his heart to act upon this word right away. I truly do not remember telling him this. The brother told me that he immediately cashed in his 401(k) s, and if he had waited any longer than he did, he would have lost $45,000. It is so important that when God gives us a prophetic word that agrees with the Scriptures, and is confirmed in our hearts, to obey immediately. I cannot tell you how many times it has saved my life because I obeyed a prophetic word I had received from God.

#23 Impartation by the Laying on of Hands

Let us now talk about the **23ʳᵈ Way** that faith will come. I do want to say this though, what I'm teaching and preaching is not formulas. These are biblical spiritual principles and truths, divine laws that God has established within his word. This is not like making a cake and following the recipe on the back of the box. Our whole emphasis is increasing our confidence, trust, reliance and dependence in **Christ,** for that the will of the **Father** will be accomplished in our life, and the earth.

#23 The **23ʳᵈ Way** that I would like to share with you is the laying on of hands. Yes, that is correct, faith comes by the laying on of hands by those who are **filled with faith** and operating in the spirit of God. Throughout the Old Testament and the New Testament, we see the importance of the hands. This is such a wonderful ministry when you look at the Scriptures that declare what God did with his **Hands**.

Hebrews 1:10 And, Thou, Lord, in the beginning hast laid the foundation of the earth; and the heavens are the works of thine hands:

Psalm 102:25 Of old hast thou laid the foundation of the earth: and the heavens are the work of thy hands.

Isaiah 64:8 But now, O Lord, thou art our Father; we are the clay, and thou our potter; and we all are the work of thy hand.

Isaiah 48:13 Mine hand also hath laid the foundation of the earth, and my right hand hath spanned the heavens: when I call unto them, they stand up together.

Even our salvation and deliverance is the result of the mighty right hand of God. Who is this mighty right hand? It is none other than **Jesus Christ**. He is the wonderful right hand of the **Father**. According to the Scriptures t it declares that **Christ** himself sits at the right hand of the heavenly **Father** upon the throne of heaven.

Exodus 15:6Thy right hand, O Lord, is become glorious in power: thy right hand, O Lord, hath dashed in pieces the enemy.

Psalm 118:15 The voice of rejoicing and salvation is in the tabernacles of the righteous: the right hand of the Lord doeth valiantly.16 The right hand of the Lord is exalted: the right hand of the Lord doeth valiantly.

Psalm 98:98 O sing unto the Lord a new song; for he hath done marvellous things: his right hand, and his holy arm, hath gotten him the victory.

Psalm 17:7 Shew thy marvellous lovingkindness, O thou that savest by thy right hand them which put their trust in thee from those that rise up against them.

Christ himself is even revealed in the book of Exodus chapter 4 when God has Moses put his hand into his shirt. And his hand became completely consumed with leprosy.

Exodus4:6 And the Lord said furthermore unto him, Put now thine hand into thy bosom. And he put his hand into his bosom: and when he took it out, behold, his hand was leprous as snow.7 And he said, Put thine hand into thy bosom again. And he put his hand into his bosom again; and plucked it out of his bosom, and, behold, it was turned again as his other flesh.

This leprosy was none other than a revelation of the right hand of God taking upon himself all of our sins, sicknesses and infirmities. **Jesus Christ** took our leprosy upon himself. When Moses stuck his hand close to his heart, in that moment his hand became leprous. And then when he stuck his hand next to his heart again, it was completely cleansed and made whole. This is what God the **Father** did to his own son **Jesus Christ**. *He made him to be sin for us who knew no sin!* But then God the **Father** raised him from the dead having removed all of our sins, sicknesses and diseases from him. God had Moses perform this amazing miracle before the children of Israel, and before all of the officials of Egypt that stood before Pharaoh. God is the one who has declared that there something special about our hands when we are full of faith and the Holy Ghost.

How Faith Comes

Please notice that as **Christ** walked the earth after he had been filled with the Holy Ghost, supernatural signs and wonders happened as he laid his hands upon the people.

Luke 4:40 Now when the sun was setting, all they that had any sick with divers diseases brought them unto him; and he laid his hands on every one of them, and healed them.

Luke 13:13 And he laid his hands on her: and immediately she was made straight, and glorified God.

Jesus sent his disciples forth telling them that they could also lay hands on the people in his holy name, and that the demons would leave, sickness and diseases would depart when they laid their hands on them.

Mark 16:18 They shall take up serpents; and if they drink any deadly thing, it shall not hurt them; they shall lay hands on the sick, and they shall recover.

Acts 28:8 And it came to pass, that the Father of Publius lay sick of a fever and of a bloody flux: to whom Paul entered in, and prayed, and laid his hands on him, and healed him.

Without a shadow of a doubt there is something that comes out of the hands of the believers as they lay them upon people. This is an invisible substance that brings about tangible results. What is this invisible substance? It is the substance of faith!

Hebrews 11:1 Now faith is the substance of things hoped for, the evidence of things not seen.

This substance is the faith which we demonstrate in **Christ Jesus**. It is a spiritual force, even as God is a spirit himself. It is beyond the explanation of the carnal natural mind. It is beyond the nucleus and the Adam molecule. It is beyond the most advanced scientific knowledge that humanity has.

2 Corinthians 4:13 We having the same spirit of faith, according as it is written, I believed, and therefore have I spoken; we also believe, and therefore speak;

This substance, this spirit of faith is released into a person, or even objects as we lay our hands upon them. Paul told Timothy to remember the laying on of hands, and the transference of this invisible substance into his life. This is the substance of faith.

2 Timothy 1:6 Wherefore I put thee in remembrance that thou stir up the gift of God, which is in thee by the putting on of my hands.

1 Timothy 4:14 Neglect not the gift that is in thee, which was given thee by prophecy, with the laying on of the hands of the presbytery.

#23rd Impartation by the Laying on of Hands

There are numerous scriptures that deal with this reality. I have included the Scriptures for your meditation. All of these realities are activated by faith in **Jesus Christ**. The early church had a revelation of the spirit of faith and its transference by the laying on of hands. May God once again resurrect this reality in our hearts and in our lives.

Acts 6:6 Whom they set before the apostles: and when they had prayed, they laid their hands on them.

Acts 13:3 And when they had fasted and prayed, and laid their hands on them, they sent them away.

Acts 19:6 And when Paul had laid his hands upon them, the Holy Ghost came on them; and they spake with tongues, and prophesied.

Acts 8:17 Then laid they their hands on them, and they received the Holy Ghost.18 And when Simon saw that through laying on of the apostles' hands the Holy Ghost was given, he offered them money,

Hebrews 6:2Of the doctrine of baptisms, and of laying on of hands, and of resurrection of the dead, and of eternal judgment.

Acts 19:11 And God wrought special miracles by the hands of Paul:12 So that from his body were brought unto the sick handkerchiefs or aprons, and the diseases departed from them, and the evil spirits went out of them.

God Touches and Heals a Mafia Man's Eyes!

I have a house where I take in and keep single men. Some of these men come from real rough backgrounds. I had one such gentleman that I was renting to who was quite large and intimidating. I would try to share **Christ** with him whenever the opportunity arrived, but he was so liberal in his thinking that it did not seem to be having any impact upon him. Everything I believe that is wrong, he proclaimed was right. And everything that I believe is right, he would argue against.

He informed me that in his past he had worked for the Mafia, and at one time he was what they called a THUMPER! I asked him what he meant by a thumper? He said that he had never physically murdered anyone, but that they would send him to rough up people, you know thump them! I have no doubt at all that what he told me was true.

One day as I was at the house where I keep these men, I saw him standing in the main front room. He seemed quite upset and distressed. I asked him what was wrong. He informed me that he had just come from the doctors because he had been having terrible problems with his eyes. After the Doctor had concluded all of the test they came back with a very disturbing report. They informed him that he had an eye disease (long medical term) that was going to cause him to go blind.

At that moment the spirit of God rose up with in me, and I proclaimed boldly that in the name of **Jesus Christ** he was not going to go blind. I told him: close your eyes! He said what? I said: close your eyes! He shut his eyes and I took my two thumbs and laid them forcefully over his two eyelids. I declared: in the name of **Jesus Christ** you lying spirit of infirmity, come out of these eyes right now! Be healed in **Jesus** name! I then removed my thumbs from his eyelids, he looked at me with questioning eyes. I said to him: it's done! He said what? I said it is done. You are healed in the name of **Jesus**. He said: really? I said: yes **Christ** has made you whole. It seemed for a minute that tears formed in his eyes as I turned around and walked away.

Approximately a week later he showed up at our thrift store that we manage. He walked into the store asking for Pastor Mike. They informed him that I was not there. Tears were rolling down his face, and they asked him what they could do for him. He told them with great joy and excitement that he had gone back to the doctors, and that his eyes were completely healed. He started hugging the people that where they're running the store. This large ex-Mafia thumper gave his heart to **Jesus Christ** that day, and became a part of the church I pastor.

As I Laid My Hands upon His Deaf Left Ear, God Instantly Opened It!

I was speaking to a gentleman one day about the reality of **Jesus Christ**. He seemed to be completely oblivious to anything about **Christ**. He informed me that as a little boy some invisible demonic entity would begin to literally push him physically. He was now approximately 58 years old, and it had been going on for 50 years. He had tried to get relief but nothing seemed to help. As he began to get older he tried to get rid of the fear that would come upon him by drinking heavily. This of course made things much worse. He said that one time he was drunk while he was driving his motorcycle. This resulted in him having a terrible accident. In this motorcycle accident his head injury was so bad that it had left him completely blind in his left eye, and deaf in his left ear. The medical world had not been able to do anything for him. For a number of years now he had been in this condition.

As he was telling me his predicament, the spirit of God Quicken to my heart to pray for him. I asked him if it would be all right for me to lay my hands upon him, and to pray over him in the name of **Jesus Christ**. He seemed to hesitate for a couple of seconds, but then he said it would be okay. I took my right hand and placed it over his left ear. Then I took my left hand and put it over his blind eye. I spoke boldly in the name of **Jesus**, commanding this spirit of blindness to come out of his eye, and commanding the spirit of deafness to come out of his left ear. I then removed my hands, and stood there looking at him.

With a complete look of shock, he declared that he heard a loud popping sound in his left ear. That he had not heard anything in that ear since he had experienced his motorcycle accident. I told him to cover his good ear, and to repeat what I said. Then I put my mouth next to his left ear and whispered **Jesus**. He came back with the word Jesus. I said it again **Jesus**. He responding by speaking the name of **Jesus**. At that moment he began to cry quite dramatically. He kept asking me what had just happened. I told him that **Jesus Christ** had opened up his deaf ear. He began to thank me profusely. I informed him it was not me, but **Jesus Christ**. He must've hugged me 2 or

3 times with great joy. I then had the wonderful opportunity to lead him in a prayer of salvation.

#24 Exalting and Magnifying Jesus Christ

We are looking at the **24th Way** in which faith will come. Let us begin this teaching by looking at Revelation chapter 12 verse 11.

Revelation 12:11 And they overcame him by the blood of the Lamb, and by the word of their testimony; and they loved not their lives unto the death.

In chapter 13 we used Revelation 12 in the emphasis of remembering what God has done for us. But now we are going to use the Scripture in order to see another truth that hast the potential of changing your life. Testimonies are given by God for you and I can proclaim boldly what **Jesus Christ** has done for us. I know many people have been taught how to witness in the sense of following some type of a script, and I'm not saying that this is always wrong, but the most powerful way to share **Christ** is in the reality of what he has done for you. Paul the apostle if you look in the book of acts constantly used his experience with **Christ** on the road to Damascus to proclaim the gospel.

Acts 9:4 And he fell to the earth, and heard a voice saying unto him, Saul, Saul, why persecutest thou me?5 And he said, Who art thou, Lord? And the Lord said, I am Jesus whom thou persecutest: it is hard for thee to kick against the pricks.

Acts 22:7 And I fell unto the ground, and heard a voice saying unto me, Saul, Saul, why persecutest thou me?8 And I answered, Who art thou, Lord? And he said unto me, I am Jesus of Nazareth, whom thou persecutest.

Acts 26:13 At midday, O king, I saw in the way a light from heaven, above the brightness of the sun, shining round about me and them which journeyed with me.14 And when we were all fallen to the earth, I heard a voice speaking unto me, and saying in the Hebrew tongue, Saul, Saul, why persecutest thou me? it is hard for thee to kick against the pricks.15 And I said, Who art thou, Lord? And he said, I am Jesus whom thou persecutest..............19 Whereupon, O king Agrippa, I was not disobedient unto the heavenly vision:

Paul's 1st desire was that men would be converted, being delivered from the power of darkness, for they could walk in the light of **Jesus Christ**.

The 24th Way in which faith will come to you and others is by exalting, boasting, magnifying, and lifting up **Jesus Christ**.

John 12:32 And I, if I be lifted up from the earth, will draw all men unto me.

John 8:28 Then said Jesus unto them, When ye have lifted up the Son of man, then shall ye know that I am he, and that I do nothing of myself; but as my Father hath taught me, I speak these things.

We know that **Jesus Christ** overcame principalities and powers. He defeated the enemy through his sufferings, sacrificial death and resurrection. That God the **Father** has given him a name that is above every name, but there is still something that must be done in order to bring about salvations and conversions. That name must be lifted up, it must be preached and declared, proclaim to all the world. We must boast, magnify, and exalt his name. It takes faith to proclaim **Jesus**, and as you lift up his name it will bring faith to yourself and to the listeners.

Mark 16:15 And he said unto them, Go ye into all the world, and preach the gospel to every creature.

It is our responsibility to exalt **Jesus Christ** because he is our Lord and Savior.

How Faith Comes

Galatians 6:4 But let every man prove his own work, and then shall he have rejoicing in himself alone, and not in another.

The world is going to exalt their gods, football, technology, sports, hobbies, vain amusements, all the things that excite them, but what is it that excites us? What is it that we take pleasure and joy in? What is it that makes us want to shout, dance and run? Is it not **Jesus Christ**, the Lamb of God, our king, our Lord and Savior!

Colossians 3:4 When Christ, who is our life, shall appear, then shall ye also appear with him in glory.

It really is not that complicated, simply share from your heart all the wonderful things that **Jesus Christ** has done for you. **Jesus** said if we are ashamed of him, then he will be ashamed of us.

Luke 9:26 For whosoever shall be ashamed of me and of my words, of him shall the Son of man be ashamed, when he shall come in his own glory, and in his Father's, and of the holy angels.

Paul the apostle declared boldly that he was not ashamed of the gospel of **Jesus Christ**. As we boast, magnify and exalt **Jesus Christ** faith will begin to enter into the hearts of the listeners. In order for salvation to come they must believe. We have the wonderful privilege of proclaiming **Jesus Christ** to a lost and dying world. He is the only hope! He is the only answer! He is the only solution! Do you believe this?

Romans 1:16 For I am not ashamed of the gospel of Christ: for it is the power of God unto salvation to everyone that believeth; to the Jew first, and also to the Greek.

2 Corinthians 7:14 For if I have boasted anything to him of you, I am not ashamed; but as we spake all things to you in truth, even so our boasting, which I made before Titus, is found a truth.

Paul declared that he boasted of **Christ** to the Corinthian's. And that he was not ashamed in his boasting. If time would permit, we could look at the

225

attitude of true believers throughout the ages. There are some wonderful and astounding Scriptures in the Old Testament of how the saints of old loved to magnify the name of God. That which we love and believe in is that which we will exalt and boast about. Too many believers are boasting on the devil, his shenanigans and his works without even realizing it. I refuse to boast on the devil and his demonic activities! **I will exalt and magnify the Lord who is worthy to be praised.**

This is the **24ᵗʰ Way** in which faith will come.

Psalm 34:2 My soul shall make her boast in the Lord: the humble shall hear thereof, and be glad.

Psalm 34:3 O magnify the Lord with me, and let us exalt his name together.

Psalm 69:30 I will praise the name of God with a song, and will magnify him with thanksgiving.

Exodus 15:2 The Lord is my strength and song, and he is become my salvation: he is my God, and I will prepare him an habitation; my Father's God, and I will exalt him.

2 Samuel 22:47 The Lord liveth; and blessed be my rock; and exalted be the God of the rock of my salvation.

Psalm 18:46 The Lord liveth; and blessed be my rock; and let the God of my salvation be exalted.

Psalm 34:3 O magnify the Lord with me, and let us exalt his name together.

Boldly preaching Jesus was about to get me pulverized!

There was a big Texan I knew in the Navy who actually rode bulls in rodeos at one time. We called him Tuck, to this day I don't know why. After

How Faith Comes

I gave my heart to **Jesus Christ**, I shared the gospel with him, his friends, and as many as I could. The Spirit of the Lord had begun to move upon one of Tuck's friends. Tuck was extremely irritated at me for causing this man to come under conviction. Up until the time I had given my heart to **Jesus**, tuck had been a good friend of mine. But now that I was in love with **Christ**, he did not want anything to do with me. Whenever he looked at me it was with great disdain.

One-night Tuck came into my room completely intoxicated with alcohol. He woke me up banging on my door like a madman. I went out to see what he wanted. When I entered the foyer he grabbed me by the neck with his large left hand. He literally picked me up off the floor by my neck and slammed me against the wall. He clenched his right hand into a fist right in front of my face pulling it back as if getting ready to hit me with all of his might. His fist literally was as big as my face. He told me that he was going to pulverize me if I did not promise to leave one of his drinking buddies alone. The man he was speaking about had taken an interest in the gospel.

In the natural, my heart should have been filled with great fear because without a shadow of a doubt he could easily beat me to death. I could literally see, and feel the devil in him. His face was all red, and his steely blue eyes were bulging, but instead of fear what rose up in my heart was a great compassion for his soul. Right there on the spot as I was hanging from my neck with his hand pinning me against the wall I began to weep for him. I told him that he could do whatever he wanted to do to me, but I would never stop preaching and exalting **Jesus Christ**. I told him that I loved him and he needed to get right with God.

He began to shake violently like a leaf in a strong wind. His fist was moving back and forth in front of my face. His mouth was moving erratically with foam coming between his teeth and hanging on his lips. During this time the other men in my barracks had heard the commotion and were all standing around watching this event unfold. After what seemed a long time Tuck finally lowered his fist and put me down. He turned around without a word and walked away from me. From that moment up until I left the Navy he never spoke to me again.

227

Many years later I was talking with Willie, the cowboy. Willie had become a master chief in the Navy and his expertise was underwater demolition. I asked what had happened to Tuck. Right after that event with me he said, Tuck lost his mind. He literally took his Colt 44 magnum pistol and walked up to our militaries base commander and put the gun against his head.

Thank God he did not shoot the man, but of course he was arrested and court-martialed. Tuck ended up being an alcoholic which caused him to lose his wife and family, and then he was diagnosed with cancer. Now the story does have a wonderful ending. Willie the cowboy told me that during his time in the Navy with me he really was not right with God. But the spirit of God had arrested him, and he had gotten right with **Jesus**. Willy the cowboy had stayed in contact with Tuck all of those years and eventually had a chance to speak to him about the Lord. Before Tuck died Willie had the opportunity to lead Tuck to **Christ**, he was gloriously born again; shortly thereafter, Tuck died and went home to be with the Lord. Someday, Lord willing, I will see him again. Only this time we will have sweet fellowship!

CHAPTER NINE

#25 Operating in the Gift of Faith

We are dealing with the **25th Way** in which faith will come. I truly believe what I am sharing in this book has been given by the divine inspiration of the Holy Ghost. Every way that faith comes which I have shared is based upon solid biblical truths. Many of us have already been operating in these truths, we simply did not realize that they produced faith. It is time for the body of **Christ** to rise up being filled with faith and the Holy Ghost to accomplish the great task which God has set before us. In order to understand the **25th Way** in which faith will come we must look at 1st Corinthians.

1 Corinthians 12:7 But the manifestation of the Spirit is given to every man to profit withal.8 For to one is given by the Spirit the word of wisdom; to another the word of knowledge by the same Spirit;9 To another <u>faith</u> by the same Spirit; to another the gifts of healing by the same Spirit;10 To another the working of miracles; to another prophecy; to another discerning of spirits; to another divers kinds of tongues; to another the interpretation of tongues:11 But all these worketh that one and the selfsame Spirit, dividing to every man severally as he will.

As you study the Scriptures you'll discover that there is 3 categories of the gifts of the spirit. The **1st** category is the utterance gifts which are revealed to us as diversity of tongues, interpretation and prophecy. The **2nd** category is the wisdom gifts which is revealed to us as the word of wisdom, the word of knowledge, and the discerning of spirits. The **3rd** category is the power gifts which is revealed to us as the gift of faith, the gift of healing, and the working of miracles. What we need to speak about in this particular chapter is one of the gifts revealed in the power gifts. This gift is called the gift of faith.

#25 Operating in the Gift of Faith

The gift of faith is not what we would call normal everyday faith, but it is a divine impartation that the Holy Spirit gives as he wills. Many of the amazing things which God has allowed me to accomplish has been when I was operating in this gift. At the end of this chapter I will share one of the amazing times that the gift of faith was operating in me. Now when this gift is in manifestation you enter into a realm that is unshakable. Your confidence, trust and reliance upon God goes through the roof. I believe that these gifts and their manifestation is to some extent determined by what office you possess within the body. In Ephesians chapter 4 Paul proclaims that when **Christ** ascended up on high, he gave gives unto men.

Ephesians 4:10 He that descended is the same also that ascended up far above all heavens, that he might fill all things.)11 And he gave some, apostles; and some, prophets; and some, evangelists; and some, pastors and teachers;

In another chapter we discussed the fact that you must begin with the faith that God has given to you.

Romans 12:3 For I say, through the grace given unto me, to every man that is among you, not to think of himself more highly than he ought to think; but to think soberly, according as God hath dealt to every man the measure of faith.

You begin to develop it, use it, increase it, and add to it by the spiritual principles which God has made available to you. You must use the faith that you have to prime the pump. In the book of James, the brother of **Jesus** declared that we must draw close to God, and then he will draw close to us.

James 4:8 Draw nigh to God, and he will draw nigh to you.

230

How Faith Comes

Hungering and thirsting after God will open the door of your heart wide for God to begin to use you in these supernatural and amazing gifts which are given to us by the Holy Ghost. And yet all of these gifts operate in us by faith in **Christ Jesus**.

Galatians 3:5 He therefore that ministereth to you the Spirit, and worketh miracles among you, doeth he it by the works of the law, or by the hearing of faith?

Operating in these gifts can only be to the same proportion of the faith that has been developed within your heart and your life. The faith I am speaking about is your faith in **Jesus Christ** and his word.

Romans 12:6
Having then gifts differing according to the grace that is given to us, whether prophecy, let us prophesy according to the proportion of faith;

1 Peter 4:10 As every man hath received the gift, even so minister the same one to another, as good stewards of the manifold grace of God.11 If any man speak, let him speak as the oracles of God; if any man minister, let him do it as of the ability which God giveth: that God in all things may be glorified through Jesus Christ, to whom be praise and dominion for ever and ever. Amen.

Remember the ultimate goal of faith is to bring us into a place of complete agreement with the Heavenly **Father** and his son **Jesus Christ**. It is the **Father's** will that we produce much fruit, for his glory and honor. Faith will bring every part of our existence into complete harmony with God and his purposes. This particular book is emphasizing the importance of faith, but this in no way diminishes the importance of love. 1st Corinthians chapter 13 emphasizes the fact that a life lived without love has no use or value.

1 Corinthians 13:1 Though I speak with the tongues of men and of angels, and have not charity, I am become as sounding brass, or a tinkling cymbal.2 And though I have the gift of prophecy, and understand all mysteries, and all knowledge; and though I have all faith, so that I could remove mountains, and have not charity, I am nothing.3 And though I bestow all my goods to feed the poor, and though I give my body to be burned, and have not charity, it profiteth me nothing.

How does the gift of faith operate? It's rather hard to explain because it just seems to happen. Many times in almost 40 years of ministry it just rises up within my heart. It takes possession of my heart, my soul, my mind, my emotions and even my feelings. It affects every part of my whole being spirit, soul, mind and body. I enter into a place where there is absolutely no doubt whatsoever, no questioning, no ifs, ands or buts. What God has spoken to my heart is absolute reality. I do not need to discuss it with anyone. You almost become like a bull in a china closet. You are coming through no matter what is in your way. You know, that you know, that you know, that you know it will happen as you obey God. Here is one example of the gift of faith operating in my life.

Broken Bones Instantly Healed as I Moved in the Gift of Faith!

One day I had to climb our 250-foot radio tower in order to change the light bulb on the main beacon. However, in order to climb the tower, I had to first find the keys; which I never did. Since I could not find the keys to get the fence open, I did the next best thing—I simply climbed over the fence.

This idea turned out not to be such a wonderful idea after all! With all of my climbing gear hanging from my waist, I climbed the fence to the very top. At this point, my rope gear became entangled in the fencing. As I tried to get free, I lost my balance and fell backwards off the fence. Trying to break my fall, I got my foot down underneath me. In which case, I came down on my foot, when it was still crooked. I hit the ground with my foot being turned on its side and I felt something painfully break in my foot. I knew instantly it was broken.

How Faith Comes

Most sane people would have climbed back over the fence, go set up a doctor's appointment, have their foot x-rayed, and then have it put into a cast. But I am not a normal-thinking person, at least according to the standards of the modern day church. When I broke my foot, I followed my routine of confessing my stupidity to God, asking Him to forgive me for my stupidity. Moreover, I spoke to my foot and commanded it to be healed in the name of **Jesus Christ** of Nazareth. When I had finished speaking to my foot, commanding it to be healed, and then praising and thanking God for the healing, there was no change in its condition. The Scripture that came to my heart was where **Jesus** declared, "The kingdom of heaven suffers violence, and the violent take it by force!" Based completely upon this scripture, I decided to climb the tower by faith, with a broken foot. Please do not misunderstand me, my foot hurt so bad I could hardly stand it. And yet, I had declared that I was healed.

There were three men watching me as I took the Word of God by faith. I told them what I was about to do, and they looked at me like as if I had lost my mind. I began to climb the 250 foot tower, one painful step at a time. My foot hurt so badly that I was hyperventilating within just twenty to thirty feet up the tower. It literally felt like I was going to pass out from shock at any moment. Whenever I got to the point of fainting, I would connect my climbing ropes to the tower, stop and take a breather. It seemed to take me forever to get to the top.

Eventually I did reach the very top of the tower, replacing the light bulb that had gone out. Usually I can come down that tower within 10 minutes, because I press my feet against the outside of the tower, and then slide down, just using my hands and arms to lower myself at a very fast pace. However, in this situation, my foot could not handle the pressure of being pushed up against the steel. Consequently, I had to work my way down very painfully and slowly. After I was down, I climbed over the fence one more time. I hobbled my way over to my vehicle, and drove up to the church office. The men who had been watching this unfold, were right behind me.

I informed some of my staff that I had broken my foot, and that I was going home to rest. At the same time, however, I told them that I believed I was healed. I was trying to activate the little bit of faith I had!

233

I went to my house, which is directly across from the church parking lot. When I finally got into my house, I made my way slowly up the stairs to our bedroom. I found my wife Kathleen in the bedroom putting away our clothes. I told her what I had done to my foot. I slowly and painfully pulled the shoe and sock off of the broken foot. What a mess! It was big and fat, swollen, black and blue all over. I put a pillow down at the end of the bed, and carefully pulled myself up onto the bed. Lying on my back, I tenderly placed my broken, extremely swollen black and blue foot onto the pillow. No matter how I positioned it, the pain did not cease. I just laid there squirming, moaning and sighing.

As I was lying there trying to overcome the shock that kept hitting my body like waves of the ocean, I heard the audible voice of God. He said to me: **"What are you doing in bed?"** Of course I was shocked at hearing Gods audible voice.

In my heart I said by saying: *Lord I'm just resting.*

Then He spoke to my heart with the still quiet voice very clearly, **Do you always rest at this time of day?**

No, Lord, I replied.

He then spoke to my heart and said this, **I thought you said you were healed?**

At that very moment the gift of faith exploded inside of me. Mind boggling an overwhelming confidence took a hold of me and I said: "Lord, I am healed!"

Immediately, I pushed myself up off of the bed, grabbed my socks and shoes, and struggled to put them back on. And what a tremendous struggle it was! My foot was so swollen that it did not want to go into my sock or my shoe. My wife was watching me as I fought to complete this task.

You might wonder what my wife was doing this whole time as I was fighting this battle of faith. She was doing what she always does, just watching me and shaking her head. I finally got the shoe on my swollen, black and blue foot. I put my foot down on the floor and began to put my

234

body weight upon it. When I did, I almost passed out. At that moment, a holy anger exploded on the inside of me. I declared out loud, "I am healed in the name of **Jesus Christ** of Nazareth!" With that declaration, I lifted my right (broken) foot as high as I could and slammed it down to the floor with all of my might.

When I did that, I felt the bones of my foot break even more. Like the Fourth of July, an explosion of blue, purple, red, and white exploded in my brain and I passed out. I came to lying on my bed. Afterward, my wife informed me that every time I passed out, it was for about ten to twenty seconds. The moment I came to, I jumped right back up out of bed. The gift of faith was working in me mightily. I got back up and followed the same process again, "In the name of **Jesus Christ** of Nazareth I am healed," and slammed my foot down once more as hard as I could! For a second time, I could feel the damage in my foot increasing. My mind was once again wrapped in an explosion of colors and pain as I blacked out.

When I regained consciousness, I immediately got up once again, repeating the same process. After the third time of this happening I came to with my wife leaning over the top of me. I remember her saying as she looked at me, "You're making me sick. I can't watch you do this." She promptly walked out of our bedroom, and went downstairs.

The fourth time I got up declaring, "In the name of **Jesus Christ** of Nazareth I am healed," and slammed my foot down even harder! Once more, multiple colors of intense pain hit my brain. I passed out again! I got up the fifth time, angrier than ever. Please realize that I was not operating in a demonic or proud anger. This was a divine gift of violent faith that said **I-will-not-take-no-for-an-answer**. I slammed my foot down the fifth time, "In the name of **Jesus Christ** of Nazareth I *am* healed!"

The minute my foot slammed into the floor, for the fifth time, the power of God hit my foot. I literally stood there under the quickening power of God. All of the pain at that moment had left my foot. I pulled back my sock, and looked at my foot and it was completely normal. There still seemed to be a little bit of bluish gray but it was disappearing. I got up praising God, I was completely healed! I went and showed my wife, and then I went back to the office showing my staff, giving glory to the Lord for my healed foot.

Dr Michael H Yeager

#26th God Will Touch Your 5 Senses

The **26th Way** in which faith will come will come as a surprise to you. The best way in order to introduce this reality is by looking at doubting Thomas. No matter what the disciples said to Thomas he would not believe that **Jesus** was raised from the dead. Finally, **Jesus** showed up and said something amazing to Thomas.

John 20:26 And after eight days again his disciples were within, and Thomas with them: then came Jesus, the doors being shut, and stood in the midst, and said, Peace be unto you.27 Then saith he to Thomas, Reach hither thy finger, and behold my hands; and reach hither thy hand, and thrust it into my side: and be not faithless, but believing.28 And Thomas answered and said unto him, My Lord and my God.

Christ wanted Thomas to literally put his finger into his hand, and his hand into his side. Every word that **Jesus** spoke was spoken out of sincerity and reality. He was not in any way jesting or fooling around with Thomas. He wanted Thomas to literally physically touch him. He was willing to let Thomas experienced him with his 5 senses in order to bring him to a Place of Faith. This is the **26th amazing way** in which faith can come.

#26th God Will Touch Your 5 Senses

I have never sought a physical touch from heaven, but I have had many encounters with God along these lines. Numerous times I have experienced, and those I have been with have experienced a wind blowing in an enclosed sanctuary where there are no Windows. A number of years ago we were conducting a women's conference when all of a sudden the room was filled with a wonderful amazing fragrance which filled the sanctuary that smelled like the fragrance which burned in the holy of holies. I think we had over 70 people that were there and experienced this fragrance. I have also experienced the Shekinah glory that was like a shimmering fog to where I could not see anyone around me. There have been times when I was ministering in the Holy Ghost and I could literally physically feel a hand on my shoulder, and I knew it was the Lord. People have heard with their own naturally ears like that of an angelic choir singing. I have also had people tell me that as they were laying on the floor under the power of God it felt like somebody's hand was going up and down their spines healing them. In those times of God physically touching people, they discovered to their own amazement and joy that faith began to rise in their hearts. I believe this is why at times **Jesus** did physical things to the blind, the sick, and the diseased in order to help them.

Mark 7:32 And they bring unto him one that was deaf, and had an impediment in his speech; and they beseech him to put his hand upon him.33 And he took him aside from the multitude, and put his fingers into his ears, and he spit, and touched his tongue;

Mark 8:22 And he cometh to Bethsaida; and they bring a blind man unto him, and besought him to touch him.23 And he took the blind man by the hand, and led him out of the town; and when he had spit on his eyes, and put his hands upon him, he asked him if he saw ought.

John 9:6 When he had thus spoken, he spat on the ground, and made clay of the spittle, and he anointed the eyes of the blind man with the clay, 7 And said unto him, Go, wash in the pool of Siloam, (which is by interpretation, Sent.) He went his way therefore, and washed, and came seeing.

Faith literally comes by the physical touch of God upon your 5 senses. In the Old Testament we have an illustration of one of the generals of the Army of Syria who had leprosy. He heard one of the Israelite slave girls talking about a prophet that was in Israel that could heal him. He received permission from his king to go visit the prophet Elisha.

3   Kings 5:9 So Naaman came with his horses and with his chariot, and stood at the door of the house of Elisha.............. 13 And his servants came near, and spake unto him, and said, My Father, if the prophet had bid thee do some great thing, wouldest thou not have done it? how much rather then, when he saith to thee, Wash, and be clean? 14 Then went he down, and dipped himself seven times in Jordan, according to the saying of the man of God: and his flesh came again like unto the flesh of a little child, and he was clean. 15 And he returned to the man of God, he and all his company, and came, and stood before him: and he said, Behold, now I know that there is no God in all the earth, but in Israel:

If you read this whole encounter you will discover that Naaman did not truly believe what Elisha said. When his servants convinced him to simply do what the prophet said, the results were miraculous. As a result of God touching this man physically in his body faith rose up in his heart. It completely set him free from idolatry from believing in any other gods. Naaman boldly declared: ***Behold, now I know that there is no God in all the earth, but in Israel:***

Another example would be King Nebuchadnezzar. God had supernaturally given him a dream about a tree that was cut down with nothing but a stump left behind. It was a warning from the Lord, but the day came when he was walking on the top of his palace full of pride and boastful of who he was. At that moment he lost his mind and for the next 7 years was like an animal. The end of those years he awoke once again to sanity, but this time he was completely transformed. God who had touched him in his 5 senses, had now brought into his heart a wonderful and powerful faith.

Daniel 4:34 And at the end of the days I Nebuchadnezzar lifted up mine eyes unto heaven, and mine understanding returned unto me, and I blessed the most High, and I praised and honoured him that liveth for ever, whose dominion is an everlasting dominion, and his kingdom is from generation to generation:

When God touched his 5 senses, He Became a Different Man!

We had a dear brother who was attending our church with his wife. He was what we would call a nominal Christian, lackadaisical in his walk with God, lukewarm in his commitment. A number of years ago God really began to move in our services with amazing manifestations. We were not seeking these manifestations, they just seemed to begin to happen as we were exalting **Christ**. The air was beginning to be filled with wonderful fragrances. Sweet-smelling oil began to flow from our hands, our fore heads, and our tear ducts. Winds began to blow in our sanctuary with no fans turned on. At times there was an invisible rain that we could literally feel hitting our faces and our bodies. People's teeth were being filled with gold.

This brother would come to our services spasmodically, sitting in the back of the sanctuary, refusing to be convinced that these manifestations were really going on. The evidence was there, but he simply could not see it, or believe it. He did not come against it, but in his heart he told us that he did not believe it. Now this brother is a truck driver and one day he stopped at a truck stop. He walked up to the counter to purchase something. As he was talking to the woman who was the attendant she made a statement. She said to him: I know it's not hot in here but for some reason you have lots of sweat rolling down your fore head. He asked her: what? You have sweat running down your fore head she declared. He reached his hand up and touched his fore head. To his shock and amazement his fore head was covered with something but it was not sweat, but with some oily substance. He brought his hand to his nose, and his sense of smell was filled with a wonderful sweet fragrance. It shook him to the very depths of his innermost being. He immediately went to the restroom to look into the mirror. Sure enough oil was flowing from his fore head, and it was increasing. His whole head began to be covered in oil. He began to weep and shake because this was an amazing miracle.

How Faith Comes

As he drove his big 18 wheel rig down the road the oil just kept coming. He said he cried and cried and cried. He decided he was not going to tell his wife anything. When he got home that night he tried to act normal. As he was standing in the bathroom, he said to the Lord, God if this is really you then fill my teeth, and all of my family's teeth as well with gold wherever there are fillings! The next morning, he got up and went to the bathroom. He opened his mouth with great trembling, and to his shock and amazement all of his fillings had been turned to gold. He called his wife and his son into the bathroom. He told them what had happened the day before. They all opened up their mouths, and sure enough there fillings had been turned to gold.

He told his wife: call up our dentist and set up an appointment to get our teeth cleaned. They went to the dentist office. The wife sat in the dentist chair, with the dentist getting ready to clean her teeth. As he looked in to her mouth he said with great surprise: who filled your teeth with gold? She said: what? He said all your fillings are filled with gold. He told her: I am your dentist, and I know I did not do this! Then she informed him that it was God who had turned their fillings into gold.

To say the least this dear brother entered into a realm of faith that he had not previously known. His Luke warmness and lackadaisical attitude disappeared. He began to share **Christ** wherever he went with as many as he could. By God touching his 5 senses, faith rose up in his heart in a wonderful and powerful way.

Dr Michael H Yeager

#27 Reading or Listening to Gods Word

There is another way in which faith comes which is very simple. We have not really taught on this particular way even though it may sound like it when I shared it with you. The **27th Way** in which faith will come is by **Simply Reading or Listening to God's Word!**

27th Way Reading or Listening to God's Word!

Yes, we know that meditation of the word brings faith, but just reading the Bible itself does bring about a steady flow of faith into your heart. I will acknowledge that at times as your reading or listening to the word of God the Holy Spirit can bring a mighty rush of faith. This is different than when you hear someone preaching **Jesus Christ**. We discussed that as the **2nd way** in which faith comes.

You can see this truth manifested in our educational system in America. Up into the 1960s Bible reading was commonplace in the public school classroom. During those years the major problems were so minor that they are not worth mentioning. What were some of these terrible things that children did? Chewing bubblegum, running in the hallways, getting a little bit loud at times, but once they took the Bible reading out of the school all hell broke loose. In the public school there is now murder, rape, shootings and knife stabbings, Gang warfare. The list is never ending of the wickedness that is transpiring in our educational system, I believe it is because they took prayer, and daily reading of the Scriptures out of the classrooms.

In 2nd Kings chapter 22 it tells us that Josiah the King was in the 18th year of his reign. He was 26 years old at this time. He sent a construction crew to work on the temple. In the mist of rebuilding the Temple they discovered the book of the law. They brought it to the King. When they began to read this book of the law to the King, something amazing happened in his heart.

2 Kings 2:10 And Shaphan the scribe shewed the king, saying, Hilkiah the priest hath delivered me a book. And Shaphan read it before the king. [11] And it came to pass, when the king had heard the words of the book of the law, that he rent his clothes.

By this young King simply hearing the word of God read out loud, faith arose in his heart. He called all the people together, putting on sackcloth and ashes, crying out to the Lord in repentance for himself and his nation. God was extremely pleased with his actions.

2 Kings 22:19 Because thine heart was tender, and thou hast humbled thyself before the Lord, when thou heardest what I spake against this place, and against the inhabitants thereof, that they should become a desolation and a curse, and hast rent thy clothes, and wept before me; I also have heard thee, saith the Lord.

Many times you'll find within the Old Testament where Moses, or the high priest, or the King or someone designated to the job would simply read the Scriptures to the people.

Deuteronomy 31:11 When all Israel is come to appear before the Lord thy God in the place which he shall choose, thou shalt read this law before all Israel in their hearing.

Joshua 8:35 There was not a word of all that Moses commanded, which Joshua read not before all the congregation of Israel, with the women, and the little ones, and the strangers that were conversant among them.

Remember it was the 1st generation that did not have enough faith to enter into the Promised Land, but as Joshua read the word of God to the 2nd generation faith rose up in their hearts and they went across the Jordan River and defeated the enemies of God. In the New Testament Paul, the apostle exhorted Timothy to read God's word. He told him that the Scripture was profitable for his spiritual growth, and maturity.

1 Timothy 4:13 Till I come, give attendance to reading, to exhortation, to doctrine.

In the epistle that Paul had written to the Saints which were in Thessalonica, he told them that they needed to read the epistle out loud to everybody.

1 Thessalonians 5:27 I charge you by the Lord that this epistle be read unto all the holy brethren.

In the epistle of Colossians, he also gave this instruction.

Colossians 4:16 And when this epistle is read among you, cause that it be read also in the church of the Laodiceans; and that ye likewise read the epistle from Laodicea.

One of the Reasons I Have Amazing Children!

I want to take just a moment and use my 3 sons and daughter as an example. You see from the time my children were born, yes even before they were born while they were still in their mother's womb, they have been listening to the word of God. To this day if you would go to their houses and walk into their bedrooms late at night or early in the morning, you would hear them listening to the word of God. My wife and I usually go to sleep listening to God's word. Many times in the morning we will listen to God's word before we get out of bed. Whenever we went on vacations or trips in the vehicle as a family we were always listening to the word of God, or some wonderful spiritual stories, like Pilgrim's progress on audio tape. I am not saying that my children are perfect, but I have not had near the heart ache, or the problems with them that most people have. My children are all grown up now in their late 20s and early 30s. I am one of those who can truly say that children are a blessing from God. But they must be raised in the nurture and admonition of the Lord.

WHY MY CHILDREN NEVER WENT ASTRAY!

Many times minister's children are the worse because of the pressures and the satanic attacks against them. I am now boasting in **Jesus Christ** about their lives. I have never preached or harped at my children. I never put ridiculous constraints upon them. I never put pressure on them to perform because they were the children of a minister. Yes, we did pray with them. Yes, my wife always had devotions with them daily, but I believe it has been the consistent flow of God's word into their lives that has caused them never to go into drugs, sexual promiscuity, or outright immorality. There is still a hunger in their hearts for God. My 2 oldest sons minister the gospel with me. My 3 sons are all in the midst of writing spiritual books. My daughter has written well over 150 spiritual songs. Faith has been maintained in their hearts because the word of God has been flowing into them from the time they were conceived in their mother's womb. We never had a TV in our house to allow their minds to become corrupted. They never complained because they did not know what they were missing. And now even if you would offer them a TV set in their houses they would boldly reject it.

CHAPTER TEN

#28 Delighting in the Word of God

As we look at the last way in which faith comes it will sound like we've already said this when we were teaching about abiding in the word. But you can abide in the word without actually delighting yourself in the word of God.

The 28th Way in which faith will come is by delighting yourself in God's word.

Let me give you an example. You can be married to your mate for 50 years or longer and still not really delight yourself or really enjoy being with your wife or your husband.

Proverbs 5:18 Let thy fountain be blessed: and rejoice with the wife of thy youth.

You can work the same job all of your life, be good at what you do, and yet never really enjoy it. I could give you many illustrations about this, but I think you get my point. We could memorize whole books of the New Testament, thousands of scriptures and yet not really delight in them. The definition for the word delight means: to rejoice, to take joy, great pleasure, to be happy in, to desire, to be blessed by. A man or woman who delights himself in the law of the Lord, is a person who takes great pleasure and joy in the truth. It is a person who loves the word of God.

Psalm 119:16 I will delight myself in thy statutes: I will not forget thy word.

You can even spend hours and days memorizing scriptures and meditating upon these truths, and yet not truly love the word of God. There are many Scriptures dealing in the Old Testament about delighting ourselves not only in God's word, but in God himself, but it will take real faith to develop a love for the truth. In the book of 2nd Thessalonians Paul warns us by the spirit of God that many in the last days will turn away from the truth because they do not love it. And because of their lack of love for God's truth the Lord will turn them over to a strong spirit of delusion. We see this happening on a massive scale in our generation right now.

2 Thessalonians 2:10 And with all deceivableness of unrighteousness in them that perish; because they received not the <u>love of the truth</u>, that they might be saved.11 And for this cause God shall send them strong delusion, that they should believe a lie:12 That they all might be damned who believed not the truth, but had pleasure in unrighteousness.

A love for God and his truth must be cultivated in us. This will be a fight of faith because the enemy of our soul wants to devour us through the deceitfulness of this world. Paul the apostle told us that we can grow by the sincere milk of the word.

1 Peter 2:2 As newborn babes, desire the sincere milk of the word, that ye may grow thereby:

I BECAME OBSESSED WITH THE DEEP HUNGER OF GOD'S WORD!

I remember giving my heart to **Jesus Christ** on February 18, 1975. As I got up from the floor born again, saved and delivered, I was a brand-new person. Immediately hunger and thirst for the Word of God took a hold of me. I began to devoured Matthew, Mark, Luke, and John.
I just could not get enough of the word of God because of my love for **Jesus Christ** and his **Father**. **Jesus** became my hero in every area of my thoughts

and daily life. He became my reason for getting up and going to work, eating, sleeping, and living. I discovered that everything I did was based on the desire of wanting to please Him. I carried my little green military Bible with me wherever I went. Whenever I had an opportunity I would open it up and study it. It wasn't very long before I believed for a larger Bible. This larger Bible gave me much more room to make notes, highlight and circle certain Scriptures. The more I fed on the Scriptures, the greater my hunger became for them. I probably was not saved even for 2 months when I was asked to speak for the 1st time at a small Pentecostal church. I believe it was called Adak Full Gospel Church. As far as I know it was the only Pentecostal church on this military base situated on a Aleutian Island in Alaska. Since 1975 I have never lost my hunger, or my thirst for God's word. I can truly say even what the psalmist said!

Psalm 104:34 My meditation of him shall be sweet: I will be glad in the Lord.

This hunger for God's word has caused me to memorize over a 3rd of the New Testament. I am not bragging or boasting, I'm just simply saying that God's word is the joy and rejoicing of my heart. There are People Who Love to Swim, People Who Love to Work out, People Who Love to Do Push-Ups and Chin-Ups and Lift Weights, but we need people who love God's word!

#28 The 28th Way in which faith will come is by delighting yourself in God's word.

Psalm 16:3 But to the saints that are in the earth, and to the excellent, in whom is all my delight.

Psalm 37:4 Delight thyself also in the Lord: and he shall give thee the desires of thine heart.

Psalm 37:23 The steps of a good man are ordered by the Lord: and he delighteth in his way.

Psalm 40:8 I delight to do thy will, O my God: yea, thy law is within my heart.

Psalm 112:1Praise ye the Lord. Blessed is the man that feareth the Lord, that delighteth greatly in his commandments.

Psalm 119:16I will delight myself in thy statutes: I will not forget thy word.

Psalm 119:24Thy testimonies also are my delight and my counselors.

Psalm 119:35Make me to go in the path of thy commandments; for therein do I delight.

Psalm 119:47And I will delight myself in thy commandments, which I have loved.

Psalm 119:70.......I delight in thy law.

Psalm 119:77Let thy tender mercies come unto me, that I may live: for thy law is my delight.

Psalm 119:92Unless thy law had been my delights, I should then have perished in mine affliction.

Psalm 119:143Trouble and anguish have taken hold on me: yet thy commandments are my delights.

Psalm 119:174I have longed for thy salvation, O Lord; and thy law is my delight.

Psalm 104:34 My meditation of him shall be sweet: I will be glad in the Lord.

This is the conclusion on this particular subject, and yet I'm sure that there is a tremendous amount more that we could say about HOW FAITH COMES. I hope and pray you begin to apply every one of these spiritual principles and truths. The greatest need we have in this generation are those who truly have faith, confidence, reliance, dependence and trust in God. Jesus boldly declared that all things are possible to them that believe in him. May this generation rise up in the power and the faith of Jesus Christ, going forth and setting the captives free.

Sincerely: Dr Michael H Yeager

LIST OF WAYS THAT FAITH COMES!

#1 Faith Given At Conception
#2 Hearing Jesus Christ Preached

#3 Meditation of the Word
#4 When You See Jesus
#5 BY Prayer and Fasting
#6 Sacrifice of Praise & Thanksgiving
#7 Assimilation by Associations
#8 Waiting upon God
#9 Being Doers of the WORD
#10 Worship in Spirit & Truth
#11 When You Cry out for Mercy
#12 By Signs, Wonders & Miracles
#13 Remembering what God has done!
#14 Instant Obedience to Gods Voice!
#15 Acknowledging Every Good Work!
#16 Eating and Drinking Jesus Christ
#17 Abiding & Dwelling in Jesus Christ!
#18 God Given Visitations, Visions & Dreams
#19 The Indwelling of Jesus Christ!
#20 by Praying in the Holy Ghost!
#21 by Seed Time and Harvest
#22 by the Prophetic Word!
#23 Impartation by the Laying on of Hands

 # 24 Exalting and Magnifying Jesus Christ
#25 Operating in the Gift of Faith
#26th God Will Touch Your 5 Senses
#27 Reading or Listening to Gods Word
#28 Delighting in the Word of God

Dr. Michael H. Yeager is a motivated speaker who would love to come and minister to your church or group. You can reach him through the following:

Address:
Jesus Is Lord Ministries International
3425 Chambersburg Rd.
Biglerville, Pennsylvania 17307

Phone: 1-800-555-4575

Websites:
www.docyeager.org
www.wordbroadcast.org
www.hellsreal.com WWW.JILMI.ORG

Books Written by Doc Yeager:

"Living in the Realm of the Miraculous #1"

"I need God Cause I'm Stupid"

"The Miracles of Smith Wigglesworth"

"How Faith Comes 28 WAYS"

"Horrors of Hell, Splendors of Heaven"

"The Coming Great Awakening"

"Sinners In The Hands of an Angry GOD, (modernized)"

"Brain Parasite Epidemic"

"My JOURNEY To HELL" - illustrated for teenagers

"Divine Revelation Of Jesus Christ"

"My Daily Meditations"

"Holy Bible of JESUS CHRIST"

"War In The Heavenlies - (Chronicles of Micah)"

"Living in the Realm of the Miraculous #2"

"My Legal Rights To Witness"

"Why We (MUST) Gather!- 30 Biblical Reasons"

My Incredible, Supernatural, Divine Experiences!

Dr Michael H Yeager

"How GOD Leads & Guides! - 20 Ways"

Phone: 1-800-555-4575

www,docyeager.com

ABOUT THE AUTHOR

Dr. Michael and Kathleen Yeager have served as pastors/apostles, missionaries, evangelist, broadcasters and authors for almost four decades. Up to this time they have authored ten books. Their three sons, daughter and daughter in law work with them in the ministry. Michael and Kathleen have been married for 36 years (1978). They have helped start over 27 churches. They flow in the gifts of the Holy Spirit, teaching the word of God, with wonderful signs & miracles following and confirming God's word. In 1983 they began **Jesus** is Lord Ministries international. The same year the Lord spoke to Dr. Yeager to go on TV. From then to now they have been actively involved in broadcast media for the propagation of the gospel. They have owned numerous radio stations through the years. They have broadcasted by satellite (with their own C band up-link system) TV stations, including low power TV stations. In the mid-90s as pastor Mike was contemplating purchasing a local TV station, the Lord spoke to his heart and said the future was the Internet. At that time **Jesus** is Lord Ministries made a sizable investment into the broadcasting of the gospel by the Internet. For a season they were the largest broadcaster in new technology that carried well-known ministers, live streaming & archiving of their programs. In the mid-70s the Lord had spoken to Dr. Mike, revealing to him that he would be a part of providing a platform by which ministers could speak to the nations. Our broadcast now reaches around the world by all the latest and modern technology.

FOR MORE BOOKS FROM DOC YEAGER VISIT:

WWW.DOCYEAGER.COM